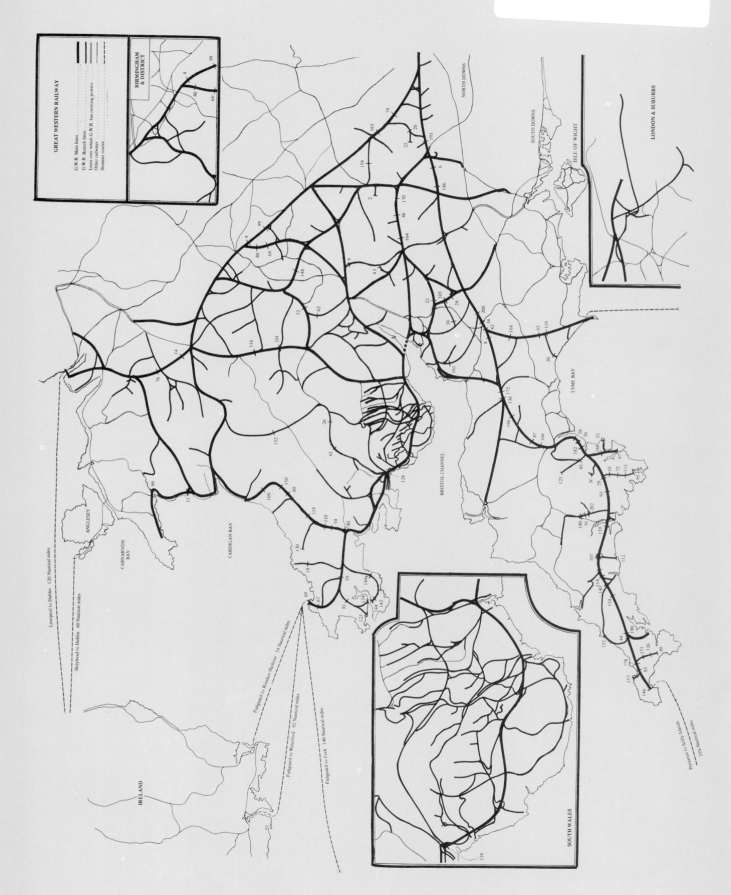

An Historical Survey of Selected

GREAT WESTERN STATIONS

Layouts and Illustrations

Volume Two

by

R.H.Clark

Oxford Publishing Co.

© 1979 Oxford Publishing Co.
SBN 860930 15 7

Acknowledgements and Bibliography

Most reference works on any subject are usually the result of the combined efforts of the sponsoring author and those who have come forward to give their valuable services in one direction or another, and particularly is this so in the preparation of a railway book because of the diversity of specialities involved.

So far as this book is concerned, my grateful thanks are extended to my sister Gwen, who has checked, re-checked, criticised, and brought to my attention the occasional anomaly in both plans and manuscript, who advised on the construction of the original MS, and who finally typed most of it; to Mr. J.W.P. Cowell for his research into obscure historical facts; to Mr. Eddie Lyons for information on certain engine sheds and early station plans; to Mr. J.F. Nayler for his help with Par station layout; to Mr. W. Vaughan-Jenkins for the use of his extensive railway library; to Mr. Brian Read for matters requiring official liaison; to Mr. J.P. Morris and Mr. G.A. Pryer for their help in identifying signals on the signalled plans; to Mr. C.J. Freezer for his helpful advice regarding the interests of modellers; and for the co-operation of the staff at the Public Record Office, Porchester Road, and British Rail (Western and Southern regions).

Individual acknowledgement to those who have kindly supplied photographs is made under each illustration.

Finally, but by no means least, my thanks go to my wife whose help and patience through our married life appeared to be unlimited, surrounded as she is by "railways" — prototype, model, documentary, literary, and social — there is never a murmur of disapproval or discouragement.

In addition to the helpful resources offered by the above, and to the books, timetables, maps, diagrams, and other documents contained in the author's own collection, the undermentioned general references have also been consulted.

"History of the Great Western Railway" by E. T. McDermott
(original and re-written versions).

"The Great Western Railway in the 19th.–20th. Centuries"
"Regional History of the Railways of Great Britain" Vols. 1, 2, and 7
"Track Layout Diagrams of the G.W.R. and B.R. (Western Region)" by R.A. Cooke
The Railway Engineer
The Great Western Railway Magazine
G.W.R. public and working timetables, and appendices
Selected articles in the railway and model railway periodicals
The R.C.H. Junction Diagram Book
Cambrian Railways and Midland & South Western Junction Railway–public timetables.

DEDICATION

To Gwen

who always likes to make a loss
on the "giving and taking account."

ERRATUM

to the first book of G.W. Stations

Page 32   Track direction arrow indication on extreme right of
main plan should read "To Whitland".

Page 43   Last line of Notes should read —
"Diagram B shows the fully signalled layout as it was
in 1940."

Page 128   Diagram "B" — "Good Shed" should read "GOODS
SHED".

Page 180   Notes, 6th line down —
". . . layout a few yards after . . ." should read —
". . . layout a few years after . . .".

Printed by Blackwells in the City of Oxford

Published by
Oxford Publishing Co.,
8, The Roundway,
Headington, Oxford.

Introduction

Since the first volume of "Great Western Stations" was completed, many more official diagrams have become available by kind permission of British Rail (Western Region), and the Oxford Publishing Company. In consequence, a wider field of selection has opened up, not only in the number of station diagrams but in the type suitable for book presentation, where there is more than one diagram for a particular station.

But however wide the field of selection may become, a decision still has to be made when one is faced with the problem of whether to include a low detailed plan of an interesting station, or a highly detailed plan of a less interesting one. Fortunately, so far, this has only arisen in isolated cases, and so far as this book is concerned, I have tried to strike a balance which (I hope) is agreeable to the reader, bearing in mind that the "interest" value of a station may not necessarily be related to its historical significance.

The selection is intended to include some of the more important stations on the Great Western system, some of those which are (or were) more interesting than important, and a few which may qualify for inclusion by reason of the historical interest of the line upon which they were located. In addition, it is cause for gratification that adequate plans of stations in Devon and Cornwall have become available in time for this book. Although nearly every Great Western enthusiast in the middle and older generations must be familiar with nearly every station that existed in these counties, the interest which these stations attract seems to increase, rather than diminish as the years progress.

Nor is interest confined merely to a station as it exists or existed. The student enthusiast wants to know "dates", and he naturally looks to an "historical survey" to supply them.

There are, of course, some well-known historical researchers of impeccable integrity who have unearthed, and recorded for posterity the results of their findings. These sources have been consulted and if they themselves have been in doubt over a date, that date has been left out. But "event" dates, particularly those of more recent years, have not been so difficult to track to source as have map, plan and illustration dates, and it will be noted that many of the plan dates have had to be qualified as being "circa". So far as the "A" diagrams are concerned, the circa date mostly refers to a longer period

before the year shown than after. In nearly all cases, the indicated year (and sometimes the month and day) appears on the original official plan, which predisposes the fact that the drawing was prepared in the office during a possible period of from a month or so to 3 or even 4 years after the survey was completed.

In the case of the signalled diagrams, and unless specifically dated, they would be current at a time during the period from (say) 1943 to 1968, or until closure if before that year, although there may have been minor alterations in the meantime. Signal box diagrams were not put in and taken out again very frequently.

The books and periodicals listed under "Further Reading" in the first volume seem to have been appreciated, and this feature has been continued here. It should be emphasised, however, that the inclusion of these references is made solely to enable the reader to follow up information on a particular station or the line upon which it is, or was, located, at his own discretion.

A study of some of the station illustrations is to be recommended as certain details can be quite revealing particularly where layouts and signalling are concerned. At any rate, a picture of a station usually reveals to the viewer its shape and style, which cannot be conveyed adequately by diagram or word-description.

The reason for the varying scales of the "A" diagrams is attributed to the fact that, for storage and file purposes, the original plans have had to be photographed "down" to a convenient and mostly standard overall size. It follows, therefore, that a station with an extensive layout finalises at a smaller scale than does a smaller station layout, and that in this process, it is impossible to adopt a uniform rate of reduction. In consequence, each separate plan has had to be individually re-scaled to fit the pages of this book, and meticulous care has been taken in the process.

Throughout this book (and as in Book 1), track direction arrows indicate either the next principal, or readily familiar station, which may not necessarily be the next ACTUAL station. This has been done to help those of us who may be less familiar with Great Western geography than some of our contemporaries. On the ORIGINAL signal box diagrams, arrow directions are always to the next signal box (by title) even though a box may not bear an associated station title.

Key to Symbols

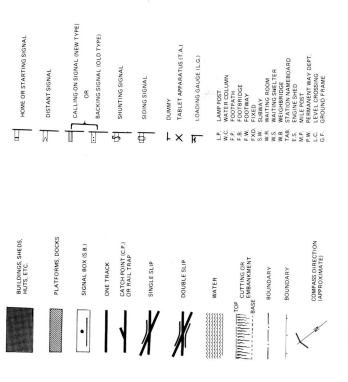

BUILDINGS, SHEDS, HUTS, ETC.

PLATFORMS, DOCKS

SIGNAL BOX (S.B.)

ONE TRACK

CATCH POINT (C.P.) OR RAIL TRAP

SINGLE SLIP

DOUBLE SLIP

WATER

CUTTING OR EMBANKMENT — TOP / BASE

BOUNDARY

BOUNDARY

COMPASS DIRECTION (APPROXIMATE)

HOME OR STARTING SIGNAL

DISTANT SIGNAL

CALLING-ON SIGNAL (NEW TYPE)
OR
BACKING SIGNAL (OLD TYPE)

SHUNTING SIGNAL

SIDING SIGNAL

DUMMY

TABLET APPARATUS (T.A.)

LOADING GAUGE (L.G.)

L.P.   LAMP POST
W.C.   WATER COLUMN
F.P.   FOOTPATH
F.B.   FOOTBRIDGE
F.W.   FOOTWAY
FXD.   FIXED
S.W.   SUBWAY
W.R.   WAITING ROOM
W.S.   WAITING SHELTER
W.B.   WEIGHBRIDGE
TAB.   STATION NAMEBOARD
E.S.   ENGINE SHED
M.P.   MILE POST
P.W.   PERMANENT WAY DEPT.
L.C.   LEVEL CROSSING
G.F.   GROUND FRAME

Notes on Layout Diagrams

1. The approximate scale of each main ("A") diagram is given below the main title of the station.

2. The official ("A") plans, while indicating most physical features concerned with the railway, including in some cases, local topography, surrounding roads and properties, some plans also show the exact position of a signal post, but the signals themselves are not illustrated or identified.

3. In the signalled diagrams, (B, C, D, etc.) and for reasons of clarity, it has been found desirable either to illustrate a signal away from its actual location, and/or to identify it by means of a 'dotted' extraction leader.

4. At the extremity of some plans it will be noted that some signals (e.g., Fixed Distants, Homes, or Advanced Starters) have been indicated with arrows pointing "off the map". This shows that such signals are well beyond the limits of the diagrams, and are included to give a complete picture of the signalling arrangements at the particular station illustrated.

5. In this book, all signalled diagrams have been based on copies of official signal box diagrams. These copies have been kindly supplied by the Signalling Record Society, but, for the benefit of the reader, the drawings have been slightly modified as follows:—

    1. Facing point locks (F.P.L's) have been excluded for reasons of clarity (in the much reduced size of the diagrams).

    2. In some cases, the signal box lever numbers which are normally shown on box diagrams, have been replaced by actual signal identities (although such titles were not necessarily uniform throughout the G.W.R. system, or in the constituent companies).

    3. "Spare" signal box lever numbers and "Spaces" have been excluded.

    4. "Dummies" have been illustrated in "semaphore" style rather than banner.

6. The lines drawn across the track at points in the "A" diagrams indicate the limits of the point blades.

7. Changes in gradient indications on the "A" diagrams should not be confused with those given in the working timetables—which are RULING gradients between stations, stop-boards, junction points or signal boxes. Those shown on the plans are actual gradient post indications.

8. On the signalled diagrams, some of the buildings (station, goods shed, overbridge, footbridge etc.) have been added for enhancement. These do *not* in any way interfere with the track and signal accuracy of the diagrams themselves, but it should be noted that while care has been taken to position these features correctly in relation to each other (and to the track itself), their size and shape are also 'diagrammatic'.

Suggested Sources of Further Information

As a means to help those who may wish to follow up information on any particular station, or the line upon which it was (or is) located, various references have been included relating to articles, illustrations, maps, and railway history books.

The references given (unless otherwise specified) refer mainly to a line of railway, and may, or may not contain specific reference to an individual station located thereon.

The list is, of course, by no means comprehensive, for there must be many more sources available, not only in the periodicals listed, but in older issues of the local press, and contemporary National magazines. In addition, the store of published railway knowledge continues to expand through the medium of our established railway journals, model and prototype, and railway books, some of which record a detailed history of a line for the first time ever.

So far as the sources mentioned in these pages are concerned, the legend and abbreviations relating to them are explained as follows:—

R. Mag. = Railway Magazine;   R.W. = Railway World (or earlier title)
R. Mod. = Railway Modeller;   T.I. = Trains Illustrated;
M.R.N. = Model Railway News (or later title);
M.R.C. = Model Railway Constructor;
R. & T.M. = Railway & Travel Monthly;
H. = Historical;   A = Article;   P = Illustration(s);   M = Map(s);
Pos. = Picture of station;   D = Descriptive;   S.B. = Signal Box.

ABINGDON

APPROX. SCALE 120 FT TO 1 INCH

(PLAN TO SHOW POSITION OF RAIL TRAPS)

C.P.
C.P.

SIDING PROJECTIONS (NOT TO SCALE)

TO RADLEY

ADV. ST.
HOME
T.P.
ENGINE SHED
P.S.
COAL BIN
T.P.
T.P.
C.P.
P.S.
T.P.
S.B.
START
T.P.
T.P.
SHEDS
L.P.
L.P.
CRANE
GOODS SHED
CANOPY
W.B.
OFFICE
T.P.
L.P.
MAIN BUILDINGS
T.P.

ABINGDON

Origin: Abingdon Railway Co.—worked by the G.W.R. from outset and taken over by that Company in 1904

Opened: 2 June 1856 (Broad gauge—converted to standard gauge 25–27 Nov. 1872)

Closed: 9 Sept. 1963 (P) (Remained open for certain goods traffic)

Plan date: 10 Dec. 1910 (Signalling 1928)

Abingdon station was built on the broad gauge single line from a junction with the main line near Nuneham, just north of the bridge over the Thames. At this point, platforms were erected for the exchange of passengers between the main line and the branch, but the "halt" never reached "station" status, although it remained in use until the new station at Radley was built. The branch line was then extended beside the main line to Radley, increasing the length of the branch from 1m. 70c. to 2m 22c. There were no intermediate stations on the branch, which had a rising ruling gradient of 1 in 200. It was (1938) worked by Train Staff, and a one class rail auto-car, and there was a maximum speed restriction for all passenger trains of 40 m.p.h. at any point with special speed restrictions of 10 m.p.h. at the junction with the main line, and of 25 m.p.h. between 57c. and 71c. The maximum (passenger) engine load was 260 tons, including auto-trains.

In the summer period of 1938, Abingdon signal box was open "for the day's train service" on weekdays, and was closed on Sundays. There was *no* switch provided.

FURTHER READING

T. I. 1954 pp. 240–241 H.A.P. Pos. (2)
R. Mag. 1956 pp. 122–124 H.A.P. Pos.
R. Mag. 1970 p. 453 Pos. (2)
"Great Western Engine Sheds, 1947" by E. Lyons. Oxford Publishing Co.

Lens of Sutton

Abingdon. From buffers, showing platform details.

Abingdon.   Signal box, water tank, gas lamps
                            and coach body.   *O.P.C.*

Abingdon.   View from buffers.   *O.P.C.*

Abingdon.   Exterior of station entrance, c.1955.   *Lens of Sutton*

Abingdon.   Terminus and goods shed.   *O.P.C.*

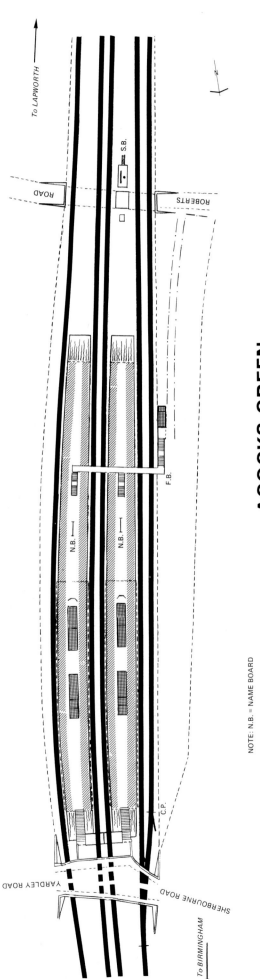

To LAPWORTH →

S.B.

ROAD

ROBERTS

ROAD

N.B.

N.B.

F.B.

C.P.

YARDLEY ROAD

SHERBOURNE ROAD

← To BIRMINGHAM

ACOCKS GREEN

DIAGRAM "A"
APPROX. SCALE : 106 FT. TO 1 INCH

NOTE: N.B. = NAME BOARD

ACOCKS GREEN

Origin: Great Western Railway (who had absorbed the Birmingham & Oxford
Junction Railway in 1848)

Opened: 1 Oct. 1852
Closed: .
Plan date: c. 1940

The station is on the G.W.R. main line to Birmingham (Snow Hill in the old days) just south of Tyseley, and on the fringe of Birmingham's suburbs. It has been chosen, not so much for any pretence at architectural appeal, but for its style as a main line through station with two island platforms, and with overbridge-access to each. It is fairly representative of the style which was adopted by many railway companies around the turn of the century for suburban stations, when there was a spate of rebuilding and "modernisation" proceeding in the outlying areas of big cities.

It is regretted that the available plan only shows the passenger station, but although the handling of passenger traffic was its prime function, there were one or two sidings to the south, and latterly a down goods loop with facing connections both to the down and up relief lines. The lines were widened and the station rebuilt in 1906/7. At the northern end of the station, the down goods loop trailed into the down relief line.

The signal box was (1938) open from 6.0 a.m. on Mondays until 11.0 p.m. on Sundays, and was provided with a switch.

FURTHER READING

R. Mag. 1905 (2) p. 445 (Rebuilding announcement)
"Victorian & Edwardian Railways" by J. G. Spence. Batsford (Photo No. 38)

O.P.C.

Acocks Green.   Exterior of entrance to station.

ACOCKS GREEN

DIAGRAM "B"
(NOT TO SCALE)

DOWN MAIN HOME

TYS

UP RELIEF START

DOWN RELIEF HOME

DOWN RELIEF TO DOWN GOODS LOOP HOME

UP

UP

MAIN

RELIEF

DOWN

DOWN

DOWN

DOWN GOODS LOOP

S.B.

F.B.

DOWN MAIN START

TYS

DOWN RELIEF START

DOWN GOODS LOOP START

TYS

TYS

UP MAIN HOME

TY

TYS

UP RELIEF HOME

TYS

DOWN RELIEF ADV. ST.

TYS

TYS

TYS

TYS

TYS

To BIRMINGHAM

NOTE: "TYS" = TYSELEY SOUTH S.B. SIGS.

OLTON

To LAPWORTH

UP RELIEF ADV. ST.

UP MAIN ADV. ST.

UP MAIN START

SOL

SOL

UP RELIEF INTERMEDIATE ST.

UP MAIN START

MA

MA

NOTE: "SOL" = SOLIHULL S.B. SIGS.

Acocks Green. Looking towards Birmingham.
O.P.C.

5

To READING

F.B.

To Newbury

To STOPS

765 FEET TO STOPS

PRIVATE SIDING

DISC.

SIG.

DISC.

GATES

GATE

CATTLE PEN

COAL PENS

GOODS SHED

OFFICE

SIG. DISC.

DISC.

SIGNAL BOX

COAL

END-LOADING BANK

GATE

T.P.

DISC.

DISC.

SHED

MAIN BUILDINGS

APPROACH ROAD

ALDERMASTON

DIAGRAM "A"
APPROX SCALE: 78 FT. TO 1 INCH

ALDERMASTON

Origin:	G.W.R. (absorbing the Berks & Hants Rly. in 1846)
Opened:	21 Dec. 1847
	Renamed "Aldermaston Halt" 5 May 1969
Closed:	6 Dec. 1965 (G) Remained open for P.S. traffic
Plan date:	c. 1928

The main buildings were typical for the period and locality, built in the "chalet" style with the roofs extending well over the structures beneath to form a platform awning right out to the edge of the platform, and uniformly so at each end. Similar styles were adopted for Theale, Midgham, Thatcham, and Pangbourne. Built of stone, they were made to last for ever, but didn't . . . .

The track layout remained much the same from early times almost down to the 2nd World War, but there was a new signal box built in 1920 near the site of the old one. With the advent of various industrial enterprises, including Government, siding and other track alterations occurred, and with the growth of commuter traffic, the platforms were extended, and the rather incongruous, though necessary, awning extension erected on the up platform.

Between the survey of the main plan and the outbreak of the last World War, there was a siding to the west of the station on the up side (opposite the goods shed) which was lifted in 1940, and the whole of the shed road and connections into the main line, together with the trailing crossover opposite the signal box were lifted in late 1967.

The down goods running loop was installed and opened on 30 Mar. 1943, and the up goods loop became redundant 20 years later. This dates the signal box diagram as being between those dates.

FURTHER READING

"Reg. History of the Railways of G.B."—Vol. 1 (The West Country)
by D. St.J. Thomas. Phoenix

Aldermaston.   General view looking West.

Author's collection

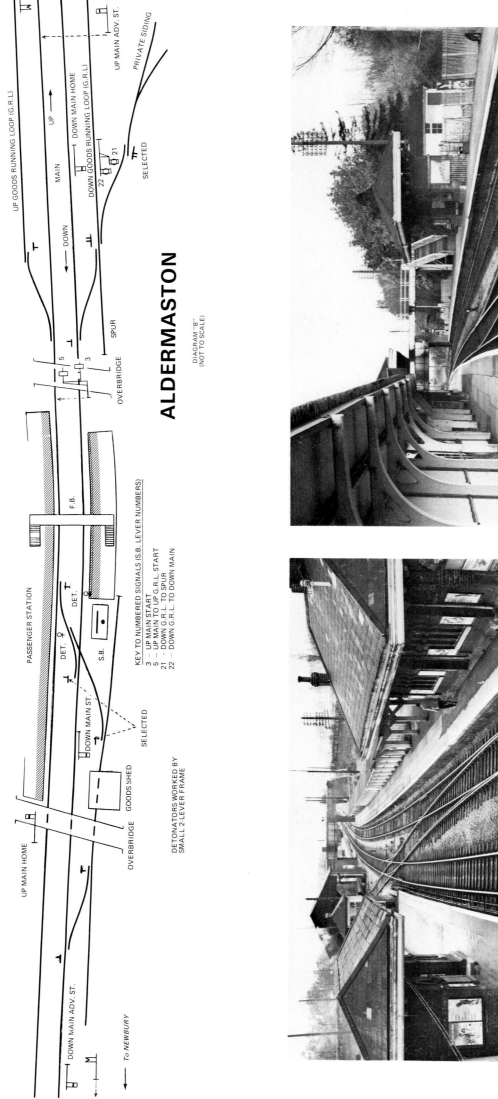

ALDERMASTON

DIAGRAM "B"
(NOT TO SCALE)

To READING →

UP GOODS RUNNING LOOP (G.R.L.)

UP MAIN

MAIN

DOWN MAIN HOME

DOWN GOODS RUNNING LOOP (G.R.L.)

UP MAIN ADV. ST.

PRIVATE SIDING

DOWN

22

21

SELECTED

SPUR

OVERBRIDGE

5

3

PASSENGER STATION

F.B.

DET.

DET.

S.B.

KEY TO NUMBERED SIGNALS (S.B. LEVER NUMBERS)

3 — UP MAIN START
5 — UP MAIN TO UP G.R.L. START
21 — DOWN G.R.L. TO SPUR
22 — DOWN G.R.L. TO DOWN MAIN

DOWN MAIN ST.

SELECTED

DETONATORS WORKED BY
SMALL 2-LEVER FRAME

UP MAIN HOME

DOWN MAIN ADV. ST.

GOODS SHED

OVERBRIDGE

To NEWBURY →

Aldermaston.   O.P.C.

Looking towards Reading.

Aldermaston.   O.P.C.

Looking towards Newbury.

7

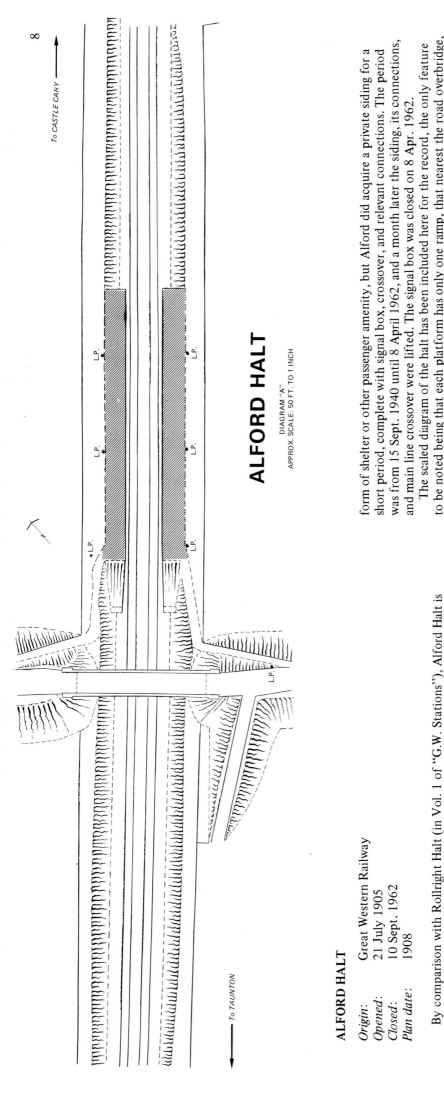

To CASTLE CARY →

← To TAUNTON

ALFORD HALT

DIAGRAM "A"
APPROX. SCALE: 50 FT. TO 1 INCH

L.P.

ALFORD HALT

Origin:	Great Western Railway
Opened:	21 July 1905
Closed:	10 Sept. 1962
Plan date:	1908

By comparison with Rollright Halt (in Vol. 1 of "G.W. Stations"), Alford Halt is twice the size—it has 2 platforms against Rollright's one. Both halts were devoid of any form of shelter or other passenger amenity, but Alford did acquire a private siding for a short period, complete with signal box, crossover, and relevant connections. The period was from 15 Sept. 1940 until 8 April 1962, and a month later the siding, its connections, and main line crossover were lifted. The signal box was closed on 8 Apr. 1962.

The scaled diagram of the halt has been included here for the record, the only feature to be noted being that each platform has only one ramp, that nearest the road overbridge, with which each platform was footpath-connected.

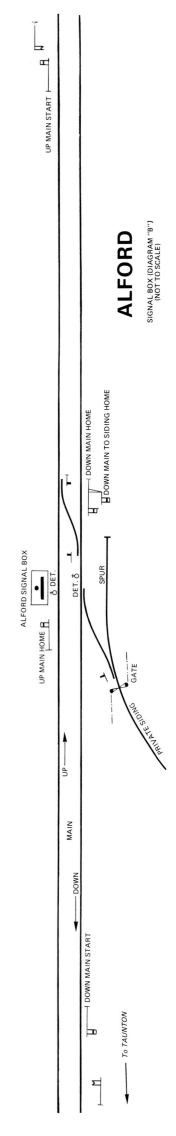

To CASTLE CARY →

UP MAIN START

ALFORD SIGNAL BOX

UP MAIN HOME

DET.

DET.

DOWN MAIN HOME

DOWN MAIN TO SIDING HOME

SPUR

GATE

PRIVATE SIDING

UP →

MAIN

← DOWN

DOWN MAIN START

← To TAUNTON

ALFORD

SIGNAL BOX (DIAGRAM "B")
(NOT TO SCALE)

ANDOVERSFORD & DOWDESWELL

Origin: M. & S.W. Jc. (Absorbed into G.W.R. in the 1923 grouping)
Opened: 1 Aug. 1891 (P) (as Dowdeswell until 1 Oct. 1892)
16 Mar. 1891 (G)
Closed: To passengers—1 April 1927
To goods—15 Oct. 1962
Plan date: 9 Dec. 1921

From December 1950, the yard was used as a coal depot only.
Until 1 October 1904, no M. & S.W. Jc. trains called at Andoversford Junction station, ½ mile north, and then only a few right down to Nationalisation. Andoversford & Dowdeswell never handled a great deal of passenger traffic, and it was one of the first casualties after grouping in the matter of station closures, but the tracks in the yard (and one track of the main line) remained in use for goods traffic down to 1962, supplementing siding accommodation at the Junction station. Full details relating to this and connections to the G.W. line at Andoversford Junction can be found in the first volume of this series.

The line south of the station to Cirencester (incl.) was singled from 8 July 1928.

The station was situated on a ruling gradient of 1 in 110 (falling) from Andoversford Junction as far as Withington.

FURTHER READING

R. Mag. 1932 (Vol. 70) pp. 157–166 H.A.P.M. Pos.
"The Midland & South Western Junction Railway" by T. B. Sands, Oakwood Press
"The Midland & South Western Junction Railway" by Colin Maggs, D. & C.
"Midland & South Western Junction Railway Time Tables" 12 July 1915 (Reprint) O.P.C.

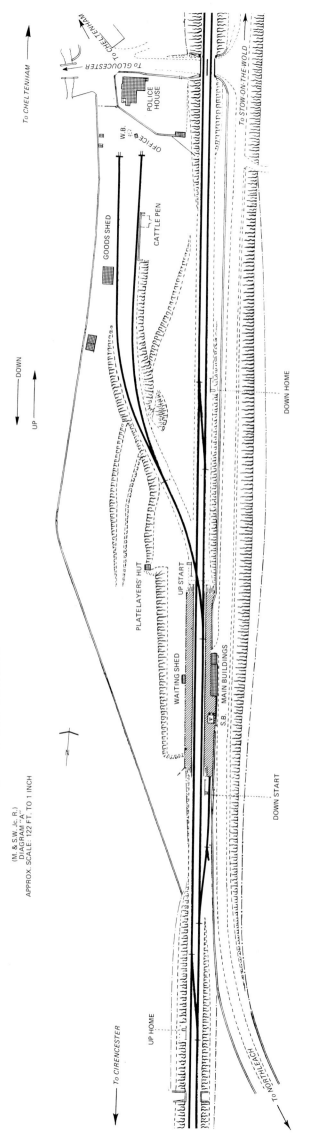

ANDOVERSFORD & DOWDESWELL

(M & S.W. Jc. R.)
DIAGRAM "A"
APPROX. SCALE: 122 FT. TO 1 INCH

AVONWICK

Origin:	Great Western Railway (by absorption of the Kingsbridge & Salcombe Rly. in 1888)
Opened:	19 Dec. 1893
Closed:	16 Sept. 1963 (P)
	11 June 1956 (G)
Plan date:	30 Dec. 1914

The station became unstaffed at the same time as goods services were withdrawn. The connection into the siding at the station end of the siding, together with the adjacent ground frame, was removed on 3 April 1955 and the siding itself, including the north end connection and cattle pen spur, was lifted on 5 Dec. 1956.

The station was the first out of Brent at 2m. 44c. therefrom and there was a ruling gradient on this section of 1 in 50 (falling), passenger and mixed trains being allowed 6 or 7 minutes, and the goods trains 9 minutes (1938), in the down direction. In the up direction, passenger trains were timed in 8 minutes, and goods trains 10 minutes. These timings refer to regular timetabled trains, not necessarily to special workings.

The branch was worked (1938) by Electric Train Staff with one crossing place (at Gara Bridge) and the maximum speed allowed was 35 m.p.h. in each direction.

It is interesting to note that at this period "A truck of cattle may be sent from Kingsbridge on any Passenger Train for Brent at which station it will be transferred to a Goods Train." (Quoted from the 1938 working time book.)

The maximum permitted loads on the branch in each direction for the undermentioned classes of engines were as follows:

44XX; 45XX; 55XX—200 tons

0-6 0; 0-6-0T; 0-6-0T ("A" group)—144 tons

2-4-0T (Metro); 0-4-2T; 48XX; 58XX; 898, 900, 908—120 tons

FURTHER READING

T.I. 1958 pp. 94—97 H.A.P.

"Reg. Hist. of the Railways of G.B." Vol. 1 (The West Country) by D. St.J. Thomas. Phoenix

Avonwick. Kingsbridge train in the platform. Note the spotless appearance of the engine, c.1900.

Lens of Sutton

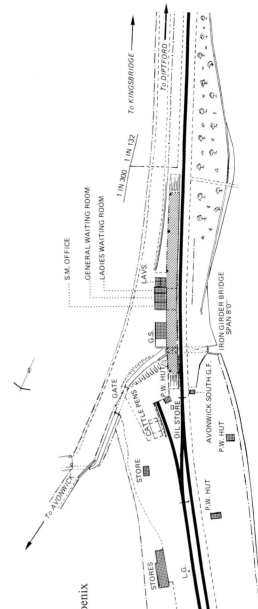

AVONWICK

Barmouth. Looking South, showing platform-side of main buildings.

Lens of Sutton

BARMOUTH

Origin: Cambrian Railways
(by absorption of the Aberystwyth & Welsh Coast Railway on 5 July 1865)

Opened: 3 June 1867 (P)
10 Oct. 1867 (G)

Closed:

Plan date: c. 1921

Barmouth found room for itself between the sheer rock face of a mountain behind it, and the sea, years before the railway appeared from around the northern corner of the Mawddach estuary, and it was wise to let it in, for the town's future prosperity as a "popular holiday resort" was assured. The Cambrian Railways (from the late 1880's onwards), and latterly the G.W.R. did brisk business from its holiday and day-tripper traffic around the Welsh coast, and developed stations' accommodation accordingly. In the case of Barmouth there were long platforms (and later, a specially long platform in addition, to provide for excursion trains), and the under-cover accommodation for passengers was by no means 'skimped'. The main buildings were on the 'up' side with the usual offices, and a verandah roof over the platforms for the whole length of these offices. On the 'down' side, there was a covered shelter nearly as long. The station itself could not have been nearer the town it served—or nearer to the sea, and the goods, cattle, coal, and stabling facilities made up in length what they were compelled to lack in width. Further-

more, at the time of preparing this book, the station is still there, though somewhat depleted in size and activity.

Although a signalled diagram of the north signal box layout has not become available to illustrate the later development of the sidings on the down side, this development nevertheless took place to cope with the peak summer periods of the years between the Wars.

Signal box opening hours for the two boxes were (1938) as follows:—

Barmouth South: Weekdays—6.30 a.m. until 10.25 p.m.
Sundays—9.0 a.m. to 7.25 p.m. with a break between 10.15 a.m. and 1.0 p.m.

Barmouth North: Weekdays—6.10 a.m. until 10.20 p.m.
Sundays—(the same as for the South box.)

The Sunday opening times during August were adjusted for the passage of goods trains.

FURTHER READING

R. & T.M. 1916 (June) pp. 353—357 D.A.P. Pos.
R. Mag. 1927 (Vol. 61) pp. 89—97 H.A.P.M. Pos.
R. Mag. 1932 (Vol. 71) pp. 27—34 D.A.P.M. Pos.
"The Cambrian Railways" (2 Vols.) by Rex Christiansen & R. W. Miller, David & Charles
"The Cambrian Railways" by R. W. Kidner, Oakwood Press

12

BARMOUTH

SIGNAL BOX
DIAGRAM "B"
(NOT TO SCALE)

TO DIAGRAM "A" (2)

UP MAIN TO SPUR START

To MORFA MAWDDACH

SPUR

(FXD)

UP EXCN. LINE START
TO UP MAIN

UP MAIN ADV. ST.

DOWN MAIN TO EXCN. LINE HOME

DOWN MAIN HOME

UP

MAIN

DOWN

EXCURSION PLATFORM

UP MAIN START

C.O.

DOWN MAIN INNER HOME

L.C.

UP MAIN HOME

SLOTTED BY NORTH S.B.

C.O.

To BARMOUTH NORTH S.B.

(FXD)

(FXD)

BARMOUTH

DIAGRAM "A" (1)
APPROX. SCALE: 120FT. TO 1 INCH

To HARLECH

N

COUNTY SCHOOLS

GAS WORKS

GAS HOLDER

STABLES ETC.

PACKERS' HUT

SIG.

PARK ROAD

FOOT BRIDGE

MARINE ROAD

S.B.

SIG.

SIG.

CATTLE PENS

WHARVES

GOODS SHED

SIG.

Barmouth.

General view through the station looking South, showing track layout. June 1949.

R.H. Clark

BARMOUTH

DIAGRAM "A" (2)
APPROX. SCALE: 130 FT. TO 1 INCH

To BARMOUTH JUNCTION

PACKERS' HUT

CHAPEL

JUBILEE ROAD

HORSE & CARRIAGE LOADING DOCK

SIG.

SUPPORTING WALL

DRINKING TROUGH

CHAPEL

CHAPEL

BEACH ROAD

CHAPEL

S.B.

TEA ROOM

WAITING SHELTER

LLANABER ROAD

SCHOOLS

CAB STAND

MAIN BUILDINGS

GATES

PORTERS' ROOM,LUGGAGE DOCK

W.B.

T.T.

TO DIAGRAM "A" (1)

13

BASCHURCH

Origin:	Shrewsbury & Chester Railway (Absorbed by G.W.R.)
Opened:	16 Oct. 1848
Closed:	12 Sept. 1960 (P)
	5 July 1965 (G)
	(Coal depot from 15 March 1965 to closure)
Plan date:	c. 1912

Baschurch was opened with the standard gauge line between Shrewsbury and Gobowen. It was a 'plain' station, the main buildings being devoid of a platform canopy of any kind, while the small building on the 'up' side had a half-width canopy attached to it. The goods yard seemed to be unnecessarily spacious as can be seen from Diagram "A", with ample dock and cattle-pen accommodation, and a through-road goods shed nearby, on the same road. This road had connections at both ends to the main line, a peculiar feature

being the siting of the cattle pens immediately opposite the lead trailing into the down main, but there was fair dock-length towards the station. In addition there were (at the period of Diagram "A") two long sidings, one of which was a crane-road. Both these sidings had disappeared by the period of Diagram "B", which was post World War 2.

Baschurch signal box opening hours in 1938 were:—

Sunday (evening) 8.40 p.m. until 7.0 a.m. the following Sunday morning, re-opening at 8.50 a.m. (Sunday) until 7.20 p.m. with a break from 12.35 p.m. until 4.20 p.m. There was no switch provided.

It was the duty of the signalman to place the level crossing gates across the railway before signing off, and to put the signals at "danger". It was obligatory for either Shrewsbury (Coton Hill) or Chester to advise if any 'specials' were to be run.

FURTHER READING

R.W. 1963 pp. 363–372 H.A.P.M.

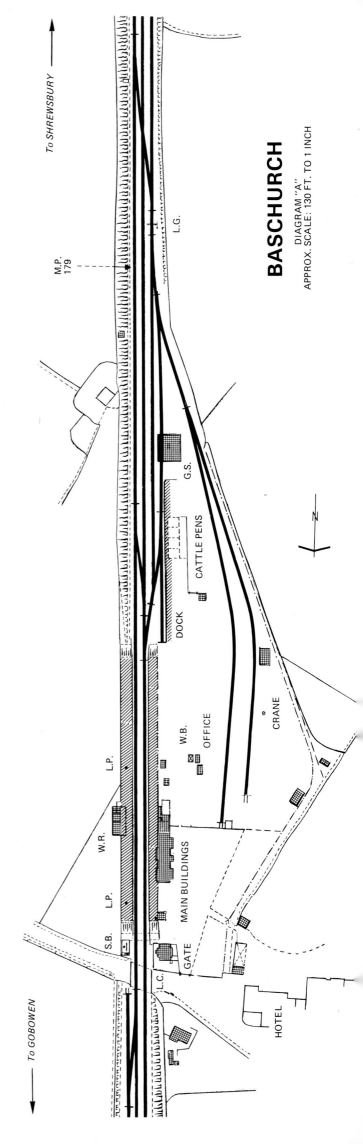

BASCHURCH

DIAGRAM "A"
APPROX. SCALE: 130 FT. TO 1 INCH

Baschurch. Looking towards Gobowen.
O.P.C.

BASCHURCH

DIAGRAM "B"
(NOT TO SCALE)

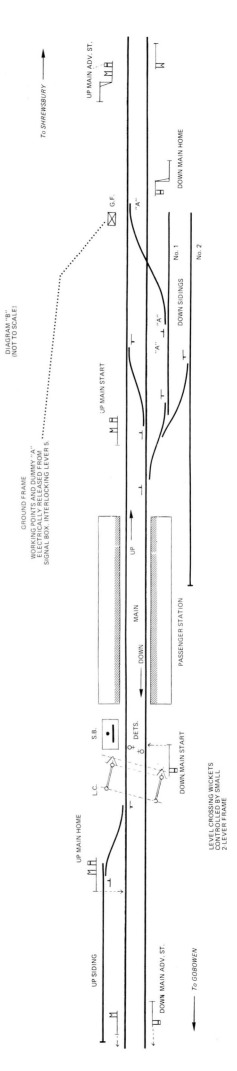

To SHREWSBURY →

UP MAIN ADV. ST.

DOWN MAIN HOME

G.F.

"A"

DOWN SIDINGS

No. 1

No. 2

"A" "A"

GROUND FRAME
WORKING POINTS AND DUMMY "A"
ELECTRICALLY RELEASED FROM
SIGNAL BOX INTERLOCKING LEVER 5.

UP MAIN START

UP

MAIN

DOWN

PASSENGER STATION

S.B.

L.C.

DETS.

DOWN MAIN START

LEVEL CROSSING WICKETS
CONTROLLED BY SMALL
2-LEVER FRAME

UP MAIN HOME

UP SIDING

DOWN MAIN ADV. ST.

← To GOBOWEN

BODMIN ROAD

Origin: Cornwall Railway
Leased from opening to G.W.R., B. & E., and S.D.R.
Absorbed by G.W.R. in 1889

Opened: 27 June 1859 (P)
2 Dec. 1859 (G)

Closed: 4 Nov. 1963 (G) to Public traffic.

Plan date: ("A") c. 1969 ("B") c. 1960

Lens of Sutton

Bodmin Road. Showing water tank and the goods shed, looking towards Lostwithiel.

Bodmin Road. Looking towards Penzance, 18 Aug. 1966. The train from Bodmin has just arrived and

John H. Meredith

Tucked in a fold of one of Cornwall's many wooded valleys, and on one of the tortuous bends which abound along the course of the main line between Plymouth and Penzance, Bodmin Road has an appeal of its own. Serving no particular town in its own right, one can feel remote and isolated when standing on its platforms, for it was essentially an exchange station between Bodmin and the rest of the G.W. Cornish system as far as the passenger was concerned, and for some of Bodmin's freight as well. Of the three leasing companies of the Cornwall Railway, the Great Western was by far the most dominating influence and, until economies had to be made in the Beeching era, every aspect of the station reflected that influence. Fortunately for posterity the station has been well documented and photographed down through the years, but I have yet to see a picture of it in broad gauge days. The Bodmin branch was opened on 27 May 1887.

While the station was in course of construction, a temporary station was used by passengers ¾ mile west (from the opening of the line on 4 May). The line from Doublebois to Bodmin Road was doubled and brought into use on 22 Dec. 1893, the section thence to Lostwithiel having been similarly doubled and used on 2 July 1893.

Before October 1892 there was no physical connection between the Bodmin branch and the main line. The siding to the clay works (beyond the goods shed) was not put in until after 1920.

The siding parallel to the goods shed road was lifted in Dec. 1966 and the shed road itself, together with the lead into the main line crossover, was taken out of use in March 1968, the crossover itself (at the western end of the platforms) becoming redundant in February of the following year.

FURTHER READING

R. Mag. 1902 (Vol. 11) pp. 441—447; 536—541 H.A.P. and G.P.
R. Mag. 1905 (Vol. 17) pp. 135—142 H.D.A.P.M. Pos. (including desc. of surrounding lines)

R. Mag. 1925 (Vol. 57) pp. 193—203 H.A.P.M. Pos.
R. Mag. 1955 p. 623 View of water tank and nameboard. Up "Cornish Riviera" approaching.
R. Mag. 1959 p. 689 Pos. (Branch platform)
"Reg. Hist. of the Railways of G.B." Vol. 1 (The West Country) by D. St.J. Thomas. Phoenix

"The Story of Cornwall's Railways" by A. Fairclough, Tor Mark Press, Truro
"The Railways of Cornwall 1809—1963" by C. R. Clinker, David & Charles

BODMIN ROAD

DIAGRAM "B"
(NOT TO SCALE)

UP MAIN START & CALLING ON

DOWN MAIN OUTER HOME & DIST.

DOWN MAIN INNER HOME

To LISKEARD

UP LOOP TO UP MAIN

UP LOOP TO SPUR

UP BRANCH TO SPUR START
UP BRANCH TO UP MAIN START

UP MAIN START

UP BRANCH TO SIDINGS START
DOWN BRANCH TO SIDINGS START

DOWN BRANCH START.

M.P. 274

DOWN — BRANCH — UP

MAIN

UP

F.B.

DOWN

S.B.

NOTE – DETONATORS WORKED BY SMALL 2 LEVER FRAME.

UP BRANCH TO PLAT HOME
UP BRANCH TO LOOP HOME

DOWN MAIN START

DOCK

CATTLE PENS

UP MAIN HOME

DOWN BRANCH ADV. ST.

To BODMIN

SIDINGS

U.M. DIST.

DOWN MAIN ADV. ST.

GATE

GOODS SHED

To PAR

BODMIN ROAD

DIAGRAM "A"
APPROX. SCALE : 120 FT. TO 1 INCH

To PLYMOUTH

To PLYMOUTH

17

CONTINUATION (NOT TO SCALE)

TANK

T.P.

SIG.

T.P.

T.P.

SIG. T.P.

M.P. 274

APPROACH ROAD

SIG.

C.P.

S.B.

S.B.

CYCLES.

C.P.

C.P.

WATER TANK

MAIN BUILDINGS

PORTER'S ROOM

GATE

DOCK

GATE

CATTLE PENS

SIG.

P.W. HUT

To BODMIN

GOODS SHED

To LOSTWITHIEL

Boncath. Looking towards Cardigan, showing the main building. 8 July 1958.

H.C. Casserley

Boncath. Looking towards Cardigan. General view of station.

Lens of Sutton

BONCATH

Origin:	Whitland & Cardigan Railway
	Absorbed by G.W.R. 1 Sept. 1886—(the day after the formal opening of the extension from Glogue)
Opened:	31 Aug. 1886 (P) (first passenger (excursion) ran over new line on
	10 Aug. 1885)
Closed:	10 Sept. 1962 (P)
	27 May 1963 (G)
Plan date:	2 June 1910 (Diagram "B" 1941)

For most country lovers, whether they be railway enthusiasts or not, there has always been a nostalgic appreciation for a remote branch railway, serving isolated communities near (and not so near) its winding route. The branch from Whitland to Cardigan was just such a branch.

Both Cardigan and Whitland were dealt with in the first volume of "G.W. Stations" and a sample (though not necessarily typical) intermediate station is not out of place in this book.

Boncath provides an example of a very modelable country station with up and down platform roads, goods siding with shed store, dock, crane and cattle pens, shunting necks and a siding to serve a private store. It also had a signal box which was a bit "nearer the ground" than some.

During the 30 years between the plans illustrated there were one or two alterations to the layout as can be seen, but the station and signal box remained faithful to their origins, as did the single lines beyond the road bridge and level crossing.

The signal box was (1938) open from 6.45 a.m. to the clearance of the last train, and was not provided with a switch.

The branch was worked by Electric Train Staff, with crossing stations at Cardigan Jc. (Whitland), Llanglydwen, Crymmych Arms, Boncath and Cardigan.

There was no Sunday service advertised in the summer of 1938.

FURTHER READING

R. Mag. 1952 pp. 481–485 H.A.P.M.
R. Mag. 1962 pp. 737–745 H.A.P.M.
"The Whitland & Cardigan Railway" by J. P. Morris, Oakwood Press
"Great Western Branch Lines, 1955–1965" by C. J. Gammell (Plate 91) O.P.C.

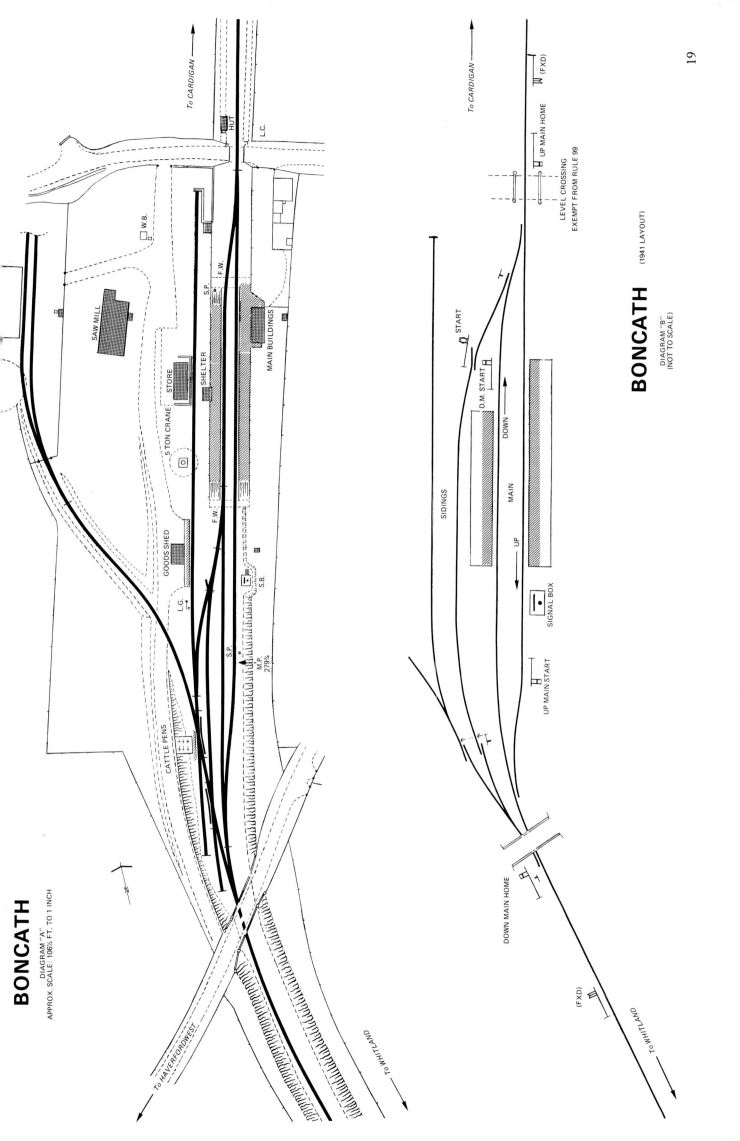

BONCATH

DIAGRAM "A"
APPROX. SCALE: 106½ FT. TO 1 INCH

To CARDIGAN →

HUT

L.C.

W.B.

SAW MILL

5 TON CRANE

STORE

SHELTER

S.P.

F.W.

MAIN BUILDINGS

F.W.

GOODS SHED

L.G.

S.B.

S.P.

M.P. 279¾

CATTLE PENS

N

To HAVERFORDWEST

To WHITLAND

BONCATH

(1941 LAYOUT)

DIAGRAM "B"
(NOT TO SCALE)

To CARDIGAN →

UP MAIN HOME

(FXD)

LEVEL CROSSING
EXEMPT FROM RULE 99

START

SIDINGS

D.M. START

DOWN

MAIN

UP

SIGNAL BOX

UP MAIN START

DOWN MAIN HOME

(FXD)

To WHITLAND

19

Lens of Sutton

Looking North.

Bourne End.

BOURNE END

Origin:	Wycombe Railway
	(Amalgamated with the G.W.R. 1 Feb. 1867)
Opened:	1 Aug. 1854 (as "Marlow Road" until Jan. 1874)
Closed:	11 Sept. 1967 (G)
Plan date:	c. 1915

Bourne End is on the section of the original Wycombe Railway, which ran between Maidenhead and High Wycombe. The northern part of this section, from Bourne End to High Wycombe (exclusive) was closed on 4 May 1970. The line was opened as broad gauge and was converted to standard gauge between the 23 Aug. and 1 Sept. 1870 (throughout from Maidenhead to Kennington Jc., Oxford).

The layout at Bourne End was unusual in that the 'up' platform was very much longer than the 'down', and that the Marlow branch platform was on a sharp curve. Also, that for such a small junction station, it was deemed necessary to have two signal boxes right down to 30 Jan. 1956, when the south signal box was closed. The north signal box was closed on 13 June 1971. The ground frame (see Diagram "B") was installed on 1 Feb. 1956. This lasted until 1968.

Rationalisation started early with the closure of the branch 'run-round' loop on 11 Dec. 1955, followed a week later by the modification of the branch connection to the main line, dispensing with the double junction and taking the outer curve of the branch direct into the down main (compare both diagrams). On 30 Jan. 1956 the crossover (opposite the south S.B.–Diagram "A") was lifted, and the up platform line trailed into the former 'down' (see Diagram "B"). Thereafter, down to the end of 1971, the layout dwindled until the station was reduced to its present form as a two road terminal with both roads converging to single line at the south end, and the Marlow branch trailing into the down platform line.

There was no switch provided in either signal box in 1938.

FURTHER READING

R. Mag. 1933 (Sept.) pp. 157–164 H.A.P.M. Pos. and (Nov.) pp. 321–326
R. Mag. 1972 p. 169 H. Para. Pos.

Bourne End. 0-4-2T No. 1442 (with W201) propelling a horse box onto a High Wycombe train. 30 July 1949.

John H. Meredith

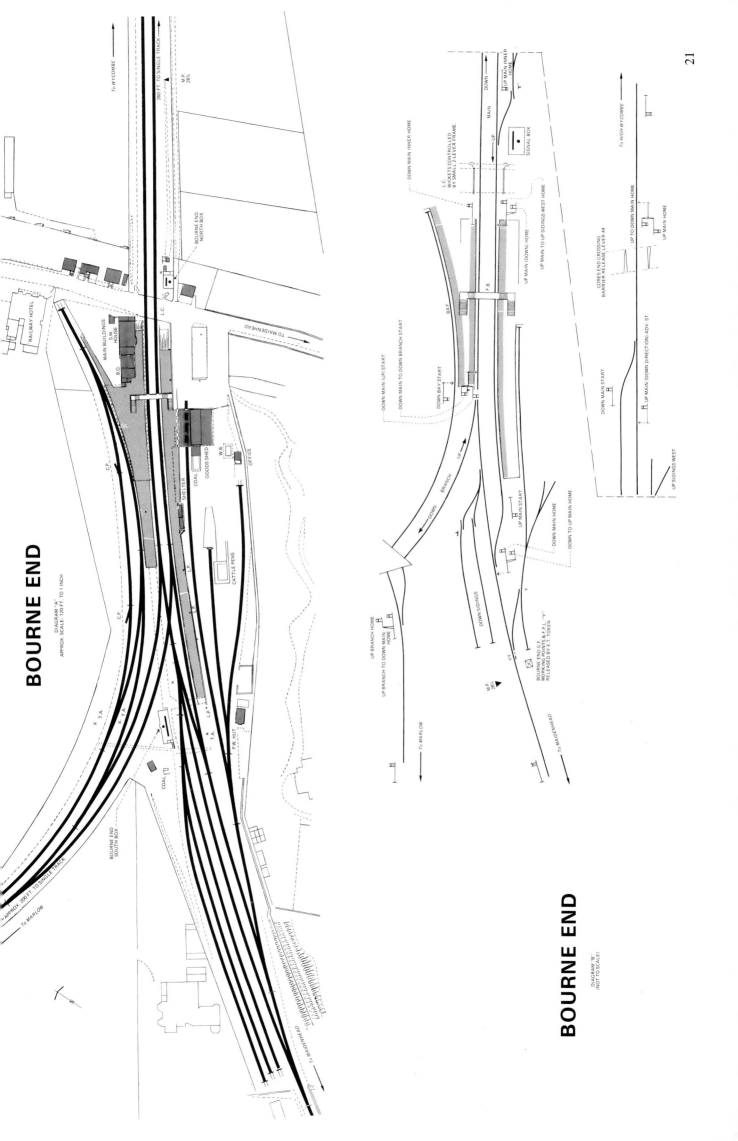

BOURNE END

DIAGRAM "A"
APPROX. SCALE: 120 FT. TO 1 INCH

To WYCOMBE →

260 FT. TO SINGLE TRACK

M.P.
28¾

BOURNE END
NORTH BOX

L.C.

TO MAIDENHEAD

RAILWAY HOTEL

MAIN BUILDINGS

S.M. HOUSE

B.O.

C.P.

C.P.

SHELTER

COAL

GOODS SHED

W.B.

OFFICE

CATTLE PENS

L.P.

L.P.

L.P.

X T.A.

X T.A.

X T.A.

P.W. HUT

COAL

BOURNE END
SOUTH BOX

APPROX. 200 FT. TO SINGLE TRACK

To MARLOW

TO MAIDENHEAD

BOURNE END

DIAGRAM "B"
(NOT TO SCALE)

DOWN MAIN INNER HOME

L.C.
WICKETS CONTROLLED
BY SMALL 2 LEVER FRAME.

MAIN

DOWN

UP

DOWN MAIN INNER
HOME

UP MAIN INNER
HOME

SIGNAL BOX

DOWN MAIN (UP) START

DOWN MAIN TO DOWN BRANCH START

DOWN BAY START

BAY

F.B

UP MAIN TO UP SIDINGS WEST HOME

UP MAIN (DOWN) HOME

DOWN BRANCH

DOWN

UP

UP MAIN START

UP MAIN INNER
HOME

DOWN MAIN HOME

DOWN TO UP MAIN HOME

UP BRANCH HOME

UP BRANCH TO DOWN MAIN
HOME

DOWN SIDINGS

Y

YY

M.P.
28¾

BOURNE END G.F.
WORKING POINTS & F.P.L. "Y"
RELEASED BY E.T. TOKEN

To MARLOW

M

M

To MAIDENHEAD

CORES END CROSSING
BARRIER RELEASE LEVER 44

UP TO DOWN MAIN HOME

UP MAIN HOME

To HIGH WYCOMBE →

DOWN MAIN START

UP MAIN (DOWN DIRECTION) ADV. ST.

UP SIDINGS WEST

BOX

Origin: G.W.R.
Opened: 30 June 1841
Closed: 4 Jan. 1965 (P)
10 June 1963 (G)

Plan date: 1908

The once attractive station of Box must have been one of Brunel's delights, for he built it in lavish style, beyond what one would deem necessary. No doubt its setting enhanced its architectural appeal as well as the coupling of the name with the famous tunnel about a mile towards the east. The station was built about the same distance from the tiny hamlet from which both station and tunnel took their names, and surely a more convenient site (for the passenger station at least) would have been where the subsequent "Mill Lane" halt was situated, between the tunnels?

The layout itself barely altered from late Victorian times to the 1960's rationalisation, except that in June 1898 the (then) East and West signal boxes were replaced by one on the up side platform, and the two platforms were slightly extended in the Bath direction. The short siding on the up side (just passing under Box Brook) was added prior to 1908 together with the double-slip and main line connection, and thereafter arrangements remained virtually static until the Beeching axe fell in the 1960's. The engine shed was closed on 24 Feb. 1919.

Box (Mill Lane) Halt (opened June 1930) was closed at the same time as withdrawal of passenger services from the main station, after a life of less than 35 years.

The 1938 working timetable (summer period) reveals the odd arrangement of the signal box being open from 8.0 p.m. on Sunday evenings until 6.0 a.m. the following Sunday morning. The box was provided with a switch.

FURTHER READING

R. Mag. 1908 (Vol. 22) p. 272 Pos.

Box. Looking towards Chippenham, exterior view of road approach and station building. *O.P.C.*

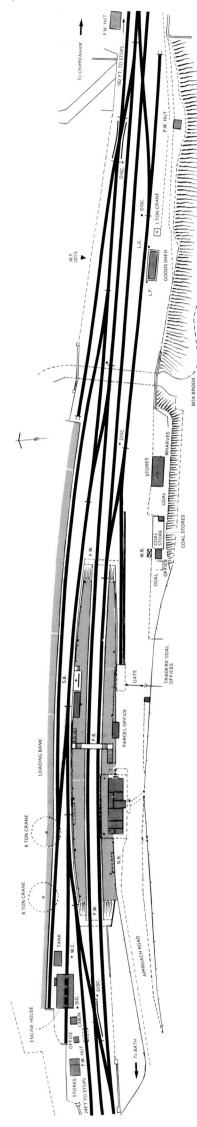

BOX

DIAGRAM "A"
APPROX. SCALE 120 FT. TO 1 INCH

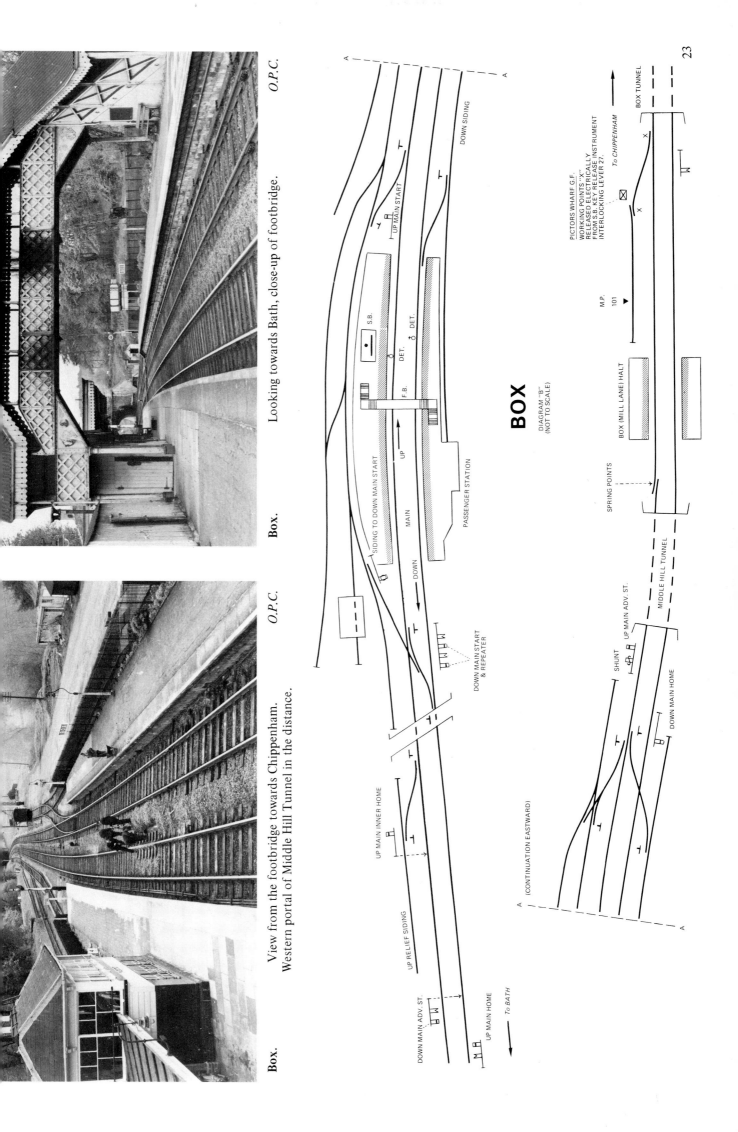

Box.   View from the footbridge towards Chippenham.   O.P.C.
Western portal of Middle Hill Tunnel in the distance.

Box.   Looking towards Bath, close-up of footbridge.   O.P.C.

DOWN MAIN ADV. ST.

UP RELIEF SIDING

UP MAIN HOME

UP MAIN INNER HOME

To BATH

DOWN MAIN START & REPEATER

SIDING TO DOWN MAIN START

UP MAIN START

DOWN SIDING

S.B.

F.B.

DET.

DET.

UP

MAIN

DOWN

PASSENGER STATION

A

A

A

BOX

DIAGRAM "B"
(NOT TO SCALE)

(CONTINUATION EASTWARD)

A

A

SHUNT

UP MAIN ADV. ST.

DOWN MAIN HOME

MIDDLE HILL TUNNEL

SPRING POINTS

BOX (MILL LANE) HALT

M.P.
101

PICTORS WHARF G.F.
WORKING POINTS "X"
RELEASED ELECTRICALLY
FROM S.B. KEY RELEASE INSTRUMENT
INTERLOCKING LEVER 27.

To CHIPPENHAM

BOX TUNNEL

X

X

23

24

Bradford-on-Avon. View taken in 1966 towards Freshford. *Lens of Sutton*

Bradford-on-Avon. Looking towards Freshford. *O.P.C.*

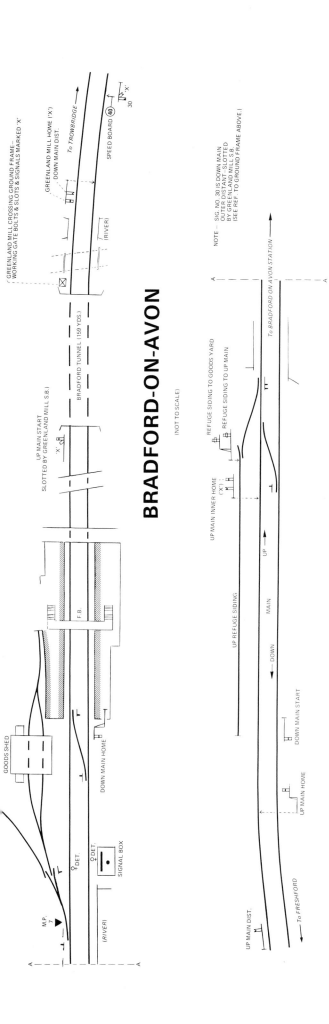

BRADFORD-ON-AVON

(NOT TO SCALE)

BRADFORD-ON-AVON

Origin: Great Western Railway (but see notes below)
Opened: 2 Feb. 1857 ("Bradford" until Jan 1899)
Closed: To goods—1 Nov. 1965 (Coal depot only from 2 Nov. 1964)

Although a suitable scaled plan has not yet become available for inclusion in this book, it was felt desirable to provide at least the layout arrangements and signalling based on the signal box diagram with a few comments.

The station really owes its origin to the Wilts, Somerset & Weymouth Railway who built it, and it was completed about 10 years before it was finally opened to passengers. In the meantime, the Wilts, Somerset & Weymouth Company was absorbed by the G.W.R. on 14 March 1850, and the station therefore became Great Western property on opening.

As might be expected, Bath stone was used in the construction of the station buildings which were attractive architecturally, and, unlike some other stations, adorned both platforms. The old 2-road goods shed (again of Bath stone) remained undisturbed for most of its life although the track layout around it altered with the development of traffic.

Sixteen months before public goods traffic was withdrawn, the goods shed lines were reduced to one track, and the two sidings at the rear (and nearest to) the shed became redundant. After the withdrawal of goods traffic the third siding at the rear, together with the other shed road became disused in Feb. 1966, and 5 months later, the same fate befell the up refuge siding and both the main line trailing crossovers. At the same time the signal box was closed.

The accompanying S.B. diagram dates from about 1946, and was current for many years before. In 1938, the box was open on weekdays from 5.30 a.m. to 9.30 p.m., and although a service is shown in the W.T.T., the box was evidently switched out on Sundays, the resultant section being between Freshford (dealt with in Book 1) and Bradford Junction boxes.

FURTHER READING

R. Mag. 1961 pp. 597—603; 640 H.A.P.M. Pos.
"Reg. Hist. of the Railways of G.B." Vol. 1 (The West Country)
by David St. John Thomas. Phoenix

BRECON
(Free Street)

Origin:	Brecon & Merthyr Railway
	Absorbed by G.W.R. in 1922
Opened:	1 Mar. 1871
Closed:	31 Dec. 1962 (P) Passenger only station
	4 May 1954 (G) Refers to WATTON goods depot.
Plan date:	c. 1914

The geographical location of the ancient town of Brecon determined its importance long before railways came anywhere near it, and a study of a road map will reveal that it is at the intersection of 5 main roads, the principal of which runs east/west from Abergavenny to Llandovery and to West Wales. It is not surprising, therefore, that at least 4 railway companies eventually tried to get their trains to it, for the potential rewards convinced the two principal competitors that the difficulties of building through the surrounding mountainous country were worthwhile.

The Brecon & Merthyr were first to arrive in May 1863, and accommodated their passengers at a 'temporary' station at Watton on the site of the later goods yard, and just below where they were to build the final "Free Street" station (which is the illustrated subject here). The Neath & Brecon were the next, who built their (also) 'temporary' terminus at Mount Street which they opened on 3 June 1867, afterwards making an end on junction with the B. & M. 12 chains eastward. With the opening of the Free Street station, Midland trains from Hereford (via Three Cocks Junction) began using the track and, later, on to Neath & Brecon metals from 2 July 1877. Mid-Wales trains used Free Street station from its opening as well.

This station cannot be said to be either attractive or imposing. Though it boasted two main platforms, an island and an eastward facing bay platform, the buildings (which also contained administrative offices, as well as the usual passenger rooms) were purely utilitarian with little pretence of architectural style. With the exception of a small arched canopy over the stretch of platform in front of the main buildings, none of the platforms were protected from the weather, and as the station was on higher ground than the town below, they could be bleak indeed.

The Neath & Brecon Railway closed their Mount Street station to passengers in 1874, using it for their own terminal goods traffic thenceforward down to Grouping.

Below the stations, extensive sidings on the Watton site appeared, and the yard included goods shed, engine shed, and offices, coaling stage and watering facilities.

A curious feature of the layout is the 50 ft. turntable, engine pit and the adjacent coaling stage on the short siding at the back of the station, all within a few feet of the end loading bank!

A further interesting historical note is that the Brecon & Merthyr Company had intended to extend their line west of Brecon to Devynock & Sennybridge, and thence through the gently graded valley to Llandovery, following the course of the main road, which would have given them lucrative access to West Wales.

Brecon station signal box was (1938) opened on weekdays at 5.55 a.m. and closed at 10.30 p.m. and was not provided with a switch. The box was closed on Sundays.

O.P.C.

Brecon. Looking West towards Devynock & Sennybridge.

FURTHER READING

R. Mag 1909 (Vol. 24) pp. 265–272 H.A.P.M. Pos. and grade profile of B. & M.
R. Mag. 1922 (Vol. 51) pp. 20; 110 (Loco & train working in latter part of 19th century)
R. Mag. 1939 (Vol. 85) pp. 185–190 H.A.P.M. Pos.
T.I. 1955 pp. 107–109 D.A.P. Pos.
R.W. 1956 pp. 73–79 H.A.P.M.
R. Mag. 1960 pp. 311–317; 375–381 H.A.P.M. Pos.
M.R.C. 1966 p. 327 Para. Track-layout (signalled), Pos. (3)
"The Brecon & Merthyr Railway" by D. S. M. Barrie, Oakwood Press
"Railway History in Pictures" Wales & Welsh Border by H. C. Casserley, D. & C.
"Great Western Engine Sheds—1947" by E. Lyons, Oxford Publishing Co.

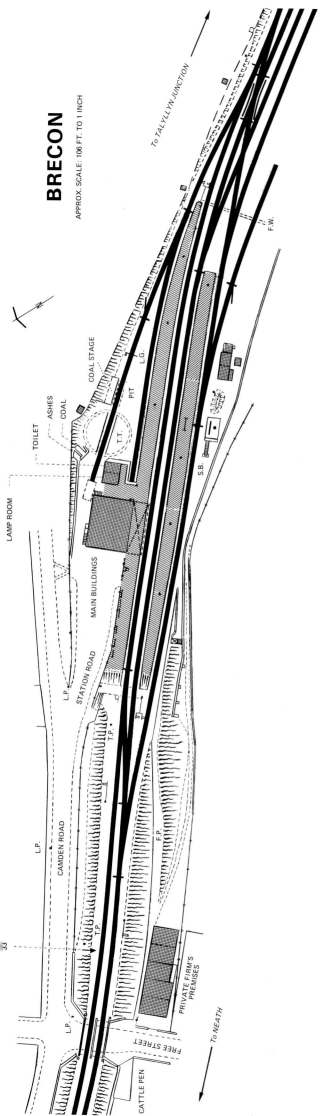

BRECON

APPROX. SCALE: 106 FT. TO 1 INCH

To TALYLLYN JUNCTION

COAL STAGE

TOILET

ASHES

COAL

LAMP ROOM

PIT

L.G.

T.T.

F.W.

S.B.

MAIN BUILDINGS

L.P.

STATION ROAD

T.P.

CAMDEN ROAD

L.P.

F.P.

T.P.

L.P.

PRIVATE FIRM'S PREMISES

To NEATH

FREE STREET

CATTLE PEN

33

Brecon. From platform looking East towards Talyllyn Junction.

O.P.C.

27

BRENT

Origin: South Devon Railway
(Absorbed by the Great Western Railway in 1878)

Opened: c. 1849
Closed: 5 Oct. 1964 (P)
6 Apr. 1964 (G)

Plan date: c. 1913 (Diagram "B" July 1950)

The South Devon Railway absorbed the Dartmouth & Torbay Railway in 1862, the South Devon & Tavistock in 1865, The Launceston & South Devon in 1869, and the Moretonhampstead & South Devon Railway in 1872.

Considering its geographical location in a thinly populated area of rural countryside on the fringe of Dartmoor, Brent was quite a substantial and well-appointed station, certainly by the time the Kingsbridge branch was opened in December 1893.

Undoubtedly the advent of this branch contributed to the station's prosperity, but also its own originating traffic warranted a more ambitious layout than its neighbouring stations westwards. For all that, however, the layout did not alter a great deal throughout the first 60 years of this century except that the "down" refuge siding (east of the station, and parallel to the main line), was converted to a loop with a facing connection into the down main line at its eastern extremity on 13 Apr. 1933. In August 1943 the loop was extended a short distance westward, and a connection put in to join the Kingsbridge branch, which gave direct access for both passenger and goods trains to the bay platform and yard from the loop without having to run via the former double slip on the "down" main.

The shed road and the parallel siding on the south side were taken out of use in July 1964, 3 months after the withdrawal of goods services. The Kingsbridge branch and the down loop referred to above were closed on 16 Sep. 1963, and the track was lifted in May of the following year. The remainder of the sidings and connections on the south side (including the bay platform loop), were taken out of use in March 1965, and the track was lifted 6 months later. The signal box remained open, though somewhat modified in its use and status until 17 Dec. 1973.

Before diesel units took over the branch, traction was provided by "45XX" and "55XX" 2-6-2T's hauling (in later steam days) a "B" set for passenger train working.

FURTHER READING

M.R.N. 1949 pp. 3—4, 8 D.A.P. Pos.(2)
T.I. 1954 p. 525 Pos.
R. Mag. 1958 p. 173 Pos.(2)
T.I. 1958 pp. 94—97 H.A.P. Pos.(3)
M.R.C. 1964 pp. 10—12 D.A.P. Pos.
"Reg. History of the Railways of G.B." Vol. 1. (The West Country) by D. St. J. Thomas.

Brent. An old view taken from the road bridge, looking west. Note the oil-lit platform lamps and the point "indicator" at the bottom left-hand. Probably taken at about the turn of the century. *Lens of Sutton*

Brent. A general view through the main line platforms *R.H. Clark*

BRENT

DIAGRAM "A"
APPROX. SCALE: 106 FT. TO 1 INCH

To TOTNES

To KINGSBRIDGE

To BUCKFASTLEIGH

M.P. 229¾

To PLYMOUTH

MAIN BUILDINGS

APPROACH ROAD

PUMP

L.P.

F.W.

LAMP HUT

CATTLE PENS

S.B.

OFFICE

GOODS SHED

DOCK

C.P.

F.B.

F.W.

KEY TO NUMBERED SIGNALS (S.B. LEVER NUMBERS)

5   UP BRANCH TO UP MAIN START
7   UP BRANCH START
59 SIDINGS START
61 DOWN BRANCH TO DOWN MAIN START
63 DOWN MAIN START
64 DOWN MAIN INNER HOME

BRENT

DIAGRAM "B"
(NOT TO SCALE)

To TOTNES

To KINGSBRIDGE

DOWN MAIN TO DOWN LOOP HOME

DOWN MAIN HOME

SPRING POINTS

UP

DOWN MAIN ADV. ST.

UP MAIN

DOWN LOOP

UP BRANCH ADV. START

BRANCH

DOWN

C.O.

R.I.   MAIN   51
        BRANCH 54
        SIDINGS 55

64

52

DOWN BRANCH HOME

DOWN BRANCH TO SIDINGS HOME

SELECTED BY 52

SELECTED BY 37

35

37

UP MAIN START

PASSENGER STATION

S.B.

DETS.

F.B.

F.B.

NO.1 SIDING

NO.2 SIDING

GOODS SHED

DOCK

BRANCH

CATTLE PENS SIDING

59

61

63

5

7

A

A

UP LOOP TO UP MAIN START

UP MAIN INNER HOME

(CONTINUATION WESTWARDS)

A

A

UP LOOP

UP MAIN HOME

DOWN MAIN ADV. START

UP MAIN TO UP LOOP HOME

SPRING POINTS

To PLYMOUTH

29

Bridport.   Main building on the up platform towards Maiden Newton.   *Lens of Sutton*

BRIDPORT

Origin:	Bridport Railway
	(Absorbed by G.W.R. in 1901)
Opened:	12 Nov. 1857
Closed:	5 May 1975 (P) (Last train ran on 3 May 1975)
	5 Apr. 1965 (G)
Plan date:	c. 1912

As can be seen from Diagram "A", the station was an odd shape, with the station buildings and signal box in a straight line with each other, and the platforms and track curving away southward towards West Bay. The 'down' platform was not opened until 1894, when substantial rebuilding was undertaken, and both platforms were given ample coverage by well balanced canopies. At this time a new signal box was provided, and the down loop (behind the platforms) was opened. On 20 Oct. 1913, the down platform was widened.

A few years before Diagram "A", the short dock siding at the south end was installed and the double slip near the engine shed, the adjacent single-slip and connection to the 'up' main line were removed in favour of a shed road to down loop connection (single-slip) and a new connection northward into the up main. At the same time a continuation of the up main to the adjacent up siding was put in, leaving the old connection from the up main into single line, as a crossover.

On 8 June 1965, all sidings, including the goods and engine shed roads, and the 'down' main through the station, were disused, and the signal box was closed. The engine shed itself had been closed in June 1959.

In 1938 (summer period), the single line branch from Maiden Newton was worked by Electric Train Staff, and Bridport signal box was opened for the first train, and closed when the last train had cleared (weekdays). The box was closed on Sundays and was not provided with a switch.

FURTHER READING

R. Mag. 1920 (Vol. 47) pp. 241–244   H.A.P.M. Pos.
T.I.   1954 p. 349 Historical article
R.W.   1955 pp. 10–12   D.AP. Pos.
R. Mag. 1957 pp. 747–751   H.A.P.M. Pos.
R. Mag. 1962 p. 71 Historical paragraph
R. Mag. 1970 p. 621 Pos.
R. Mod. 1972 p. 147 (Full signal box diagram)
"The Bridport Branch" by B. L. Jackson & M. J. Tattershall,   O.P.C.
"G.W. Branch Lines 1955–1965" by C. J. Gammell   O.P.C.
"G.W. Engine Sheds—1947" by E. Lyons   O.P.C.

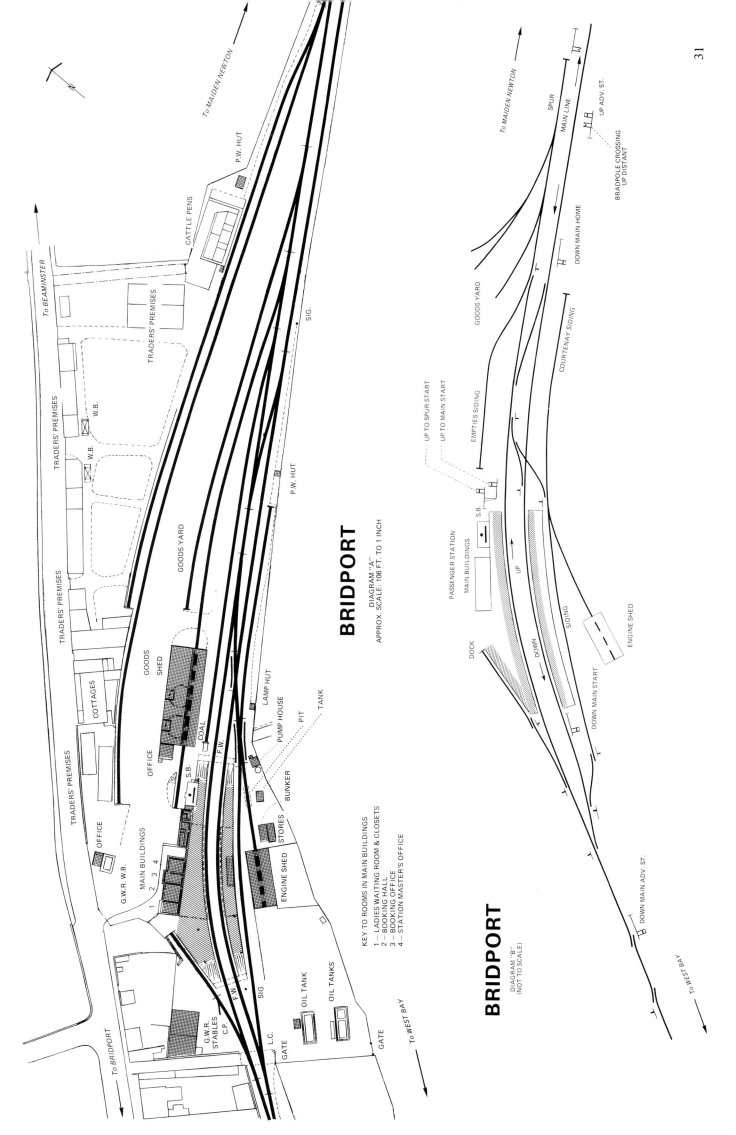

BRIDPORT

DIAGRAM "A"
APPROX. SCALE: 106 FT. TO 1 INCH

KEY TO ROOMS IN MAIN BUILDINGS

1 — LADIES WAITING ROOM & CLOSETS
2 — BOOKING HALL
3 — BOOKING OFFICE
4 — STATION MASTER'S OFFICE

BRIDPORT

DIAGRAM "B"
(NOT TO SCALE)

BRIXHAM

Origin: Torbay & Brixham Railway
(Absorbed by G.W.R. in 1883)
Opened: 28 Feb. 1868 (P)
1 May 1868 (G)
Closed: 13 May 1963
Plan date: 4 Jan. 1910

The 2m. 1c. branch from Churston to Brixham must be one of the shortest branches on the G.W. system as it was. In fact, had Brixham not been a fishing port of some importance it is doubtful if the little line would ever have been built, for there were many towns and villages which were more than 2 miles from a railway, and from the stations which bore their name, even from early times.

The station itself was a small 'squat' affair and neat without architectural embellishments, and the layout provided reasonable accommodation for the traffic it handled. Perhaps it might be expected that a town of Brixham's size deserved a more elaborate rail terminal, but it had always enjoyed good road communication with the outside world, and being above the town it was not totally convenient for its passengers.

The little engine shed was closed from 22 July 1929, but the track remained as a siding, the lead thereto being transferred to the 'down' road in Dec. 1931. This siding was eventually lifted in Sept. 1959.

In 1938, the branch was worked by Electric Train Token, and an interesting feature was that on approaching both Brixham and Churston, all trains had to draw to a stand at each station's home signal before proceeding to the respective termini.

For just over a mile and a quarter, the line rose at 1 in 95 from Churston, and thereafter fell at 1 in 79 to Brixham.

Brixham signal box was opened on weekdays for the first train and closed after the last train had cleared, and was not provided with a switch. The box was opened on Sundays as required.

FURTHER READING

R. Mag. 1963 p. 483 Pos.
"Reg. Hist. of the Railways of G.B." Vol. 1. (The West Country)
by D. St. J. Thomas. Phoenix

Brixham. Towards terminus.
O.P.C.

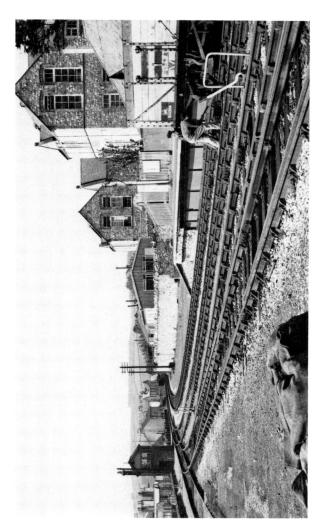

Brixham.
View of rail approach looking towards Churston.
O.P.C.

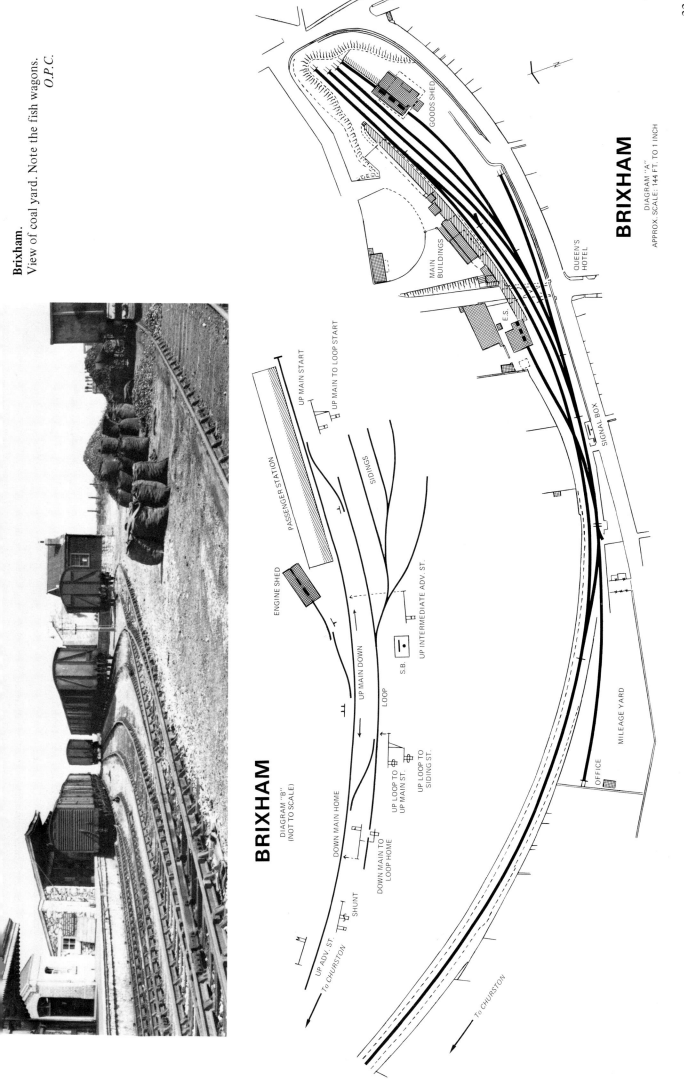

Brixham.
View of coal yard. Note the fish wagons.
O.P.C.

BRIXHAM

DIAGRAM "A"
APPROX. SCALE: 144 FT. TO 1 INCH

GOODS SHED

MAIN BUILDINGS

E.S.

QUEEN'S HOTEL

SIGNAL BOX

MILEAGE YARD

OFFICE

To CHURSTON

BRIXHAM

DIAGRAM "B"
(NOT TO SCALE)

PASSENGER STATION

ENGINE SHED

UP MAIN START

UP MAIN TO LOOP START

SIDINGS

UP INTERMEDIATE ADV. ST.

S.B.

UP MAIN DOWN

LOOP

UP LOOP TO UP MAIN ST.

UP LOOP TO SIDING ST.

DOWN MAIN HOME

DOWN MAIN TO LOOP HOME

UP ADV. ST.

SHUNT

To CHURSTON

33

Bruton. A close view of main buildings on the up side. May 1966. *R.H. Clark*

Bruton. Looking West towards Castle Cary. May 1966. *R.H. Clark*

Bruton. Looking East towards Witham in May 1966. *R.H. Clark*

BRUTON

Origin:	Great Western Railway (who had absorbed the Wilts., Somerset & Weymouth Railway in 1851)
Opened:	1 Sept. 1856
Closed:	5 Apr. 1965 (G)
Plan date:	1908

Lying as it does, on the 10 mile long Brewham bank with gradients of 1 in 93 on the eastern end, and 1 in 98 westward, Bruton usually provided an opportunity to witness some high speed in the 'down' direction, and some spectacular exhausts in the 'up' direction.

Although the station was in a rural and thinly populated area, its stone buildings were large and strong in construction with obvious intent to "last for ever".

The sidings layout behind the signal box on the 'down' side was revised c. 1912.

The track through the goods shed, and connection into the up main line near the platform end was removed the same year as withdrawal of goods traffic (1965), the connections at the western end having been taken out in Dec. 1963.

The down refuge siding was extended in Sept. 1896 and further extended in October 1906. It was lifted in Dec. 1963.

The signal box was (1938) open from 6.0 a.m. on Mondays to 6.0 a.m. Sunday mornings, and reopened at 11.0 a.m. to close at 7.0 p.m., and *was* provided with a switch.

The passenger station became an unstaffed halt from 6 Oct. 1969.

FURTHER READING

"A Reg. Hist. of the Railways of Great Britain" Vol. 1. (The West Country) by D. St. J. Thomas. Phoenix

BRUTON

DIAGRAM "A"
APPROX. SCALE: 140.8 FT. to 1 INCH

To WITHAM

M.P. 126

DITCH

OCCUPATION BRIDGE

F.W.

F.W.

MAIN BUILDINGS

SHELTER

F.B.

F.W.

S.B.

DOCK

CATTLE PEN

OFFICE

G.S.

STATION APPROACH

CRANE

STABLES

W.B.

OFFICE

GATE

GATE

PUMP HOUSE

To CASTLE CARY

N

BRUTON

DIAGRAM "B"
(NOT TO SCALE)

To FROME

UP MAIN ADV. ST.

M.P. 126

DOWN MAIN HOME

DOWN REFUGE SIDING

C.P.

UP MAIN START

PASSENGER STATION

UP

MAIN

DOWN

F.B.

DET.

DET.

S.B.

GOODS SHED

DOWN MAIN START

DOWN SIDINGS

UP MAIN HOME

C.P.

C.P.

DOWN MAIN ADV. ST.

To CASTLE CARY

DETONATORS WORKED
BY SMALL 2-LEVER FRAME

35

Buckfastleigh. General view through the station towards Ashburton. August 1956.

Buckfastleigh. Looking towards Totnes through the station.

R.H. Clark

Lens of Sutton

BUCKFASTLEIGH

Origin: Buckfastleigh, Totnes & South Devon Railway. Worked by the South Devon Railway until that company became part of G.W.R. in 1878. (Absorbed by G.W.R. on 1 July 1897).

Opened: 1 May 1872 (opened throughout to Ashburton). Trains used station from 1868.

Closed: 3 Nov. 1958 (P)
10 Sept. 1962 (G)
Re-opened by Dart Valley Railway Co. on 5 Apr. 1969 (formal opening by Lord Beeching on 21 May 1969).

Plan date: 1912

Thanks to the enterprise of the Dart Valley Railway Preservation Society, Buckfastleigh station continues to thrive as the northern terminus of the branch from Totnes.

The Totnes-Ashburton branch was built as broad gauge and was converted to standard gauge on 23 May 1892.

Down to the time of official closure, the layout at Buckfastleigh had altered little, except that the former double-slip at the Ashburton end had been replaced by a hand-operated lead into the far siding, and a box-operated crossover connection to the main line.

The branch was worked by South Devon Block Telegraph instruments and Train Staff & Ticket, with Staff Stations at Totnes, Buckfastleigh and Ashburton. Staverton was an intermediate Block Post. Two goods trains, or passenger and goods, were allowed to cross at Buckfastleigh "when absolutely necessary" (quoting instructions to staff) provided that the passenger train was held at the main platform.

The signal box hours were (1938): Weekdays— 7.50 a.m. to 9.15 p.m. (11.15 p.m. Sats.), and was closed on Sundays. The box was not provided with a switch.

The loop and main line to the left of Diagram "A" converge a short distance beyond the limit shown.

FURTHER READING

R. Mag. 1913 (Vol. 32) p. 133 H. paragraph
R. Mod. 1950 p. 217
R. Mag. 1955 p. 809 H. Paragraph
R.W. 1957 p. 174 H. Paragraph
R.W. 1966 pp. 396–399 H.D.A.P.M. Pos.
R.M. 1969 pp. 372–374 H.D.A.M. (description of re-opening by Lord Beeching.)
"Reg. History of the Railways of G.B." Vol. 1. (The West Country) by D. St. J. Thomas. Phoenix

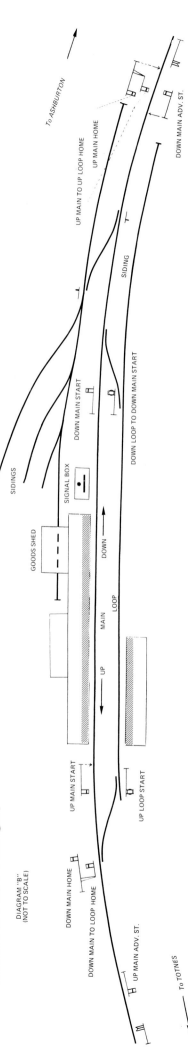

BUCKFASTLEIGH

DIAGRAM "A"
APPROX. SCALE: 120 FT. TO 1 INCH

RIVER DART

To ASHBURTON

S.M. OFFICE
PARCELS OFFICE
BOOKING OFFICE
GENERAL WAITING ROOM
LADIES WAITING ROOM
GENTS. LAV.
STORES

To BUCKFASTLEIGH

N

S.M. HOUSE

L.P.

DOCK

L.P.

DOCK

DOCK

G.S.

W.B.

5 TON CRANE
RAD. 12'0"

SAND BUNKER

30 CWT TRUCK CRANE
RAD. 12'0"

P.W. HUT

SIG.

SIG.

SIG.

LG

SIG.

SIG.

S.B.

M.P.
7

SIG.

To TOTNES

BUCKFASTLEIGH

DIAGRAM "B"
(NOT TO SCALE)

To ASHBURTON

UP MAIN TO UP LOOP HOME

UP MAIN HOME

DOWN MAIN ADV. ST.

SIDING

SIDINGS

GOODS SHED

SIGNAL BOX

DOWN MAIN START

DOWN LOOP TO DOWN MAIN START

UP

MAIN

DOWN

LOOP

UP MAIN START

UP LOOP START

DOWN MAIN HOME

DOWN MAIN TO LOOP HOME

UP MAIN ADV. ST.

To TOTNES

CAMERTON

Origin: Bristol & North Somerset
(Absorbed by G.W.R. in 1884)
Opened: 1 Mar. 1882
Closed: 21 Sept. 1925 (P)
15 Feb. 1951 (G)
Plan date: 23 June 1910

Camerton station will be remembered by older readers as being the one used in the filming of "The Ghost Train" in the early 1930's, and it is interesting to note that the station at Monkton Combe, at the other end of this 1909 rail link between Limpley Stoke and Hallatrow, was used 20 years later for filming "The Titfield Thunderbolt".

The whole station at Camerton did not alter hardly at all from the time that the line was opened to Limpley Stoke until total closure, and even 5 years after passenger services ceased, a reliable contemporary source states that everything was still complete, including all signals, brick-built signal box (opened on 3 May 1910 and replaced by two

ground frames from 23 Feb. 1938), buildings and platform. The same source states that there were no facing point locks.

The Limpley Stoke and Hallatrow branch was worked by electric tablet.
Camerton Colliery closed on 15 Apr. 1950. The last train on the branch ran on 14 Feb. 1951 and consisted of a Dean 0-6-0 (No. 2444) and three vans and brake.

FURTHER READING

R. Mag. 1911 (Vol. 29) pp. 33–37
R. Mag. 1953 (Vol. 99) pp. 163–167; 193 (Filming the "Titfield Thunderbolt")
R. Mag. 1953 (Vol. 99) pp. 265–269 H.A.P.M. Pos.
R. World 1965 pp. 309–311 H.A.P. Pos.
"The Somerset Coal Canal and Railways" by K. R. Chew, David & Charles
"Reg. Hist. of the Railways of Great Britain" Vol. 1. (The West Country) by D. St. J. Thomas. Phoenix

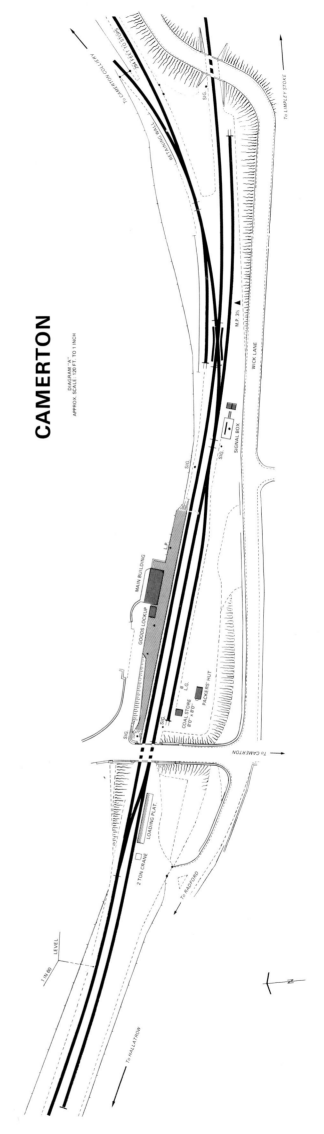

CAMERTON

DIAGRAM "A"
APPROX. SCALE: 120 FT. TO 1 INCH

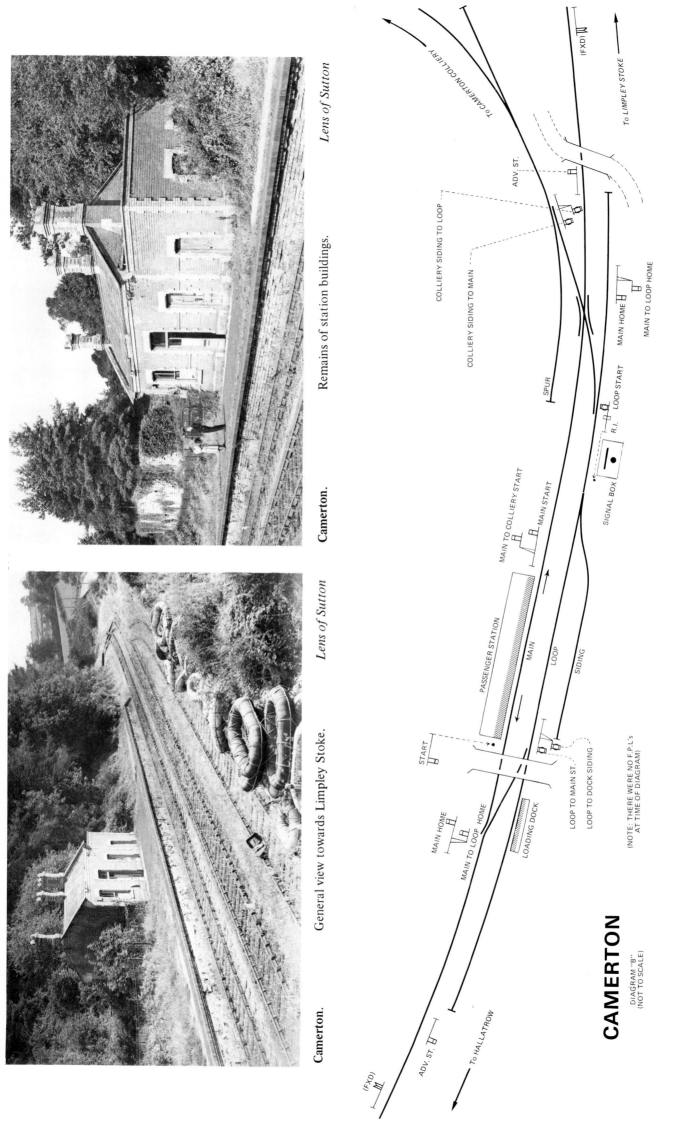

Camerton.   *Lens of Sutton*   Remains of station buildings.

Camerton.   *Lens of Sutton*   General view towards Limpley Stoke.

CAMERTON

DIAGRAM "B"
(NOT TO SCALE)

(NOTE: THERE WERE NO F.P.L.'s
AT TIME OF DIAGRAM)

To CAMERTON COLLIERY

To LIMPLEY STOKE

ADV. ST.

COLLIERY SIDING TO LOOP

COLLIERY SIDING TO MAIN

SPUR

MAIN HOME

MAIN TO LOOP HOME

LOOP START

R.I.

SIGNAL BOX

MAIN TO COLLIERY START

MAIN START

PASSENGER STATION

MAIN

LOOP

SIDING

START

MAIN HOME

MAIN TO LOOP HOME

LOADING DOCK

LOOP TO MAIN ST.

LOOP TO DOCK SIDING

ADV. ST.

To HALLATROW

(FXD)

(FXD)

Carmarthen. A view through the station in Edwardian days.

H.C. Casserley Collection

Carmarthen. Looking South towards the junction.

Lens of Sutton

CARMARTHEN

Origin: Carmarthen & Cardigan Railway
(Absorbed by the Great Western Railway 22 Aug. 1881)

Opened: 1860 (1st. station)
1902 (2nd. station) —but see notes.

Closed: —

Plan date: c. 1912

The South Wales Railway was extended as a broad gauge single line from Pembrey to a temporary railhead near the later Carmarthen Junction on 11 Oct. 1852, and further extended to Haverfordwest (as a broad gauge single line with Barlow rails) on 2 Jan. 1854. The line was doubled on 1 July 1857. The South Wales station was named "Carmarthen" until 1 July 1860 when the Carmarthen & Cardigan Company opened the first part of its line from the South Wales line to Conwil, when the station then became "Carmarthen Junction". The first station of the former Carmarthen & Cardigan Railway, near the town, was closed on 1 July 1902 when a new station was opened about a ¼ mile south. Carmarthen Junction station was closed to passengers on 27 Sept. 1926, and to goods on 7 June 1965.

Diagram "A" shows the passenger station layout and northern rail approach, and Diagram "B" shows the signalled layout from the south. The complementary diagrams have not (so far) been obtainable, but certain modifications which occurred in the inter-

At the time of the scaled survey illustrated, the modest buildings on the 'up' side, had no canopy attached, and the platform was otherwise bare and wide, but in contrast, the main buildings (which were long and substantial), on the 'down' side helped to support a full width canopy, extending well beyond their normal limit as far as the first step of the footbridge.

In later years, the level crossing was replaced by a road-overbridge, but the date of this is not known. The track down the middle, between the platform lines could be used as a passing loop for either lines, for freight trains—the "middle" siding on Diagram "B".

Carmarthen Station signal box was (1938) open from 3.50 a.m. Mondays, until 8.10 a.m. on the following Sunday morning, re-opening at 11.0 a.m. until 10.0 p.m. (or after clearance of the 3.55 p.m. Paddington) with a provisional break between 2.35 p.m. and 5.0 p.m.

FURTHER READING

R. Mag. 1939 (Vol. 85) pp. 197–202 H.A.P. Pos.
T.I. 1959 pp. 39–42, 44–45 H.A.P.M. (Article on the Aberystwyth–
Carmarthen branch)
T.I. 1963 (Vol. 18) p. 298 Pos.
R. Mag. 1964 pp. 404–412, 512–516 H.A.P.M. (Article on the Central Wales Line.)

CARMARTHEN

DIAGRAM "A"
APPROX. SCALE: 120 FT. to 1 INCH

To LAMPETER

PENSARN ROAD

S.B.

L.C.

DOCK

STATION APPROACH

MAIN BUILDINGS

ROADWAY

GATE

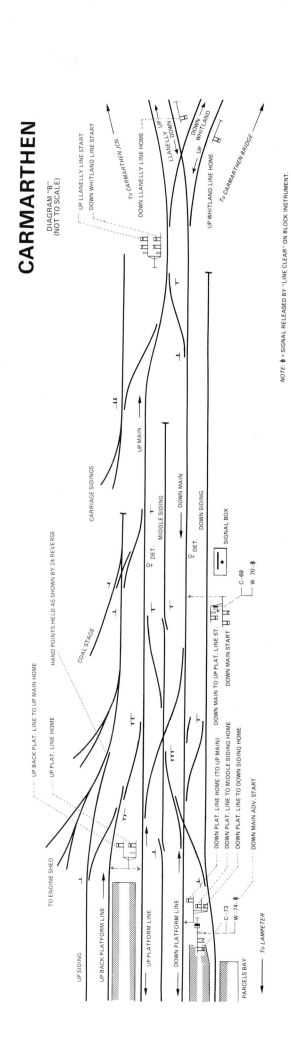

CARMARTHEN

DIAGRAM "B"
(NOT TO SCALE)

UP LLANELLY LINE START

DOWN WHITLAND LINE START

To CARMARTHEN JCN.

DOWN LLANELLY LINE HOME

LLANELLY UP
DOWN

UP WHITLAND LINE HOME

DOWN WHITLAND

To CARMARTHEN BRIDGE

CARRIAGE SIDINGS

UP MAIN

MIDDLE SIDING

DET.

DOWN MAIN

DET.

DOWN SIDING

SIGNAL BOX

C-69

W. 70-

DOWN MAIN TO UP PLAT. LINE ST.

DOWN MAIN START

HAND POINTS HELD AS SHOWN BY 24 REVERSE

COAL STAGE

UP BACK PLAT. LINE TO UP MAIN HOME

UP PLAT. LINE HOME

TO ENGINE SHED

UP SIDING

UP BACK PLATFORM LINE

UP PLATFORM LINE

DOWN PLATFORM LINE

C-73

W-74-

C-73

DOWN PLAT. LINE HOME (TO UP MAIN)

DOWN PLAT. LINE TO MIDDLE SIDING HOME

DOWN PLAT. LINE TO DOWN SIDING HOME

DOWN MAIN ADV. START

PARCELS BAY

To LAMPETER

NOTE: ꝑ = SIGNAL RELEASED BY "LINE CLEAR" ON BLOCK INSTRUMENT.

CASTLE CARY

Origin: Great Western Railway (Wilts., Somerset & Weymouth)

(Absorbed by G.W.R. in 1851)

Opened: 1 Sept. 1856

Closed: 3 Oct. 1966 (G)

Plan date: c. 1906 ("A") (Diagram "B" refers to old box)

There was never anything spectacular about Castle Cary, but it provided a convenient jumping off point for the remainder of the Great Western's "new direct route to the West" through Somerton, and Langport (East) to join the old main line (so called "the Great Way Round") at Cogload. This was completed throughout and ready for use on 11 June 1906 for through goods traffic, and on 2 July 1906 for through passenger trains. With th the additional traffic, which had hitherto gone via Swindon and Bristol, activity at Castle Cary was somewhat increased, but only by the passing through of non-stop expresses, for the pattern of local stopping services was altered but little, and the effect on local goods traffic was minimal. The opening dates of the intermediate sections of the new line were as follow:–

Castle Cary to Charlton Mackrell   1 July 1905 (as a single line)

Curry Rivel Jc. to Somerton   20 May 1906 (as a single line and for local goods only)

Athelney to Cogload Junction   2 April 1906 (goods trains only at first)

By the time that through goods and passenger trains passed over it to and from the West, the whole section had been doubled.

The goods shed road was lifted towards the end of June 1969, and the adjacent (back) siding shortly after, together with the short spur. The connection into the down main line was disconnected in May 1968. The up siding on the Weymouth branch was taken out of use in mid-December 1963, as was the connection from the down loop into the down main. The Weymouth branch at Castle Cary was finally singled on 12 May 1968.

The former S.B. (which was opened on 11 April 1905) was damaged in the late World War, and the new (present) box was opened on 27 Oct. 1942.

Castle Cary signal box (1938) open continuously, and was provided with a switch. An interesting fact is that when the box was switched out the junction was set for the Weymouth line, referred to as the "Main Line" in the Summer 1938 W.T.T.

FURTHER READING

R. Mag. 1905 (Vol. 17) pp. 89–96   H.A.P.M.

R. Mag. 1969 p. 150 Pos.

"Reg. Hist. of the Railways of Great Britain" Vol. 1. (The West Country)

by D. St. J. Thomas Phoenix

Castle Cary. Looking West through the station from the footbridge. Feb. 1964.

R.H. Clark

Castle Cary. General view of station and yard looking East. Feb. 1964.

R.H. Clark

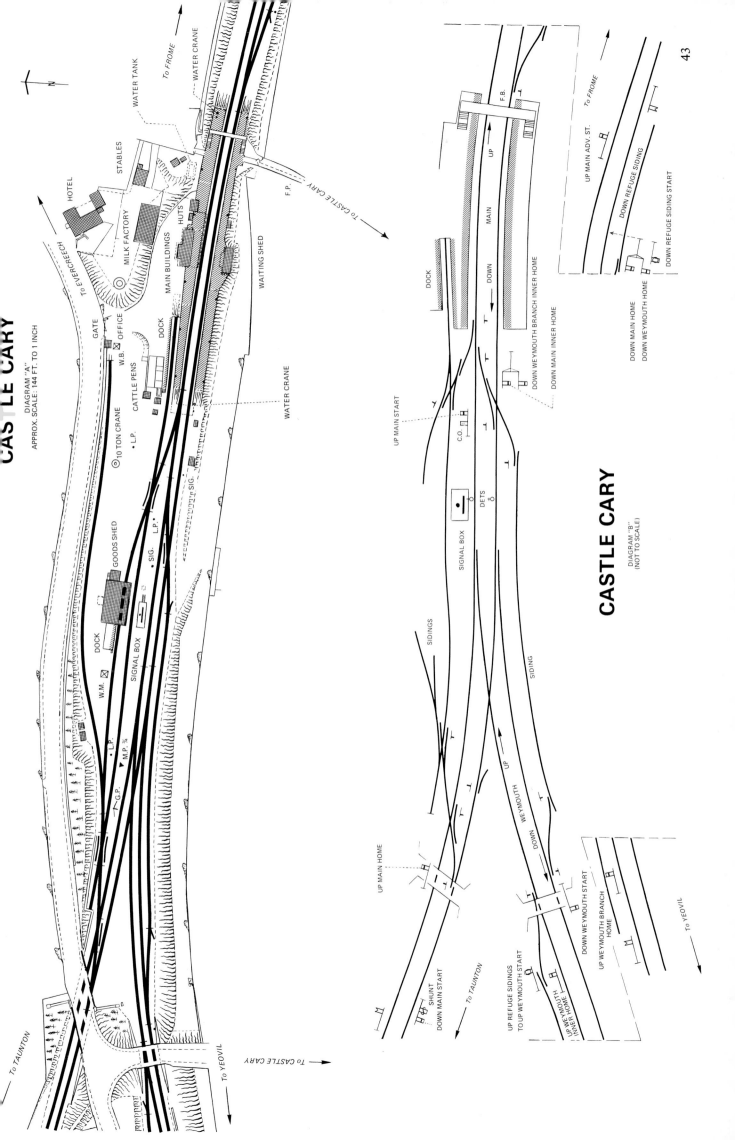

CASTLE CARY

DIAGRAM "A"
APPROX. SCALE: 144 FT. TO 1 INCH

To TAUNTON

To CASTLE CARY

To YEOVIL

To EVERCREECH

HOTEL

STABLES

WATER TANK

WATER CRANE

To FROME

MILK FACTORY

MAIN BUILDINGS

HUTS

WAITING SHED

WATER CRANE

F.P.

To CASTLE CARY

GATE

OFFICE

W.B.

CATTLE PENS

DOCK

10 TON CRANE

L.P.

SIG.

L.P.

GOODS SHED

DOCK

W.M.

SIGNAL BOX

L.P.

M.P. ¾

G.P.

CASTLE CARY

DIAGRAM "B"
(NOT TO SCALE)

To FROME

UP MAIN ADV. ST.

DOWN REFUGE SIDING

DOWN REFUGE SIDING START

DOWN MAIN HOME

DOWN WEYMOUTH HOME

F.B.

UP

MAIN

DOWN

DOCK

DOWN WEYMOUTH BRANCH INNER HOME

DOWN MAIN INNER HOME

UP MAIN START

C.O.

SIGNAL BOX

DETS

SIDINGS

SIDING

UP

WEYMOUTH

DOWN

UP MAIN HOME

SHUNT

DOWN MAIN START

To TAUNTON

UP REFUGE SIDINGS

TO UP WEYMOUTH START

UP WEYMOUTH INNER HOME

DOWN WEYMOUTH BRANCH HOME

UP WEYMOUTH BRANCH START

To YEOVIL

43

CHACEWATER

Origin: West Cornwall Railway
Leased from opening to G.W.R., B. & E., and S.D.R.
(Absorbed by G.W.R. in 1878)

Opened: 25 Aug. 1852
Closed: 5 Oct. 1964 (P)
5 Oct. 1964 (G) Remained open for P.S. traffic, now withdrawn

Plan date: 1913

Chacewater came into the railway scene long before the rails had left Paddington by the building of the 4 ft. gauge line of the Redruth & Chacewater Railway which was opened on 30 Jan. 1825 to serve the rich copper mines of the period in this part of Cornwall. The station with which we are concerned here, however, arrived with the opening of the railway from Truro, but the intermediate history of developments which cannot be dealt with here, is well worth following up by those interested. In addition to those sources listed below, there are other reliable works on the subject contained in more general histories of Cornish industry.

The 18½ mile branch to Newquay (which served no less than 10 intermediate halts) formerly joined the main line at the Blackwater Junctions (east and west) in both directions forming a triangle thereat. The west curve here was disused from 5 May 1919, and from 9 Nov. 1924 the north and east signal boxes, as were the junctions with the main line and the Newquay branch extended as an independent line to join the up platform loop at Chacewater station, as revealed in Diagram "B". The west signal box at Blackwater Junction was closed on the 18 Sept. 1924. The whole branch, including the platform loop and trailing connections into the up main, was closed entirely from 4 Feb. 1963 and the track lifted at Chacewater 2 years later.

The 'up' loop and main line trailing crossover had been brought into use in 1912.

The Newquay branch was a single line, worked by Electric Train Staff with crossing places at St. Agnes, Perranporth, Shepherds and Tolcarn Junction.

In 1938, Chacewater signal box was open from 5.15 a.m. to 10.0 p.m. on weekdays, and 9.10 a.m. to 9.0 p.m. (with 2 breaks) on Sundays, and the box was provided with a switch.

FURTHER READING

R. Mag. 1903 (Vol. 13) pp. 38–42 D.A.P.M. Article on line to St. Agnes & Perranporth
"The Hayle, West Cornwall & Helston Railways" by G. H. Anthony, Oakwood Press
"Reg. Hist. of the Railways of Great Britain" Vol. 1. (The West Country)
by D. St. J. Thomas. Phoenix

CHACEWATER

DIAGRAM "A"
APPROX. SCALE: 120 FT. TO 1 INCH

TO TRURO · LEVEL · 1 in 124 · M.P. 306 · S.M. HOUSE · 1 in 124 · 1 in 70 · S.B. · CRANE · COAL · OIL · TO REDRUTH · IRON GIRDER BRIDGE SPAN – 26' 0"

KEY TO STATION ROOMS

1. LAV.
2. LADIES W.R.
3. GENERAL W.R.
4. PORTERS' ROOM
5. GENERAL W.R.
6. PARCELS OFFICE
7. S.M. OFFICE
8. BOOKING OFFICE

(UP SIDE)

Chacewater.

Looking West towards Penzance.

Lens of Sutton

Chacewater.

Looking East towards Truro.

Lens of Sutton

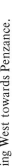
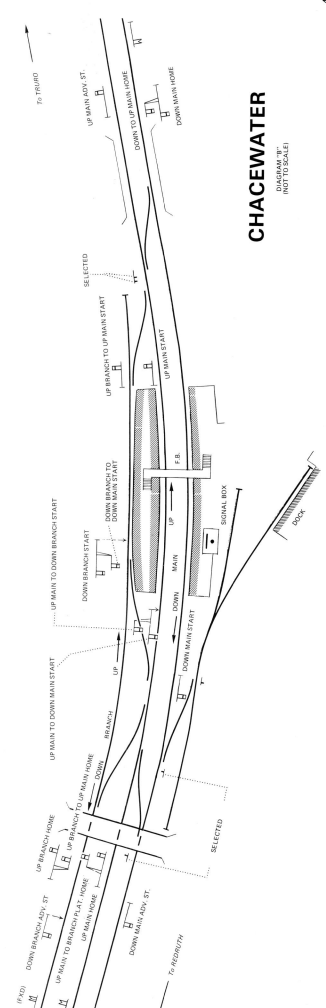

CHACEWATER

DIAGRAM "B"
(NOT TO SCALE)

TO TRURO

UP MAIN ADV. ST.

DOWN TO UP MAIN HOME

DOWN MAIN HOME

SELECTED

UP BRANCH TO UP MAIN START

UP MAIN START

DOWN BRANCH TO DOWN MAIN START

F.B.

UP MAIN TO DOWN BRANCH START

DOWN BRANCH START

UP

MAIN

DOWN

SIGNAL BOX

UP

DOWN MAIN START

DOCK

UP MAIN TO DOWN MAIN START

BRANCH

DOWN

UP BRANCH HOME

UP BRANCH TO UP MAIN HOME

SELECTED

(F.XD)

DOWN BRANCH ADV. ST

UP MAIN TO BRANCH PLAT. HOME

UP MAIN HOME

DOWN MAIN ADV. ST.

TO REDRUTH

45

CHALLOW

Origin: Great Western Railway
Opened: 20 July 1840
Closed: 7 Dec. 1964 (P)
29 Mar. 1965 (G) Final closure
(Diagram "B" old box)

Plan date: c. 1934

Until 1 June 1864, the station title was "Faringdon Road", and from 19 May 1965 the yard handled coal only until final closure.

The original station buildings were of timber construction, and the whole station was virtually demolished and rebuilt in 1932, when the line was quadrupled. The new station buildings were of ordinary brick construction, but neat and by no means unattractive. In the course of quadrupling, the down side was completed first and brought into use on 4 Dec. 1932, and the up side on 22 Jan. 1933, the former by the extension of the down refuge siding through to Wantage Road, and the latter by upgrading the up goods road (opened for goods traffic in November 1907) to passenger status on 10 Oct. 1932, and extended to Wantage Road on 4 Dec. of that year. Both roads were taken out of use a week after the final withdrawal of goods services.

The old signal box was replaced by a new one on 4 Dec. 1932 which, itself, was closed on 30 May 1965. This box was (1938) open continuously, and was provided with a switch.

There was a maximum speed limit of 20 m.p.h. for all trains passing to and from the down main and down relief lines.

The facing connection from the up main to the up platform line was discontinued from 5 Apr. 1965, and the goods shed roads (and connections) on 30 May 1965.

In the 1890's there was a small turntable to the east of the goods shed, which served the (curved) dock road, and a short siding at right angles to the running road, but this was removed shortly after the turn of the century, together with the "right-angled" siding and replaced by a point for the dock roads only.

Challow. View of main building from the platform side.

O.P.C.

CHALLOW

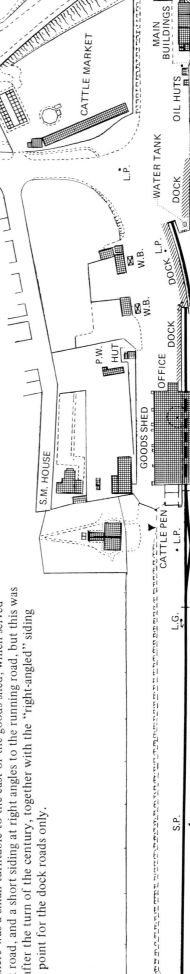

CHALLOW

DIAGRAM "A"
APPROX. SCALE: 130½ FT. TO 1 INCH

To DIDCOT →

← To DIDCOT

CHALLOW ROAD BRIDGE
SQUARE SPAN 67' 9"
SKEW SPAN 78' 4¼"

M.P. 63¾

N.B.

SHELTER

F.B.

GATES

OIL HUT

CATTLE MARKET

MAIN BUILDINGS

OIL HUTS

OIL HUTS

WATER TANK

DOCK

D.

D.

F.W.

S.P.

DOCK

L.P.

W.B.

W.B.

L.P.

DON

CHALLOW

DIAGRAM "B"
(NOT TO SCALE)

To DIDCOT →

UP AVOIDING LINE

UP MAIN HOME

UP MAIN ADV. ST.

DOWN MAIN HOME

DOWN REFUGE SIDING

DOWN REFUGE SIDING START

UP MAIN TO UP AVOIDING LINE START

UP MAIN START

PASSENGER STATION

F.B.

GOODS SHED

DOCK

UP

MAIN

DET.

DET.

DOWN

SIGNAL BOX

UP MAIN TO UP AVOIDING LINE HOME

UP MAIN HOME

UP REFUGE TO UP MAIN START

UP REFUGE TO UP MAIN HOME

DOWN MAIN START

DOWN MAIN ADV. ST.

DOWN MAIN ADV. ST.

← To SWINDON

47

John H. Meredith

Cirencester Town. Looking from buffers. 3 Dec. 1949.

Lens of Sutton

Cirencester Looking towards terminus

CIRENCESTER

Origin: Cheltenham & G.W. Union
(Absorbed by G.W.R. in 1843)
31 May 1841 (Renamed "Cirencester Town" on 1 July 1924)

Opened: 6 Apr. 1964 (P)
Closed: 4 Oct. 1965 (G)

Plan date: 1909

The 4m 17c. broad gauge single line from Kemble to Cirencester was one of the earliest to appear on the system, and was leased to and worked by the G.W.R. until it was absorbed by that company on 1 July 1843.

Cirencester originally had a small overall roof, but this was removed in 1874, and replaced by a standard platform canopy, but the original tall buildings remained for the whole of the station's life, except for a partial rebuilding in 1956 when great care was taken to use the same Bath stone to tone in with the surrounding original structure, and to maintain the old style.

Before the 1923 Grouping, 4 additional sidings, and a pig dock neck, parallel with the main line were built to the east of the original yard, together with the two double-slip connections (Diagram "B").

Early in 1959, when the threat of closure loomed, the Western Region made valiant efforts to popularise the branch, withdrawing steam and replacing with a diesel rail bus, but in spite of considerable support by the town's inhabitants, the branch passenger services finally succumbed in April 1964, followed by total closure 18 months later. The engine shed (which had been used by the railbus since steam was withdrawn on 2 Feb. 1959), was finally closed on the same day as withdrawal of passenger services, followed by the closure of the signal box on 14 June 1964, when all the tracks west of the station platforms became redundant and disused.

In 1938 (summer period), the signal box opening hours were from 5.35 a.m. to clearance of the last train on weekdays, and from 1.20 p.m. until 8.20 p.m. with an afternoon break between 3.45 and 5.25 p.m. on Sundays. There was no switch provided.

FURTHER READING

R.W. 1958 pp. 367–369 H.A.P. Pos.
T.I. 1960 pp. 365–366; 384 D.A.P.
R. Mag. 1964 pp. 742–748 H.A.P.M. Pos.
"Gone with Regret" Plate 43 by George Behrend, Lambarde Press
"Great Western Branch Lines, 1955–1965" by C. J. Gammell. O.P.C.

CIRENCESTER

DIAGRAM "A"
APPROX. SCALE: 106½ FT. TO 1 INCH

N

To KEMBLE →

GATE

GATE

OFFICE
W.B.

OFFICE

OFFICE
W.B.

STORE

GATE

GATE

GATE

GATE
W.B.

OFFICE

CRANE

C.P.

C.P.

C.P.

SIGNAL BOX

ENGINE SHED

PACKERS HUT

REFUSE BINS

PUMP & ENGINE SHED

TANK & COAL STAGE

GOODS SHED

CHECKERS' HUT

GRAIN SHED

CATTLE PENS

C.P.

OIL HUT

PORTERS' HUT

MAIN BUILDINGS

1
2

3
4

DOCK

GATE

GATE

KEY TO STATION ROOMS
1.   STATION MASTER'S OFFICE
2.   BOOKING & PARCELS OFFICE
3.   LADIES WAITING ROOM
4.   GENERAL WAITING ROOM

CIRENCESTER

DIAGRAM "B"
(NOT TO SCALE)

To KEMBLE →

(FXD)

UP ADV. ST.

G.F.

XX

PIG DOCK

X
X
X
X

DOWN HOME

ENGINE SHED

UP INTERMEDIATE START

PADLOCKED WHEEL STOP
(KEY KEPT IN SIGNAL BOX)

YARD

CRANE ROAD

DOWN INNER HOME

SIGNAL BOX

CATTLE PENS

UP START

GOODS SHED

PASSENGER STATION

DOWN   MAIN   UP

LOOP

SIDINGS

DOCK

GROUND FRAME
WORKING POINTS
F.P.L. & DISC. "X"
RELEASED BY KEY
ON E.T. STAFF

49

CLYNDERWEN

Origin: South Wales Railway
Worked by G.W.R. locos and rolling stock from opening.
(Amalgamated with the G.W.R. & West Midland on 1 Aug. 1863)

Opened: 2 Jan. 1854 (as "NARBERTH ROAD")
Renamed "Clynderwen" 1 Dec. 1875; "Clynderwen Halt"
from 6 Sept. 1965; and "Clynderwen" 5 May 1969

Closed: 6 Sept. 1965 (G)
Plan date: c. 1910

Clynderwen station in West Wales, literally straddles the boundary between the former counties of Carmarthenshire and Pembrokeshire, 364¼ miles from Paddington. The old line that served Maenclochog, Rosebush and thence to Letterston ran parallel with the main line, westward from Clynderwen for about 1¼ miles before turning northward.

In Diagram "A", the up side platform extends beyond its limit to a distance of 100 ft., and the down refuge siding (opposite the up platform) extends similarly for 850 ft. to the stops. As can be seen from the diagrams, no footbridge connected the two platforms, foot communication being provided by means of a ramp across the tracks at the platforms' extremities nearest to each other.

In 1938, the signal box was open from 7.30 a.m. on Mondays to 6.30 a.m. on Sundays, and was provided with a switch. Bearing in mind the almost continuous scheduled opening time of the box, it should also be borne in mind that right down to recent times, and particularly between 1906 and (say) 1960, this main line has handled a great deal of night traffic, both goods and passenger, as well as the considerable daytime train service. From 6.30 a.m. on Sundays to 7.30 a.m. on Mondays, when the box was obviously switched out, there must have been a 12¾ mile section between Whitland West box and Clarbeston Road Junction box, and longer on Sunday mornings for about 5 hours when the two last mentioned were "out". It was, in fact, possible to create a section about 24 miles long between Whitland East signal box and Manorowen, beyond Letterston Junction.

FURTHER READING

R. Mag. 1899 (Vol. 5) pp. 252–260
R. Mag. 1939 (Vol. 85) pp. 197–202   H.A.P. Pos.
R.W. 1950 p. 206 Hist. notes on Rosebush line
"The North Pembrokeshire & Fishguard Railway" by J. P. Morris, Oakwood Press

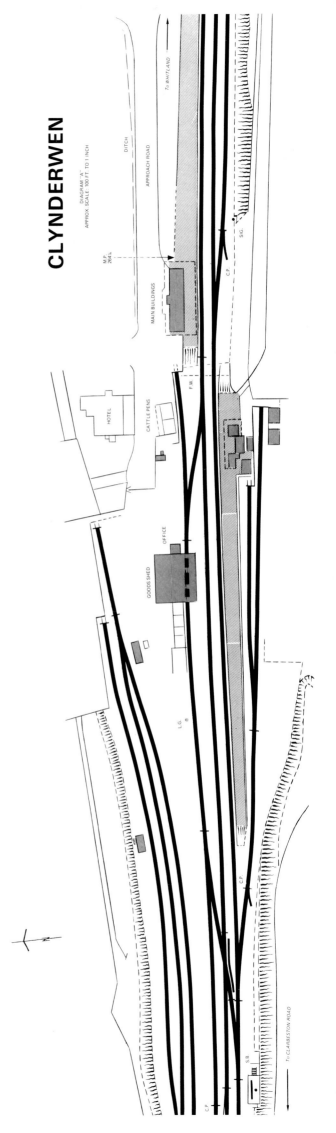

CLYNDERWEN

Clynderwen.

Looking West towards Fishguard. c.1920.

J.P. Morris Collection

Clynderwen.

Looking East towards Whitland. 30 July 1958. Down express entering the station.

M. Hale

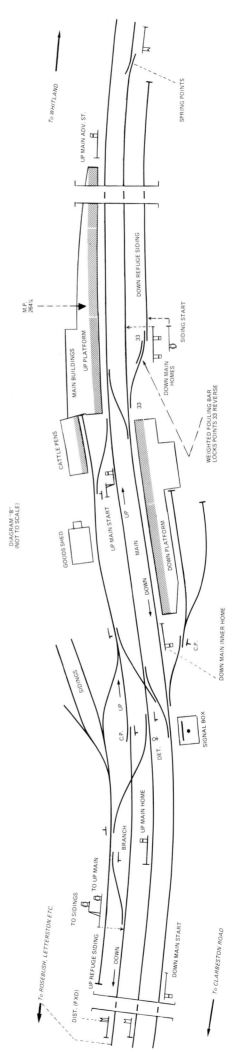

CLYNDERWEN

DIAGRAM "B"
(NOT TO SCALE)

To WHITLAND

UP MAIN ADV. ST.

SPRING POINTS

M.P. 264¼

MAIN BUILDINGS

UP PLATFORM

DOWN REFUGE SIDING

SIDING START

33

DOWN MAIN HOMES

CATTLE PENS

33

WEIGHTED FOULING BAR
LOCKS POINTS 33 REVERSE

GOODS SHED

UP MAIN START

UP

MAIN

DOWN PLATFORM

DOWN

C.P.

DOWN MAIN INNER HOME

SIDINGS

C.P.

UP

SIGNAL BOX

DET.

BRANCH

UP MAIN HOME

TO UP MAIN

TO SIDINGS

To ROSEBUSH, LETTERSTON ETC.

DIST. (FXD)

UP REFUGE SIDING

DOWN

DOWN MAIN START

To CLARBESTON ROAD

51

Colwall.	Looking towards Malvern.	*Lens of Sutton*

Colwall.	Looking towards Malvern.	*O.P.C.*

COLWALL

Origin: West Midland Railway

By amalgamation of the Newport, Abergavenny & Hereford Railway; Oxford, Worcester & Wolverhampton Railway; Worcester & Hereford Railway;—1 July 1860.

Absorbed by the Great Western Railway in 1863.

Opened: 13 Sept. 1861
Closed: 2 Nov. 1964 (G)
Plan date: c. 1922

Colwall was opened with the standard gauge line of the West Midland Railway between Malvern Wells and Shelwick Junction (north of Hereford—on the Shrewsbury & Hereford Railway). With the exception of Malvern and Ledbury tunnels, the line was doubled in July 1868.

Colwall station is located almost at the watershed of the line as it passes through the Malvern Hills, with a gradient of 1 in 80 climbing from Great Malvern (and beyond at lesser grades), and falling towards Ledbury less steeply, but with a 1 in 80 grade approaching Ledbury and beyond.

The layout underwent some development, and alteration in its time, and even the (nearly) mile-long Malvern Tunnel immediately to the East of the station was closed and

a new tunnel bored, in the mid-1920's. The new tunnel was brought into use on 2 Aug. 1926.

At the time of the survey illustrated, there was a short 'neck' trailing into the up main line to the west of the station, but this was removed at an unknown date in later years. It could have been put there to derail 'runaways' on the wrong line, bearing in mind the gathering steepness of the falling grade towards Ledbury. A week after the opening of the new tunnel, the old signal box was replaced by a new one (opened 11 Aug. 1926) which, itself, was closed when all sidings and connections had been discontinued (in stages), and the line singled to Ledbury (exclusive) on 1 Oct. 1967.

Diagram "B" would be current (circa) 1945–1955.

Colwall signal box was (1938) open from 1.30 a.m. Mondays until 6.0 a.m. the following Sunday morning (subject to advice from Worcester Control) re-opening at 9.40 a.m. until 8.45 p.m. with two intermediate breaks. The box was not provided with a switch.

FURTHER READING

R. Mag. 1908 (Vol. 22) pp. 410–418   H.A.P. + Grade profile.
R. Mag. 1959 pp. 445–450, 455; pp. 533–538   H.A.P.M.

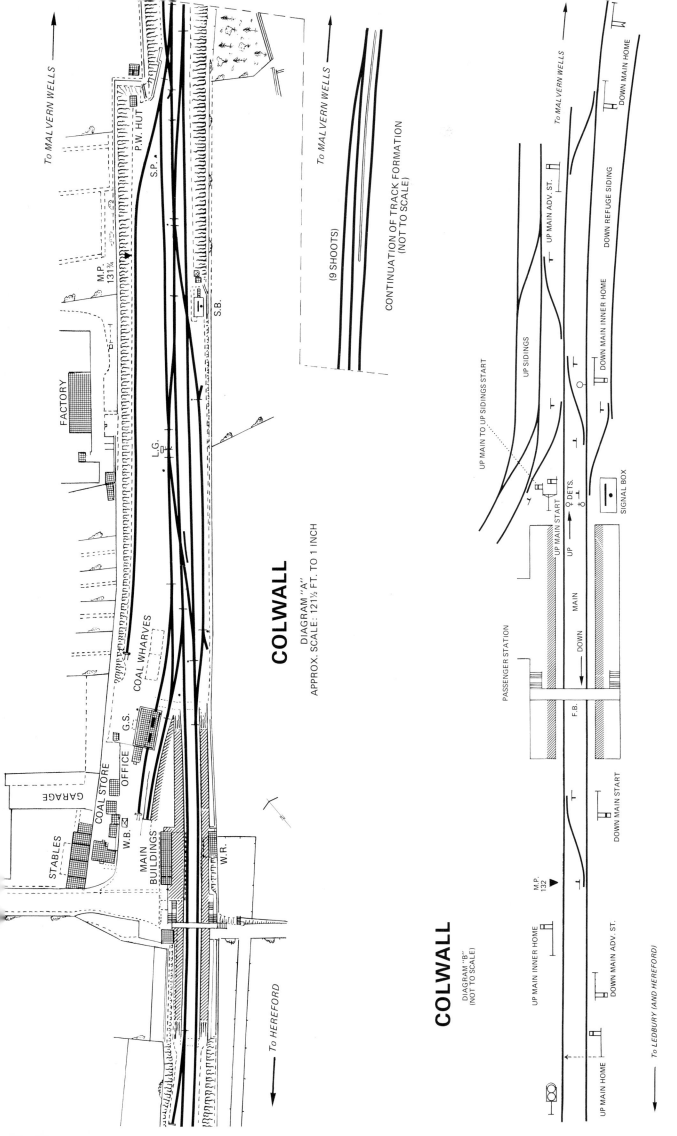

COLWALL

DIAGRAM "A"
APPROX. SCALE: 121½ FT. TO 1 INCH

To MALVERN WELLS →

To HEREFORD →

To MALVERN WELLS →

(9 SHOOTS)

CONTINUATION OF TRACK FORMATION
(NOT TO SCALE)

FACTORY

STABLES

GARAGE

COAL STORE

OFFICE

G.S.

MAIN
BUILDINGS

W.B.

W.R.

COAL WHARVES

L.G.

S.B.

P.W. HUT

S.P.

M.P.
131¾

COLWALL

DIAGRAM "B"
(NOT TO SCALE)

To MALVERN WELLS →

To LEDBURY (AND HEREFORD) →

PASSENGER STATION

UP SIDINGS

UP MAIN TO UP SIDINGS START

UP MAIN ADV. ST.

UP MAIN START

UP

MAIN

DOWN

F.B.

DETS.

SIGNAL BOX

DOWN MAIN INNER HOME

DOWN REFUGE SIDING

DOWN MAIN HOME

DOWN MAIN START

UP MAIN INNER HOME

DOWN MAIN ADV. ST.

M.P.
132

UP MAIN HOME

53

CONWIL

Origin: Carmarthen & Cardigan
(Absorbed by G.W.R. in 1881)
Opened: 3 Sept. 1860 (From reliable sources but open to confirmation)
Closed: 22 Feb. 1965 (P)
2 Dec. 1963 (G)
Plan date: 18 June 1912

This little station, (serving the tiny hamlet of Conwil Elvet, about a mile northwards) nestles snugly in the deep Swili valley, which provided just enough room for the railway, river and the winding road, and, although the prime purpose of this book is as its title indicates, I make no apology for extolling the station's pretty and topographical setting. It was situated about 6¾ miles from Carmarthen, and was the second station up the line towards Pencader, (Newcastle Emlyn) and Aberystwyth.

As can be seen from the diagrams, the layout remained undisturbed for nearly all its life except for operational refinements which could apply to any station.

The line from Carmarthen to Pencader was part of the Carmarthen & Cardigan Railway, and was opened as a broad gauge line, though not until 28 Mar. 1864 did it reach Pencader—on 1 Jan. 1866 making an end on junction with the Manchester & Milford line from Lampeter. On the same day, (1 Jan. 1866) a third rail completed the task of mixing the gauge, allowing standard gauge trains to operate over this section. The section was eventually converted to standard gauge only on 1 June 1872.

The signal box was (1938) open from 5.30 a.m. to the clearance of the last train on weekdays, and it was closed on Sundays at that time, there being no advertised service. It was not provided with a switch.

FURTHER READING

R. Mag. 1939 (Vol. 85) p. 198 (Article on "The G.W.R. in West Wales" by T.R. Perkins)

T.I. 1959 pp. 39–42; 44–45 H.A.P.M. (Article on Aberystwyth Carmarthen branch)

R.W. 1973 pp. 76–77 H.A.P.M. (Short history of the Carmarthen & Cardigan Railway)

"The Teifi Valley Railway" by Roger Padfield & Barry Burgess Laidlaw-Burgess, Haverfordwest

Conwil.
Looking towards Llanpumpsaint. 15 June 1962.

M. Hale

CONWIL

DIAGRAM "B"
(NOT TO SCALE)

To CARMARTHEN

SIDING

HOME

START

UP

MAIN

SIGNAL BOX

DOWN

PASSENGER STATION

START

SHUNT

HOME

To PENCADER

To CARMARTHEN

N

SHELTER

T.P

T.P

T.P

O.H. IND.

C.P.

GOODS SHED

WEIGH BRIDGE

CRANE

OFFICE

To CARMARTHEN

120 FT. TO STOPS

55

PUBLIC HOUSE

S.B.

SIG

MAIN BUILDINGS

ROCK

To CONWIL VILLAGE

To PENCADER

CONWIL

DIAGRAM "A"
APPROX. SCALE: 80 FT. TO 1 INCH

DAWLISH

Origin:	South Devon Railway
	(Absorbed by G.W.R. in 1878)
Opened:	30 May 1846
Closed:	17 May 1965 (G)
Plan date:	Diagram "A" c. 1970

No station could be nearer the sea and the town it serves, than Dawlish, and it is not impossible that the predominant enthusiasm for the Great Western Railway was conceived in the very young of each generation by the close proximity between moving train and bucket and spade holiday maker on the adjacent beach.

Like Teignmouth, 6 miles down the line, Dawlish station had little room to accommodate itself, let alone a yard complex which would have been more in keeping with the developing town. But for all that, its historical, physical and operational interest qualifies it for more attention than it has so far received in the printed word.

As can be seen, Diagram "A" shows the arrangements well after the rationalisation programme had had its full effect, and after the former goods yard had been converted to a car park, but Diagram "B" is more informative as it shows most of the layout and all the signalling arrangements under the control of Dawlish Signal Box before rationalisation.

The old signal box. which was on the 'down' platform, was closed and a new one opened on the 'up' platform on 9 Sept. 1920.

Before 1961, the shed road passed right through the goods shed, but was shortened in that year, and progressively in the course of the succeeding years the yard sidings and connections became redundant, and were eventually cleared away, but the trailing crossover opposite the goods yard lead was not discontinued until Jan. 1974. The crossover at the south end of the station had been lifted 8 years earlier.

The signal box was (1938) open on weekdays from 4.30 a.m. (SX) and closed at 11.0 p.m. (Mons. to Thurs.), remaining open on Friday nights until 11.30 p.m. Saturdays. On Sundays, the box was open from 10.0 a.m. until 10.30 p.m. with a break between 5.0 p.m. and 6.30 p.m. The box *was* provided with a switch.

Dawlish. An old view, probably taken at about the turn of the Century, looking South, and showing a railmotor at the up platform.

H.C. Casserley Collection

FURTHER READING

R.W.   1955 pp. 187–190   H.A.P. Pos.
"Reg. Hist. of the Railways of Great Britain"
Vol. 1. (The West Country) by D. St.J. Thomas. Phoenix

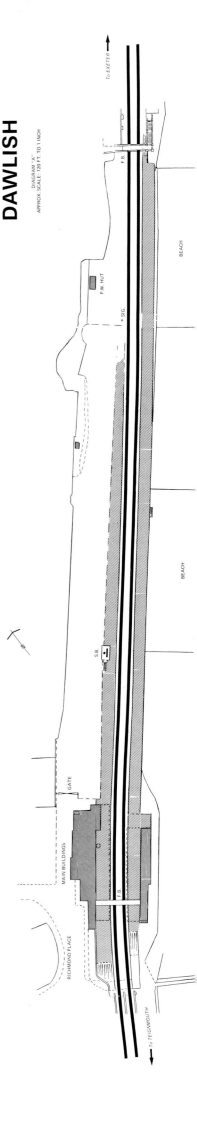

DAWLISH

DIAGRAM "A"
APPROX. SCALE: 120 FT. TO 1 INCH

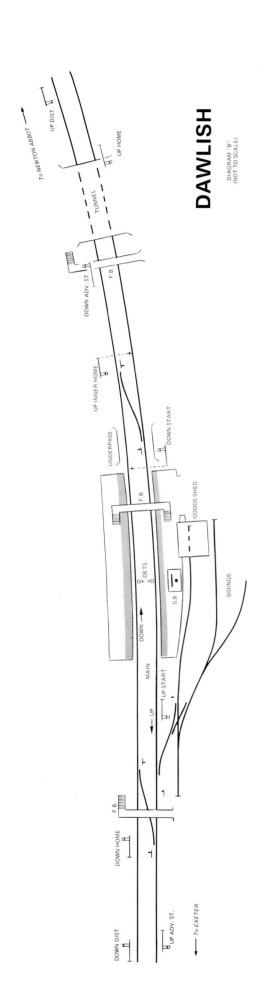

DAWLISH

DIAGRAM "B"
(NOT TO SCALE)

To NEWTON ABBOT →

UP DIST.

UP HOME

TUNNEL

DOWN ADV. ST.

F.B.

UP INNER HOME

UNDERPASS

F.B.

DOWN START

GOODS SHED

DETS.

S.B.

DOWN

MAIN

UP

UP START

SIDINGS

F.B.

DOWN HOME

DOWN DIST.

UP ADV. ST.

← To EXETER

Lens of Sutton

Dawlish. Looking towards Exeter, showing signal box and timbered down platform.

Lens of Sutton

Dawlish. An early view before the main line was doubled.

Dawlish Warren.   An old view looking towards Exeter.   *Lens of Sutton*

DAWLISH WARREN

Origin: Great Western Railway
Opened: 1st. station—1905
             2nd. station—23 Sept. 1912
Closed: 1 Jan. 1917 until 1 May 1919 (Station temporarily closed to P. and G.)
             5 Aug. 1963 (G)

With the Edwardian growth in popularity of seaside resorts throughout the country, Dawlish Warren soon found itself on the railway map, and although it may not have ever reached the classical status of "holiday resort", such was the demand, the G.W.R. found it necessary to replace the first station by a second (a short distance to the north) on 23 Sept. 1912.

The original station was named "Warren Halt", which was renamed "Dawlish Warren" from 1 Oct. 1911 until closure and replacement.

The S. Devon line between Exeter and Newton Abbot was originally built as a single line, and this was doubled between Starcross and Dawlish in Feb. 1874, 31 years before Warren Halt appeared.

Dawlish Warren signal box was (1938) open continuously, and was provided with a switch.

FURTHER READING

"Reg. Hist. of the Railways of Great Britain" Vol. 1. (The West Country)
             by D. St. J. Thomas. Phoenix

"The Great Western at the Turn of the Century" by A. R. Kingdom (Pos.) O.P.C.

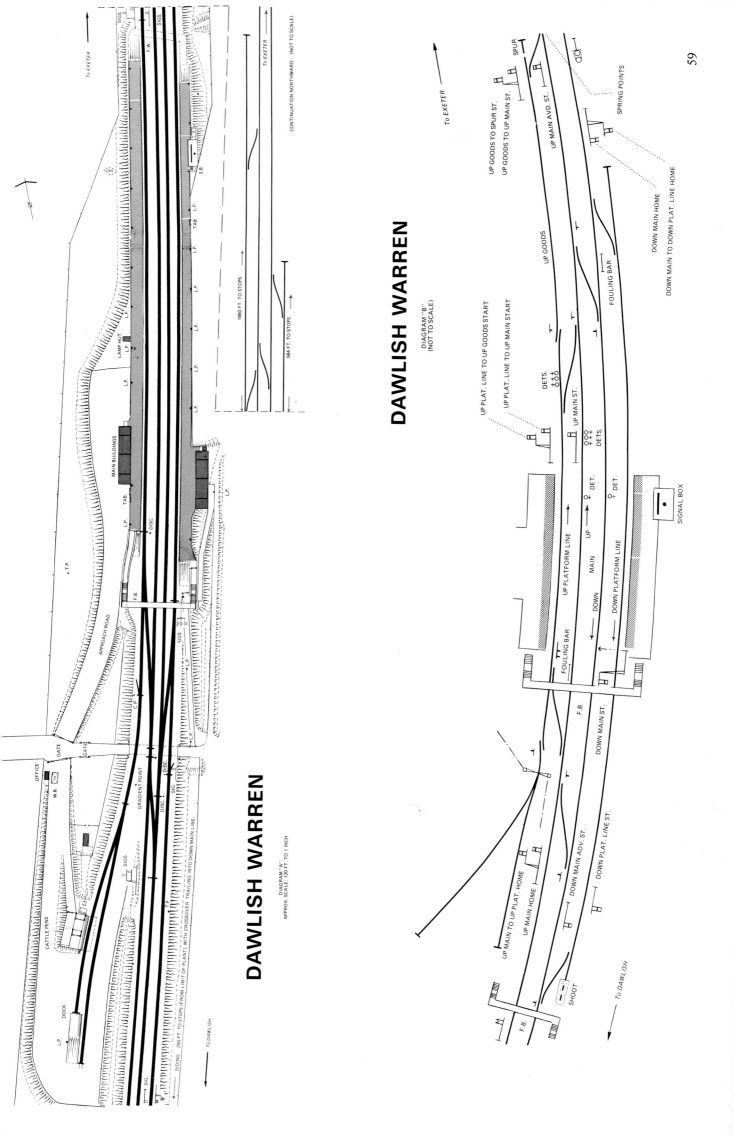

DAWLISH WARREN

DIAGRAM "A"
APPROX. SCALE: 120 FT. TO 1 INCH

DAWLISH WARREN

DIAGRAM "B"
(NOT TO SCALE)

59

Derry Ormond. Looking towards Pencader. (Note oil lamps.)

Lens of Sutton

DERRY ORMOND

Origin: Manchester & Milford
(Leased to the G.W. in 1906 and absorbed in 1911)

Opened: 1866 (opened as "BETTWS" and renamed in July 1874)

Closed: 22 Feb. 1965 (P)
2 Dec. 1963 (G)

Plan date: 1908

Derry Ormond station lies about a mile north of Aberayron junction. It would be interesting to know the reason behind the change of name, for its original title obviously refers to the much nearer village of Bettws Bledrws, which lies on the main road half way between the station and the 'estate' of Derry Ormond. Perhaps it was in deference to the local landowner of the time.

As can be seen, there was no alteration in the track layout between 1908 (3 years before the G.W. took over the Manchester & Milford Co.) and the post-war signal box diagram.

The station lies on the 7 mile long incline, which rises all the way from Llanybyther to Llangybi. The signal box opened on weekdays at 6.40 a.m. and closed after the clearing of the last train (1938) and was closed all day on Sundays. There was no switch provided.

A point worth noting is that in 1877, and at least down to 1893, the yard crane was 3 ton capacity, but the 1908 plan reveals a 2 ton power-operated crane.

FURTHER READING

T.I. 1959 pp. 39—42; 44—45 H.A.P.M.

"The Teifi Valley Railway" by Roger Padfield & Barrie Burgess
Laidlaw-Burgess (Haverfordwest)

DERRY ORMOND

A view through the station looking towards Neath. May 1955. *R.H. Clark*

Origin:	Neath & Brecon
	(Absorbed by the G.W.R. on 1 July 1922)
Opened:	3 June 1867
Closed:	15 Oct. 1962 (P)
	15 Oct. 1962 (G)
Plan date:	c. 1923

Although the plan seems somewhat bare of detail, Devynock station was an interesting outpost of the South Wales railway system, being opened by the Neath & Brecon Railway and retaining its title to 1 Aug. 1913 when "& Sennybridge" was added.

The station was built at a point where the main road and the railway from Brecon part company, the former winding off along the valley towards Llandovery, and the latter turning south to make the long climb over the Black Mountains to Neath. The main buildings were of neat stone construction with a platform canopy. A solidly built goods shed of irregular shape was at the north end of the platform, and a large water tank immediately opposite the station buildings.

From Neath Yard signal box to Brecon Station signal box the line was (1938) single with crossing places at Cadoxton (a goods train and passenger train only), Cilfrew, Crynant, Ynisdawley, Onllwyn, Craig-y-nos, Devynock & Sennybridge and Brecon Station signal box, and was worked by Electric Train Token.

The passenger trains serving the station were few and far between numbering 3 each weekday with an additional service terminating and starting from and to Brecon on Fridays only. There was no Sunday service.

The signal box was open between 8.15 a.m. and 6.50 p.m. The closing time was dependent upon advice from the signal box in advance that an up or down train had cleared. The box was closed on Sundays, and no switch was provided.

Devynock & Sennybridge.

FURTHER READING

R. Mag. 1939 (Vol. 85) pp. 185–190 H.A.P.M. Pos.
R.W. 1956 pp. 73–79 H.A.P.M.
"The Brecon & Merthyr Railway" by D. S. M. Barrie, Oakwood Press

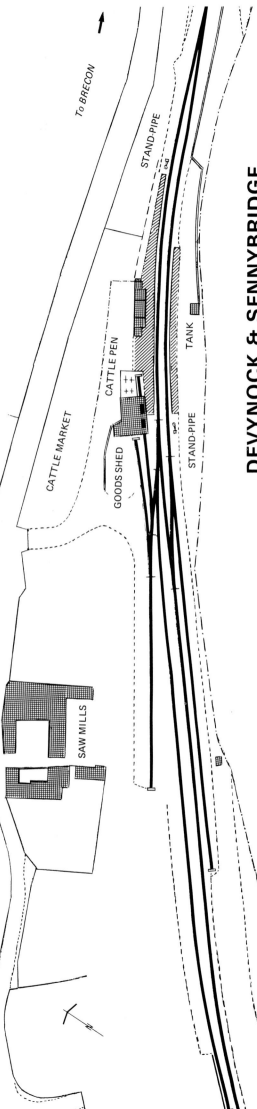

DEVYNOCK & SENNYBRIDGE

APPROX. SCALE: 121½ FT. to 1 INCH

To BRECON

STAND-PIPE

CATTLE MARKET

CATTLE PEN

GOODS SHED

TANK

STAND-PIPE

SAW MILLS

To NEATH

Dymock. Close-up of main buildings. *O.P.C.*

Dymock. View North, main buildings on right. *O.P.C.*

DYMOCK

Origin: Newent Railway
(Absorbed by the G.W.R. in 1892)

Opened: 27 July 1885 (by the Great Western Railway)
Closed: 13 July 1959 (P)
1 June 1964 (G)

Plan date: 1908

Dymock. General view looking South. *O.P.C.*

This once attractive and well groomed rural station was on the line from Over junction (near Gloucester) to Ledbury, which followed a general north-westerly direction, as did its neighbour only a few miles to the south west—the Hereford, Ross & Gloucester line (dealt with in the first volume of "G.W. Stations"). The 12¾ mile line from Over to Dymock was built as a single line on earthworks which had allowed for double track if required (but never was). The remaining 4¾ miles to Ledbury were double-track from the outset, but the line was singled from 4 January 1917 when, at the same time, an additional signal box was provided at Ledbury junction and titled "Ledbury Branch" Signal Box. (This box was closed in 1925). Thereafter the line was single throughout with intermediate crossing and staff stations at Newent and Dymock. The branch was worked by Electric Train Staff (in 1938).

The signal box was open on weekdays only from 9.40 a.m. to 9.0 p.m. with a break between 5.40 p.m. and 8.0 p.m. The box was provided with a switch.

Dymock had full goods and passenger facilities, and a 5 ton crane in its heyday, but from the day of withdrawal of passenger services, the signal box was reduced in status to that of a ground frame, and the branch was cut at the Ledbury end of the platforms—resulting in goods services arriving from the Gloucester direction only, for the next 5 years. The track between Dymock and Ledbury was lifted in easy stages between 14 Aug. 1960 and 29 Apr. 1962, and that between Over junction and Dymock on 15 June 1964—a fortnight after goods services ceased.

FURTHER READING

R. Mag. 1958 pp. 228—232   H.A.P.M. Pos.
R. Mag. 1959 p. 843 Pos.

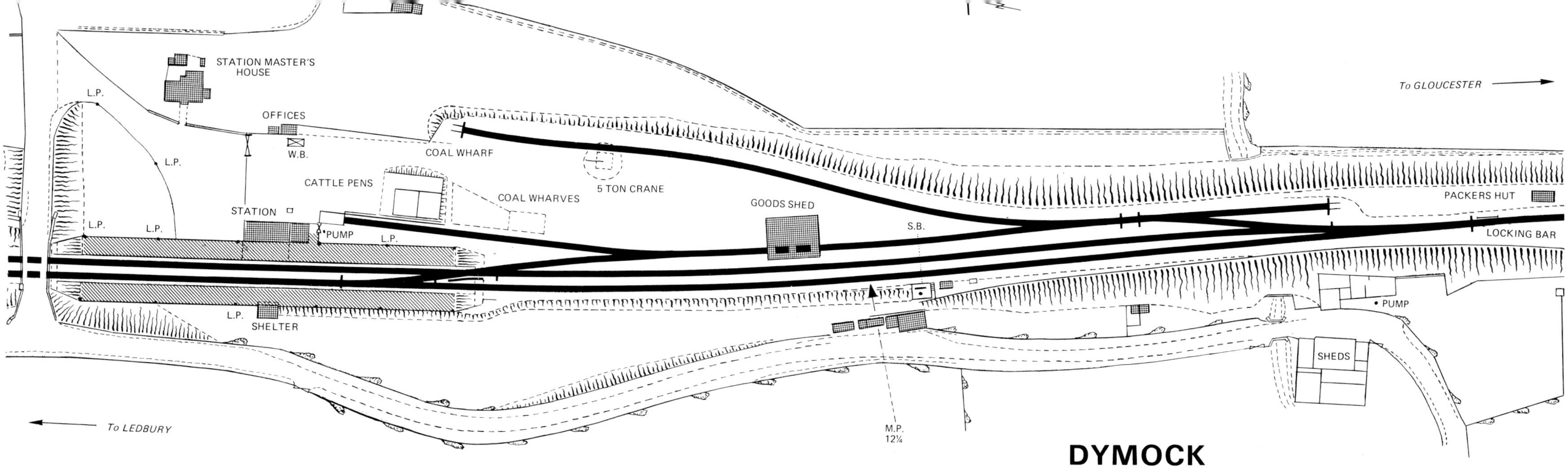

DYMOCK

DIAGRAM "A"
APPROX. SCALE: 106 FT. TO 1 INCH

To GLOUCESTER →

PACKERS HUT

LOCKING BAR

PUMP

SHEDS

S.B.

M.P.
12¼

GOODS SHED

5 TON CRANE

COAL WHARF

COAL WHARVES

STATION MASTER'S HOUSE

OFFICES

W.B.

CATTLE PENS

PUMP

L.P.

STATION

L.P.

L.P.

L.P.

L.P.

L.P.

L.P.

L.P. SHELTER

← To LEDBURY

DYMOCK

DIAGRAM "B"
(NOT TO SCALE)

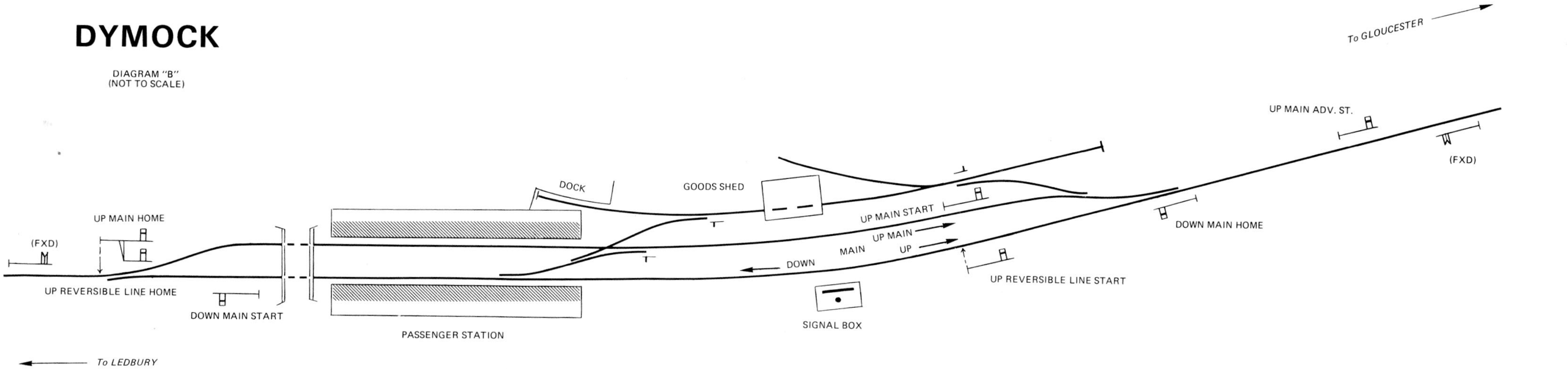

To GLOUCESTER →

UP MAIN ADV. ST.

(FXD)

DOWN MAIN HOME

UP REVERSIBLE LINE START

UP MAIN START

UP MAIN

UP

GOODS SHED

MAIN

DOWN

SIGNAL BOX

DOCK

PASSENGER STATION

UP MAIN HOME

UP REVERSIBLE LINE HOME

(FXD)

DOWN MAIN START

← To LEDBURY

63

EARLSWOOD LAKES

Origin: Great Western Railway
(By absorption of the Birmingham & North Warwickshire Railway on 30 July 1900)

Opened: 1 July 1908 (P) (Renamed "Earlswood" 6 May 1974)
       9 Dec. 1907 (G)
Closed: 6 July 1964 (G)
Plan date: 1908

The station is at the summit of the long bank from the direction of Stratford-on-Avon, and the gentler slope on the Birmingham side down to Bordesley.

The line from Bearley West Junction (near Stratford-on-Avon) to Tyseley was—by railway history standards—a late addition to the Great Western system, and, with the opening of the 18 mile line, 10 intermediate stations were opened, including Earlswood Lakes. In early Edwardian times, the country to the south of Birmingham was becoming increasingly attractive to the city workers (later to be dubbed "commuters") and the whole line was well patronised from the outset. The stations were wisely constructed to handle such passenger traffic, and Earlswood Lakes itself was built substantially, with neat brick buildings on both the long platforms, which were connected by a standard steel footbridge.

The scaled diagram shows the layout of the station and spacious yard as it was at opening, the yard containing a single long siding for coal traders, a short dock, and a 'loop' siding. A small structure on the main platform served as a goods shed.

In the summer period of 1938, the signal box was open continuously, and was provided with a switch.

FURTHER READING

R. Mag. 1908 (Vol. 22) pp. 116–120; 243–251   H.A.P.M. Pos. + grade profile of line
R. Mag. 1968 pp. 382–387; 482–487   H.A.P.M. Pos. + grade profile
"Reg. Hist. of the Railways of Great Britain" Vol. 7. (The West Midlands)
       by R. Christiansen. David & Charles

Earlswood Lakes.   Looking towards Henley-in-Arden.   *Lens of Sutton*

KEY TO STATION ROOMS

1. GENTS TOILET
2. LADIES WAITING ROOM
3. BOOKING HALL
4. BOOKING OFFICE
5. PARCELS & CLOAKROOM
6. S.M. OFFICE
7. PORTERS ROOM
8. GENTS LAV.
9. LADIES LAV.
10. LADIES WAITING ROOM
11. GENERAL WAITING ROOM

EARLSWOOD LAKES

APPROX SCALE: 108 FT TO 1 INCH

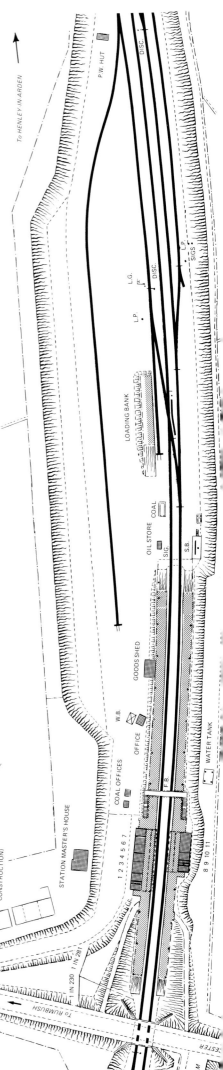

Evershot. View towards Maiden Newton. General view through station. *O.P.C.*

Evershot. Towards Castle Cary from the footbridge. *O.P.C.*

Evershot. Looking towards Maiden Newton. View from the South end of the station showing the signal box and goods yard. *O.P.C.*

EVERSHOT

Origin: Great Western Railway (who had absorbed the Wilts, Somerset, & Weymouth Railway in 1851)

Opened: 20 Jan. 1857
Closed: 3 Oct. 1966 (P)
7 Sept. 1964 (G)

Plan date: c. 1912

The broad gauge single line from Yeovil to Dorchester was opened on 20 Jan. 1857, Evershot being one of the intermediate stations from the outset. During 1858, the section from Yeovil to Evershot was doubled.

The station was small and well balanced, with both 'up' and 'down' platforms of almost equal length, and exactly opposite each other, and with the buildings on each platform of roughly equal size. It will be noticed in Diagram "A" that at the time of survey, there was no footbridge, and the old signal box was at the end of the 'up' siding. This box was closed and replaced by a new one nearer the station on the 'down' side between then and the end of the 1st War. The short siding parallel to the old 'up' siding (Diagram "B") was added in 1914. Little was done to the layout down to the Beeching rationalisation programme, when the old 'up' siding became redundant on 18 Dec. 1963, and the remaining sidings with connections on 7 Jan. 1965, 4 months after the withdrawal of freight facilities. The signal box was closed on the same day. On 26 May 1968 the line was singled, trains using the 'up' line only.

In the summer period of 1938, the signal box was open from 6.0 a.m. on Mondays to 6.0 a.m. the following Sunday morning, re-opening the same morning at 12.0 noon to close at 10.30 p.m. with an afternoon break between 3.30 p.m. and 5.0 p.m. There was no switch provided.

FURTHER READING

"The Railways of Dorset" by J. H. Lucking.   R.C. & T.S.
"Reg. History of the Railways of Great Britain." Vol. 1. (The West Country)
by D. St. J. Thomas. Phoenix

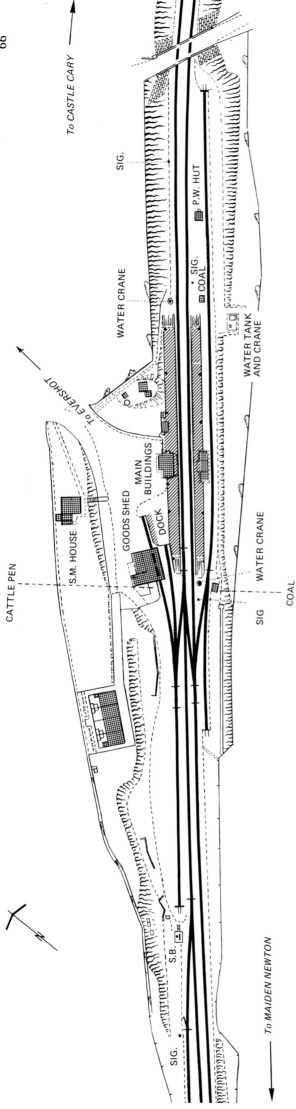

To CASTLE CARY

SIG.

WATER CRANE

To EVERSHOT

SIG.
COAL

P.W. HUT

WATER TANK
AND CRANE

MAIN
BUILDINGS

GOODS SHED

DOCK

S.M. HOUSE

CATTLE PEN

WATER CRANE

SIG

COAL

S.B.

SIG.

To MAIDEN NEWTON

EVERSHOT

DIAGRAM "A"
APPROX. SCALE: 130 FT. TO 1 INCH

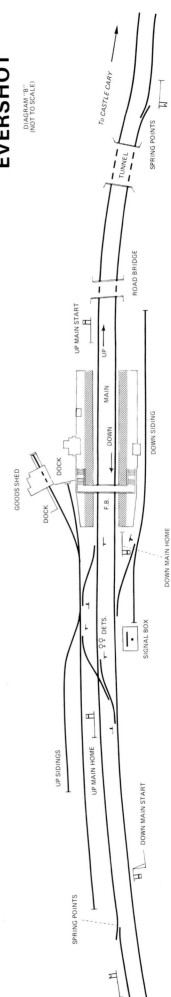

EVERSHOT

DIAGRAM "B"
(NOT TO SCALE)

To CASTLE CARY

TUNNEL

SPRING POINTS

ROAD BRIDGE

UP MAIN START

UP

DOWN

MAIN

DOWN SIDING

GOODS SHED

DOCK

DOCK

F.B.

DOWN MAIN HOME

UP SIDINGS

UP MAIN HOME

DETS.

SIGNAL BOX

DOWN MAIN START

SPRING POINTS

To MAIDEN NEWTON

**Fishguard &
Goodwick.**   View through the station towards Fishguard Harbour.   O.P.C.

FISHGUARD & GOODWICK

Origin: Great Western Railway
Opened: 1 July 1899 (G) ("Goodwick" until 1 May 1904)
                1 Aug. 1899 (P)
Closed: 6 Apr. 1964
Plan date: 1910

**Fishguard &
Goodwick.**   Looking East showing signal box and the engine shed
                    in the background.

**Fishguard &
Goodwick.**   View of the rail approach on the Western side of the   O.P.C.
                    station, taken from the road overbridge.

The station was first opened by the North Pembrokeshire & Fishguard Railway on
14 March 1895 for goods, and for passengers on 11 April 1895. (For full details, see
Mr. J. P. Morris's book referred to below, and in Vol. 2 of "The History of the G.W.R.",
both the original and revised editions).

The station proper did not occupy much land space, being an ordinary 2-road through
station with a short dock one side and a throat for the engine shed sidings on the other.
Through the close proximity of the Harbour station, opened 7 years later, and that
station's space restrictions, it was inevitable that the layout at Fishguard & Goodwick
should considerably develop, and that it did quite quickly, as a glance at the scaled
diagrams (from a 1910 survey) will reveal.

There was a large 2-road engine shed which was opened in the same year as the
Harbour station, and which survived until 1963.

The signal box opening hours in the summer period of 1938 were similar to those
applying at Fishguard Harbour box (overleaf) with adjustment to the Sunday afternoon
re-opening time (4.15 p.m.) and provisions, one of the latter being that Fishguard Harbour
box should advise other boxes concerned when they were required to open beyond their
official scheduled times. There was no switch provided at Fishguard & Goodwick signal
box.

FURTHER READING

"The North Pembrokeshire & Fishguard Railway" by J. P. Morris. Oakwood Press
"Great Western Engine Sheds—1947" by E. Lyons. Oxford Publishing Co.   O.P.C.
"The G.W.R. in the 20th Century" by O. S. Nock. Ian Allan Ltd.

FISHGUARD & GOODWICK

DIAGRAM "A"
APPROX. SCALE: 132 FT. TO 1 INCH

68

To CLARBESTON ROAD

ENGINE SHED

T.T.

CRANE

L.P.

CRANE

PIT

COAL STAGE

CATTLE PENS

MILEAGE SIDINGS

SIG.

SIG.

F.W.

CRANE

G.S.

MAIN BUILDINGS

W.B.

GATES

SIG.

CRUSHER

To FISHGUARD HARBOUR

N

FISHGUARD & GOODWICK

DIAGRAM "B"
(NOT TO SCALE)

To CLARBESTON ROAD

BRICKWOODS GROUND FRAME

YARD GROUND FRAMES
LEVERS RELEASED
BY KEY ON E.T. STAFF

WEIGHTED POINTS
SLOTTED BY 23

37 35

UP MAIN START

UP

DOCK

MAIN

DOWN

LOCO SIDINGS

ENGINE SHED

S.B.

36

31

UP MAIN HOME

DOWN GOODS RUNNING LOOP

SIDINGS

To FISHGUARD HARBOUR

DOWN MAIN
ADV. ST.

(FISHGUARD HARBOUR SIGNALS)

KEY TO NUMBERED SIGNALS

31 – DOWN MAIN TO DOWN GOODS RUNNING LOOP START
35 – DOWN MAIN TO DOWN GOODS RUNNING LOOP HOME
36 – DOWN MAIN STREET
37 – DOWN MAIN HOME

FISHGUARD HARBOUR

Origin: Fishguard Bay Railway & Pier Company—title changed in 1894 to Fishguard & Rosslare Railways. Eventually under control of G.S. & W.R. and G.W.R. who built the station.

Opened: 30 Aug. 1906

Closed:

Plan date: c. 1910 (Signalled diagram—c. 1947)

A terminus at Fishguard was the original intention of the South Wales Railway, but this scheme was abandoned in 1851 in favour of one at Neyland. The project was revived in 1897 by the G.W.R. who in 1898 acquired control of the North Pembrokeshire & Fishguard Railway (who had reached Letterston in March 1895). In May 1899 it was agreed that the Fishguard & Rosslare Railways and Harbours Company would complete the harbours at both ports, building a railway between Rosslare and Waterford, and to supply the cross channel steamers. It was agreed also, that the G.W.R. should make an entirely new line from Clarbeston Road to Fishguard (Goodwick). This line was opened on 1 July 1899. Work proceeded on the extension to the harbour, and the new route to Ireland was opened on 30 Aug. 1906.

Such were the origins of the Fishguard Harbour station—in brief summary. A more detailed description of events can be found in the "History of the G.W.R." Vol. 2.

The station can best be described as a 'through' terminal, and is one of the few of this type to be found in these Islands. A prominent feature of the station is the large area of covered cattle-pen accommodation which was provided—necessary for the considerable amount of cattle traffic between the ports.

Regarding the track and platform usage within the station itself, it will first be noted that the two island platforms between them, serve all four platform lines, but that only the two served by the island platform furthest from the harbour are passenger lines. This is how the station was first arranged and signalled when first opened, but the layout was so designed as to allow the other lines (shown as No. 1 and No. 2 sidings on the signalled diagram illustrated) to be used as passenger lines if required later.

During the time that the station was busy with Cunarder traffic from 1908 onwards, it became necessary to use No. 1 siding as a running line—the platform becoming No. 3. This arrangement lasted until about 1926, by which time the Cunarder traffic had been lost, and the line then reverted to 'siding' status, except for occasional special passenger-workings.

The ground frame between Nos. 1 and 2 platform lines replaced two earlier ground frames (one for each catch-point) during the resignalling of the station in 1926. At the same time, the single-slip points outside the signal box (these points were previously compound points) were installed.

For the modeller, Fishguard Harbour station offers definite potentialities, and, being an "open-ended" terminal, convenience of operation in particular.

Signal box opening hours in the summer period of 1938 were—Mondays 6.0 a.m. until 6.25 a.m. the following Sunday morning (or after clearance of the train departing at 6.05 a.m.), re-opening at 12.0 noon, closed at 2.0 p.m. (or after clearance of the 1.25 p.m. 'up' train) and if the 4.25 p.m. ex-Fishguard Harbour was running—opened again at 3.30 p.m. to finally close at 5.0 p.m. The box was not provided with a switch.

FURTHER READING

R. Mag. 1906 (Vol. 19) pp. 217–226   H.D.A.P.M. Pos. (under construction)
    + grade profile.

R. Mag. 1910 (Vol. 26) p. 411   H.A.P.

"The G.W.R. in the 20th Century" by O. S. Nock. Ian Allan Ltd.

"The Great Western at the Turn of the Century" by A. R. Kingdom. O.P.C.

Great Western Railway Magazine. 1905 Jan. and Feb.: 1906 Feb. and Sept.

Fishguard Harbour. 'Country' end of station and road approach. *O.P.C.*

Fishguard Harbour. General view of station. *R.H. Clark*

FISHGUARD HARBOUR

DIAGRAM "A"
APPROX. SCALE: 132 FT. TO 1 INCH

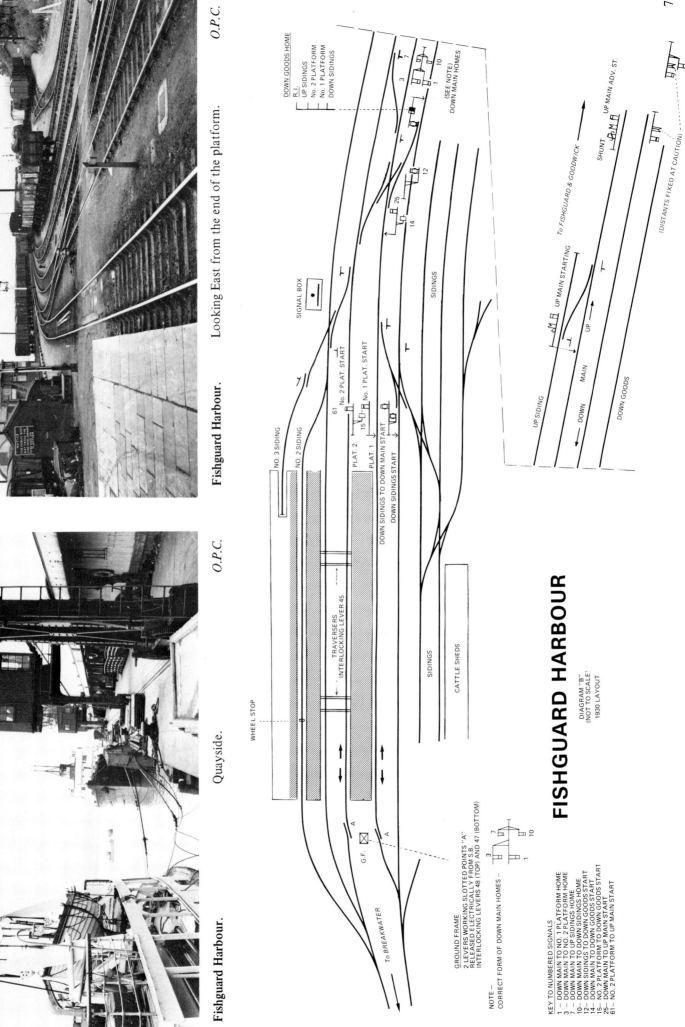

Fishguard Harbour. O.P.C. Quayside.

Fishguard Harbour. Looking East from the end of the platform. O.P.C.

DOWN GOODS HOME

R.I.
UP SIDINGS
No. 2 PLATFORM
No. 1 PLATFORM
DOWN SIDINGS

(SEE NOTE)
DOWN MAIN HOMES

SIGNAL BOX

SIDINGS

NO. 3 SIDING
NO. 2 SIDING

No. 2 PLAT. START
No. 1 PLAT. START

PLAT. 2
PLAT. 1

DOWN SIDINGS TO DOWN MAIN START
DOWN SIDINGS START

SIDINGS

CATTLE SHEDS

WHEEL STOP

TRAVERSERS
INTERLOCKING LEVER 45

G.F.

GROUND FRAME
2 LEVERS WORKING SLOTTED POINTS "A"
RELEASED ELECTRICALLY FROM S.B.
INTERLOCKING LEVERS 48 (TOP) AND 47 (BOTTOM)

NOTE—
CORRECT FORM OF DOWN MAIN HOMES—

To BREAKWATER

To FISHGUARD & GOODWICK

UP MAIN ADV. ST.

SHUNT

UP MAIN STARTING

UP SIDING

DOWN

MAIN

UP

DOWN GOODS

(DISTANTS FIXED AT CAUTION)

FISHGUARD HARBOUR

DIAGRAM "B"
(NOT TO SCALE)
1930 LAYOUT

KEY TO NUMBERED SIGNALS
1 — DOWN MAIN TO NO. 1 PLATFORM HOME
3 — DOWN MAIN TO NO. 2 PLATFORM HOME
7 — DOWN MAIN TO UP SIDINGS HOME
10— DOWN MAIN TO DOWN SIDINGS HOME
12— DOWN SIDINGS TO DOWN GOODS START
14— DOWN MAIN TO DOWN GOODS START
15— NO. 2 PLATFORM TO DOWN GOODS START
25— DOWN MAIN TO UP MAIN START
61— NO. 2 PLATFORM TO UP MAIN START

71

GARA BRIDGE

Origin: Great Western Railway
(by absorption of the Kingsbridge & Salcombe Railway in 1888)
Opened: 19 Dec. 1893
Closed: 16 Sept. 1963 (P & G)
Plan date: 1912

Gara Bridge was the principal of the three intermediate stations on the Kingsbridge branch, and the only passing station. Apart from the up platform and the passing loop through it, the basic layout was almost identical with those of Avonwick to the north and Loddiswell on the south except that the siding and dock were at the Kingsbridge end of the station, whereas at the other two aforementioned stations, the sidings were at the Brent end. As can be seen from the illustrations, the style of the three stations' buildings were similar, and each one was on a curve in the line.

The ruling gradient from Avonwick was 1 in 82 (falling) and the station enjoyed the same train service as at both its neighbouring stations.

At some time after the survey of the main plan shown here, the trailing lead into the up line from the siding, together with its single slip point trailing into the down line at the southern end of the down platform, was taken out of use and removed, being replaced with a facing lead into the siding in the down main at the same spot.

Unlike Avonwick and Loddiswell, Gara Bridge boasted a signal box as well as a ground frame, and the signal box, open from 7.0 a.m. to 9.25 p.m. (SX), 10.5 p.m. (SO), was not provided with a switch.

FURTHER READING

T.I.   1958 pp. 94–97   H.A.P.
M.R.C.   1965 p. 101 Detailed picture of signal box
"A Great Western Gallery" by B. L. Davis and A. I. Rivers (Pos.)
Great Western Society Ltd.
"Reg. Hist. of the Railways of Great Britain" Vol. 1. (The West Country)
by D. St. J. Thomas. Phoenix

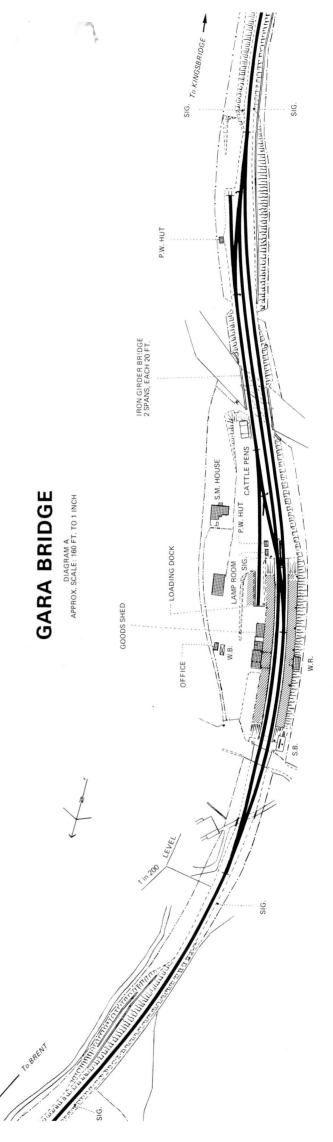

GARA BRIDGE

DIAGRAM A
APPROX. SCALE: 160 FT. TO 1 INCH

Gara Bridge. Looking towards Brent. Camping coach on right.
May 1956.

R.H. Clark

Gara Bridge. Looking towards Kingsbridge.

Lens of Sutton

GARA BRIDGE

DIAGRAM "B"
(NOT TO SCALE)

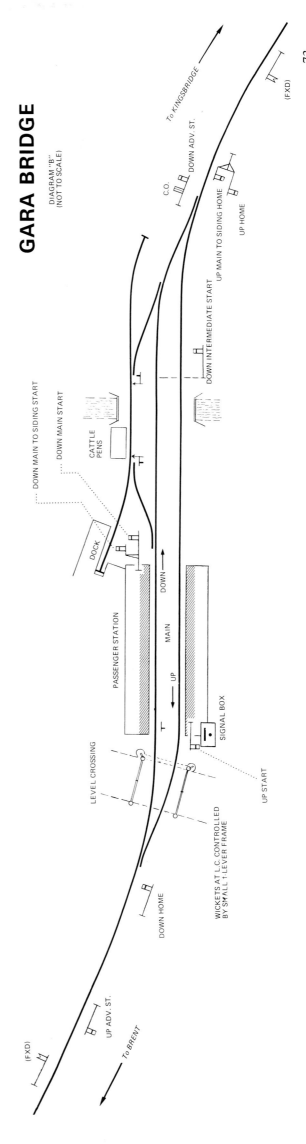

To KINGSBRIDGE

DOWN ADV. ST.

C.O.

UP MAIN TO SIDING HOME

UP HOME

DOWN INTERMEDIATE START

DOWN MAIN TO SIDING START

DOWN MAIN START

CATTLE
PENS

DOCK

DOWN

MAIN

UP

PASSENGER STATION

SIGNAL BOX

UP START

LEVEL CROSSING

WICKETS AT L.C. CONTROLLED
BY SMALL 1-LEVER FRAME

DOWN HOME

UP ADV. ST.

(FXD)

To BRENT

73

GERRARDS CROSS

Origin: Great Western & Great Central Joint

Opened: 2 April 1906 (P)
20 Nov. 1905 (G)

Closed: 6 Jan. 1964 (G)

Plan date: 1910 (Diagram "B" 1924)

The joint line from Northolt Junction to High Wycombe was opened first to goods traffic on 20 Nov. 1905, and for passengers on 2 April 1906, and the intermediate stations at opening were Ruislip, Denham, Gerrards Cross and Beaconsfield.

Gerrards Cross was built as a 4-road station with the 'up' and 'down' through lines passing down the centre, between the 'up' and 'down' platform loops. In relation to the station buildings provided, the platforms are long and spacious, having been built with 'commuter' traffic in mind.

Between 1910 and 1920, the two short sidings on the 'up' side, opposite the signal box, were installed, as well as the extension of the 'up' platform loop westward to form

a longer siding, and protecting catch point (see Diagram "B").

On 11 Nov. 1923 the East signal box was closed, and the West signal box lost its "West", to become "Gerrards Cross" signal box. The platform loops were extended eastward and the old connections to the main lines taken out on 2 May 1942, the platforms themselves being extended in the same direction in 1960.

Although goods facilities had been withdrawn in January of 1964, it was not until November of the same year that the sidings, and all connections to the main and 'up' loop lines were discontinued for use.

In the summer of 1938, the signal box was open continuously, and was provided with a switch.

FURTHER READING

R. & T.M.   1911 (Jan.) p. 38 Pos.
R. & T.M.   1912 (Oct.) pp. 293–298   D.A.P. Pos.
R. & T.M.   1920 (Nov.) p. 285 Pos.

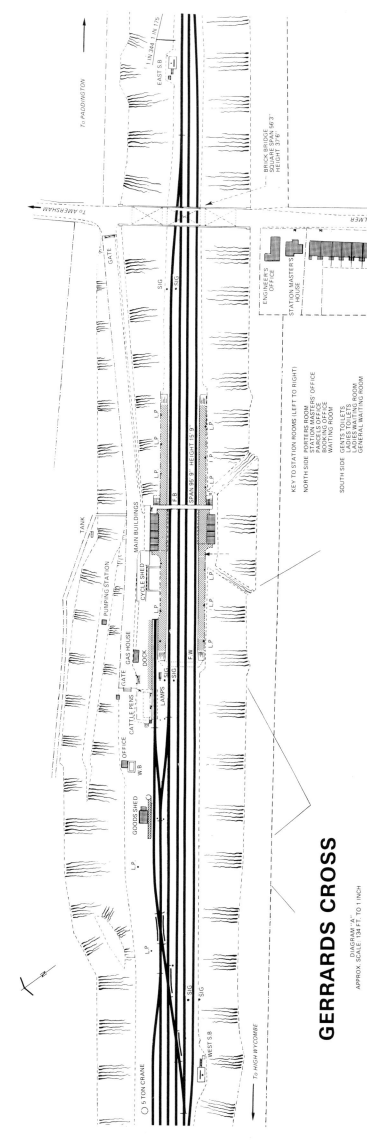

GERRARDS CROSS

DIAGRAM "A"
APPROX. SCALE 134 FT. TO 1 INCH

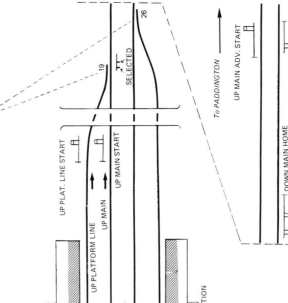

Gerrards Cross. Looking towards Princes Risborough. *H.C. Casserley*
14 June 1958.

Gerrards Cross. Looking towards Paddington on a misty day. *Lens of Sutton*

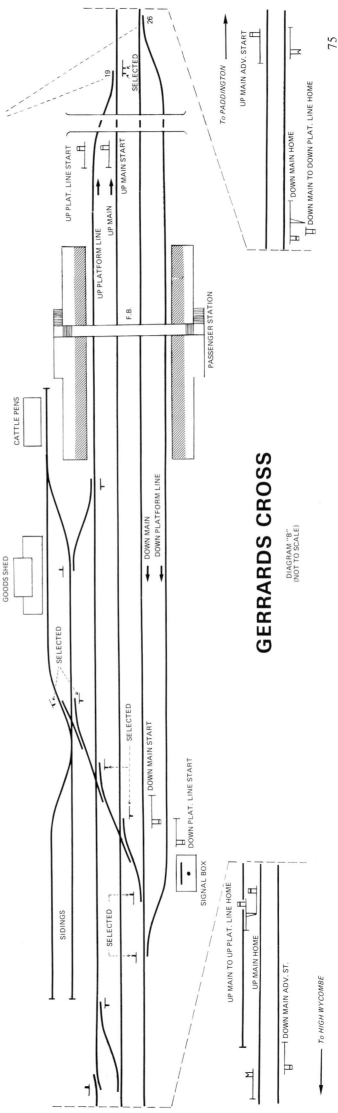

POINTS 19 AND 26 WORKED
BY MOTOR (HAND GENERATOR)

To PADDINGTON →

UP PLAT. LINE START

UP MAIN START

UP MAIN ADV. START

DOWN MAIN HOME

DOWN MAIN TO DOWN PLAT. LINE HOME

UP PLATFORM LINE

UP MAIN

F.B.

PASSENGER STATION

CATTLE PENS

GOODS SHED

DOWN MAIN

DOWN PLATFORM LINE

SELECTED

SELECTED

DOWN MAIN START

DOWN PLAT. LINE START

SIGNAL BOX

SELECTED

SIDINGS

SELECTED

UP MAIN TO UP PLAT. LINE HOME

UP MAIN HOME

DOWN MAIN ADV. ST.

DOWN MAIN ADV. ST.

← To HIGH WYCOMBE

GERRARDS CROSS

DIAGRAM "B"
(NOT TO SCALE)

GOBOWEN

Origin:	Shrewsbury & Chester Railway
	(Absorbed by G.W.R. on 1 Sept. 1854)
Opened:	16 Oct. 1848
Closed:	2 Nov. 1964 (G)
Plan date:	c. 1913

Gobowen was opened with the standard gauge line from Shrewsbury to Ruabon on the date shown above, and was quickly followed by the branch to Oswestry on 23 Dec. 1848.

It was a straight two-road 'through' main line station, and, before the 1960's rationalisation programme had 'up' and 'down' bay roads and extensive sidings.

The platforms are long with extensive canopies. Actual terminal goods facilities, however, were limited with a small 'through' road goods shed containing a 2-ton capacity crane, adjacent cattle pens with a sizeable platform dock, and a "back" siding—that was all. The main unusual feature of the layout on the yard side was that the only access to the "back" siding was via (and into) the loco shed! This loco shed had a pit extending almost the whole of its length, plus a shorter pit at the northern end, outside.

The branch to Oswestry lost its passenger services on 7 Nov. 1966.

In the summer period of 1938, the opening hours for the two signal boxes were:—

Gobowen South: Mondays, 4.15 a.m. to 8.0 a.m. the following Sunday morning, re-opening at 11.45 a.m. (Sunday) until 6.50 p.m. with a break from 12.45 p.m. to 5.40 p.m.
The box was provided with a switch.

Gobowen North: Sunday 8.30 p.m. until 8.10 a.m. the following Sunday, re-opening at 8.40 a.m. until 6.45 p.m. with a break from 12.30 p.m. to 4.10 p.m.
The box was NOT provided with a switch.

Before leaving duty, the signalmen were obliged to put the level crossing gates across the railway, and to put the signals at danger. It was obligatory for either Shrewsbury (Coton Hill) or Chester to advise if any 'specials' were to be run.

Gobowen. Looking towards Ruabon. Oswestry branch train in the bay platform on the left. *M. Hale*

Gobowen. View through station towards Shrewsbury *O.P.C.*

FURTHER READING

R.W. 1963 pp. 363–372 H.A.P.M.

"The Cambrian Railways" (Vol. 1) by R. Christiansen & R. W. Miller. David & Charles

GOBOWEN

DIAGRAM "A"
APPROX. SCALE: 174 FT. TO 1 INCH

To SHREWSBURY →

To OSWESTRY →

S.B.

ENGINE SHED

WATER TANK

CATTLE PENS

G.S.

W.B.

OFFICE

MAIN BUILDINGS

S.M. HOUSE

To OSWESTRY

L.C.

IRON GIRDER F.B. SPAN 43'

SIDING
41' TO STOPS

To LLANGOLLEN

S.B.

To RUABON

N

GOBOWEN

SOUTH S.B.

ENGINE SHED

UP PLAT.

DOWN PLAT.

ENLARGEMENT (NOT TO SCALE) TO SHOW POINTWORK NORTH OF STATION

Gobowen. Looking towards Ruabon.
O.P.C.

GWINEAR ROAD

Origin: West Cornwall Railway
Leased from opening to G.W.R., B. & E., and S.D.R. and
absorbed by G.W.R. in 1878

Opened: 11 Mar. 1852 (First opened by Hayle Railway Co. 22 May 1843)

Closed: 5 Oct. 1964 (P)
9 Aug. 1965 (G)

Plan date: c. 1908

Like many other junction stations in the British railway system, Gwinear Road was rather remote and "out in the wilds" being about 3 miles by road from the small village of Gwinear its nearest settlement of human habitation. But when the Helston branch was decided upon, Gwinear Road was the most convenient junction point with the main line, and the station's importance increased accordingly, necessitating the subsequent building of the complex of sidings on the down side of the main line and to the east of the junction.

The signal box at the eastern end of the up platform was closed on 30 Nov. 1916 when the new 'West' box was opened on the opposite side of the station, at the eastern end of the down platform. From Camborne to Gwinear Road the main line was doubled from 21 Jan. 1900, and thence to Angarrack on 13 June 1915, the platforms were extended at the same time.

The East signal box was (1938) open on weekdays from 2.15 p.m. to 10.5 p.m. with a break between 5.15 and 7.55 p.m. and was provided with a switch. It was closed on Sundays. The West box (at the station itself) was open from 4.45 a.m. to 10.50 p.m. (or as soon as the last train had cleared)—12.5 a.m.S O (Sunday mornings), and on Sundays from 5.45 a.m. to 10.45 p.m. with breaks between 2.15 and 4.55 p.m. and 5.40 and 7.45 p.m. The West box was not provided with a switch.

The main line between Truro and Penzance was opened as "narrow gauge", but on 6 Nov. 1866 a broad gauge rail was added and brought into use for goods trains, passenger trains following on 1 Mar. 1867.

FURTHER READING

R. Mag. 1925 (Vol. 57) pp. 193–203   H.A.P.M.
T.I.   1952 pp. 203–207   D.A.P. Pos.
R.W.   1964 pp. 424–428   H.A.P.M. Pos.

"The Hayle, West Cornwall & Helston Railways" by G. H. Anthony. Oakwood Press
"The Story of Cornwall's Railways" by A. Fairclough. Tor Mark Press
"Reg. Hist. of the Railways of Great Britain" Vol. 1. (The West Country)
   by D. St. J. Thomas. Phoenix

"The Railways of Cornwall, 1809–1963" by C. R. Clinker. David & Charles

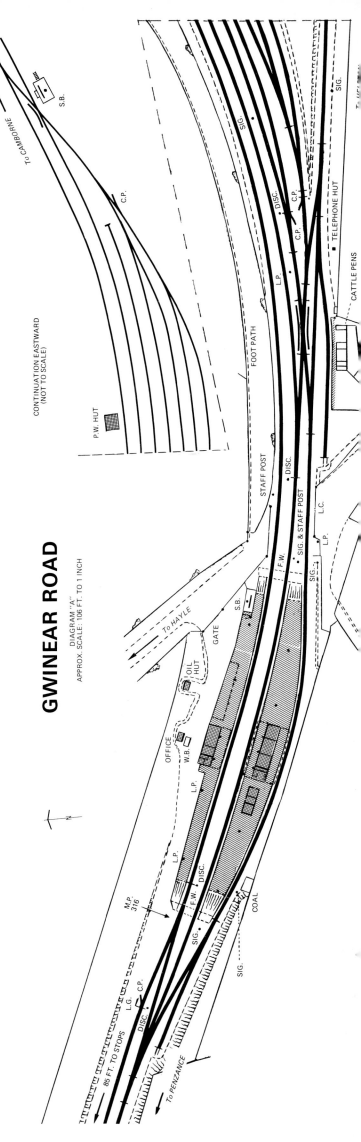

GWINEAR ROAD

DIAGRAM "A"
APPROX. SCALE: 106 FT. TO 1 INCH

GWINEAR ROAD

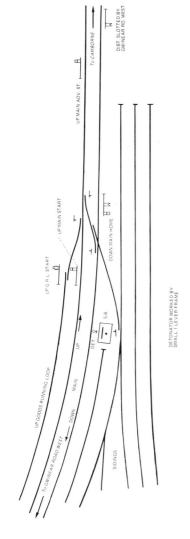

EAST SIGNAL BOX
DIAGRAM "C"
(NOT TO SCALE)

DIST. SLOTTED BY
GWINEAR RD. WEST

To CAMBORNE

UP MAIN ADV. ST.

UP MAIN START

UP G R L START

DOWN MAIN HOME

UP

DET. S.B.

DOWN MAIN

To GWINEAR ROAD WEST

UP GOODS RUNNING LOOP

SIDINGS

DETONATOR WORKED BY
SMALL 1 LEVER FRAME

Gwinear Road. The station building on the down side, and the nameboard. *Lens of Sutton*

GWINEAR ROAD
FOR HELSTON
THE LIZARD, MULLION
AND PORTHLEVEN

GWINEAR ROAD

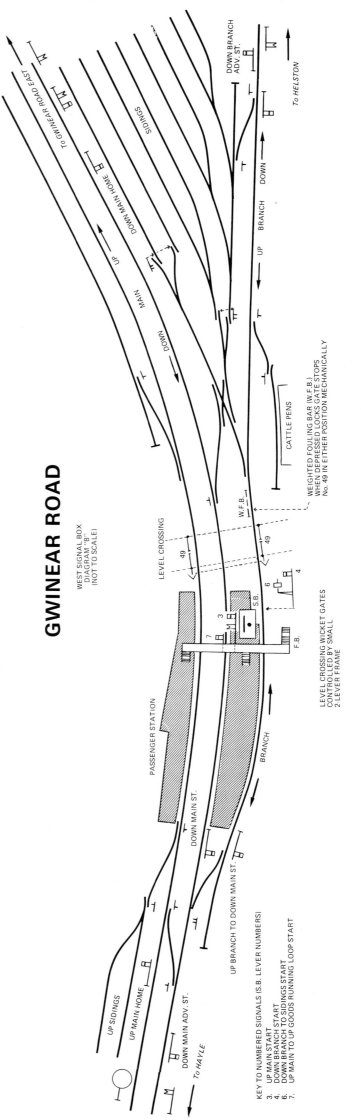

WEST SIGNAL BOX
DIAGRAM "B"
(NOT TO SCALE)

To GWINEAR ROAD EAST

DOWN BRANCH
ADV. ST.

To HELSTON

SIDINGS

DOWN MAIN HOME

UP MAIN

DOWN MAIN

UP BRANCH

DOWN BRANCH

CATTLE PENS

WEIGHTED FOULING BAR (W.F.B.)
WHEN DEPRESSED LOCKS GATE STOPS
No. 49 IN EITHER POSITION MECHANICALLY

LEVEL CROSSING

W.F.B.

49

49

PASSENGER STATION

7

3

M

S.B.

6

4

F.B.

DOWN MAIN ST.

UP BRANCH TO DOWN MAIN ST.

BRANCH

LEVEL CROSSING WICKET GATES
CONTROLLED BY SMALL
2-LEVER FRAME

UP SIDINGS

UP MAIN HOME

DOWN MAIN ADV. ST.

To HAYLE

KEY TO NUMBERED SIGNALS (S.B. LEVER NUMBERS)

3. UP MAIN START
4. DOWN BRANCH START
6. DOWN BRANCH TO SIDINGS START
7. UP MAIN TO UP GOODS RUNNING LOOP START

80

HALL GREEN

Origin:	Great Western Railway (By absorption of the Birmingham & North Warwickshire Railway on 30 July 1900)
Opened:	1 July 1908 (P) 9 Dec. 1907 (G) (Opening of line from Tyseley to Bearley West Jc. for goods traffic)
Closed:	6 May 1968 (G)
Plan date:	c. 1913

Hall Green is on the same line as Earlswood Lakes and, at opening, the general layout followed a similar pattern, with neat and substantial main buildings (106 feet long), and long platforms, connected near the centre by a footbridge. The latter had a continuation on the 'down' side to a footpath to the main road which passed over the railway on a skew bridge.

It will be seen from Diagram "B" that the siding accommodation had developed, with a 'down' siding near the signal box and additional sidings on the 'up' side.

A point worth noting is that the access to the station offices can only be made from the platform side.

In the summer period of 1938, Hall Green signal box was open from 5.30 a.m. on Mondays until 1.0 a.m. the following Sunday morning, re-opening at 7.0 a.m. and closing at 11.0 p.m. with a long break from 1.0 p.m. to 7.30 p.m. The box was provided with a switch.

FURTHER READING

R. Mag. 1968 pp. 382–387; 482–487 H.A.P.M. and grade profile.
"Reg. Hist. of Rlys. of G.B.—The West Midlands" by Rex Christiansen. David & Charles

Hall Green. Looking towards Shirley. An old view through the station with local railmotor approaching.

Lens of Sutton Collection

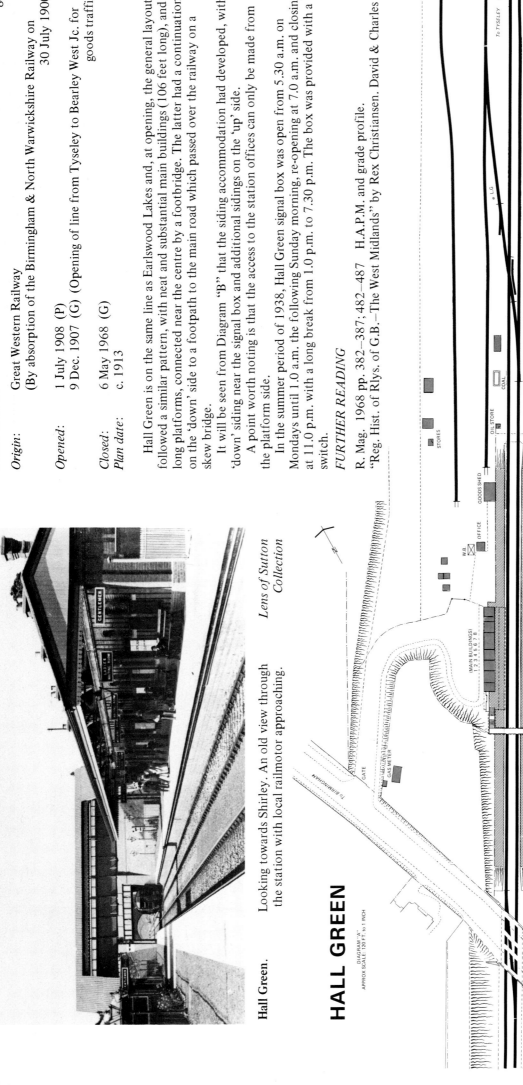

HALL GREEN

DIAGRAM "A"
APPROX SCALE: 120 FT. to 1 INCH

KEY TO STATION ROOMS (MAIN BUILDINGS)
1. STATION MASTER'S OFFICE
2. PARCELS & CLOAKROOM
3. BOOKING OFFICE
4. BOOKING HALL
5. GENERAL WAITING ROOM
6. LADIES WAITING ROOM
7. LADIES LAV.
8. GENTS. LAV.

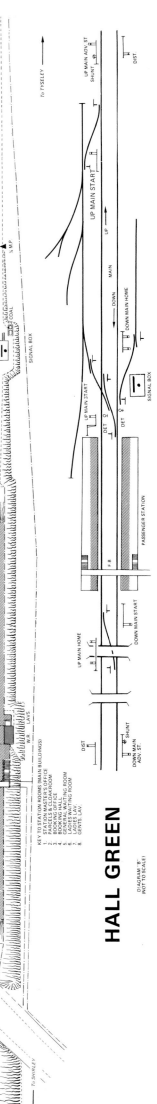

HALL GREEN

DIAGRAM "B"
(NOT TO SCALE)

HAVERFORDWEST

Origin: South Wales Railway
         (Amalgamated with the G.W.R. and West Midland 1 Aug. 1863)

Opened: 2 Jan. 1854
Closed:
Plan date: c. 1910

The South Wales Railway extended their broad gauge single line from Carmarthen to Haverfordwest on 2 Jan. 1854. Barlow rails were initially used in its construction, but this pattern was discontinued (wherever they had been used) a few years later as being totally unsatisfactory on account of "track-spreading tendencies".

As with most original stations, that at Haverfordwest was a humble affair, containing the barest minimum of facilities but subsequent development eventually produced the layout illustrated in Diagram "A". In this, evidence can be seen of the former broad gauge in the wide "6 foot" way between the tracks.

However, few stations in such rural areas have seen such alterations in their layouts which occurred as 'recently' as 1938, when the goods yard was virtually transferred from one side of the main line to the other, including the goods shed itself. A new footbridge was built facing the opposite way from the old, the platforms were extended, and buildings modernised. A curious feature of the new goods yard layout is that no shunting necks were provided, and those on the old 'down' siding were discontinued. The old dock siding and its shunting neck (west of the 'up' platform) was taken out, as was the long "ladder" crossover from the 'down' main to the goods shed road, and the 'middle' siding was converted to an 'up' goods loop. This re-arrangement allowed for the handling of longer trains without fouling neighbouring tracks.

The 1938 signal box opening hours were:—

Haverfordwest: Mondays: 5.30 a.m. until 7.20 a.m. Sunday mornings (or after clearance of last 'down' train)

          Sundays: 12.40 p.m. until clearance of last train.
                    There was no switch provided.

Haverfordwest Bridge West:

               Weekdays: 6.0 a.m. to 10.0 p.m.
               A switch was provided.

FURTHER READING

R. Mag. 1914 (Vol. 35) July & Aug. issues (Articles on "Little England beyond Wales" by G. W. Potter)

R. Mag. 1939 (Vol. 85) pp. 197–202   H.A.P.

Haverfordwest.   Looking towards Clarbeston Road. 30 July 1958.   *M. Hale*

Haverfordwest.   General view of whole station and goods yard looking towards Johnston.

J.P. Morris

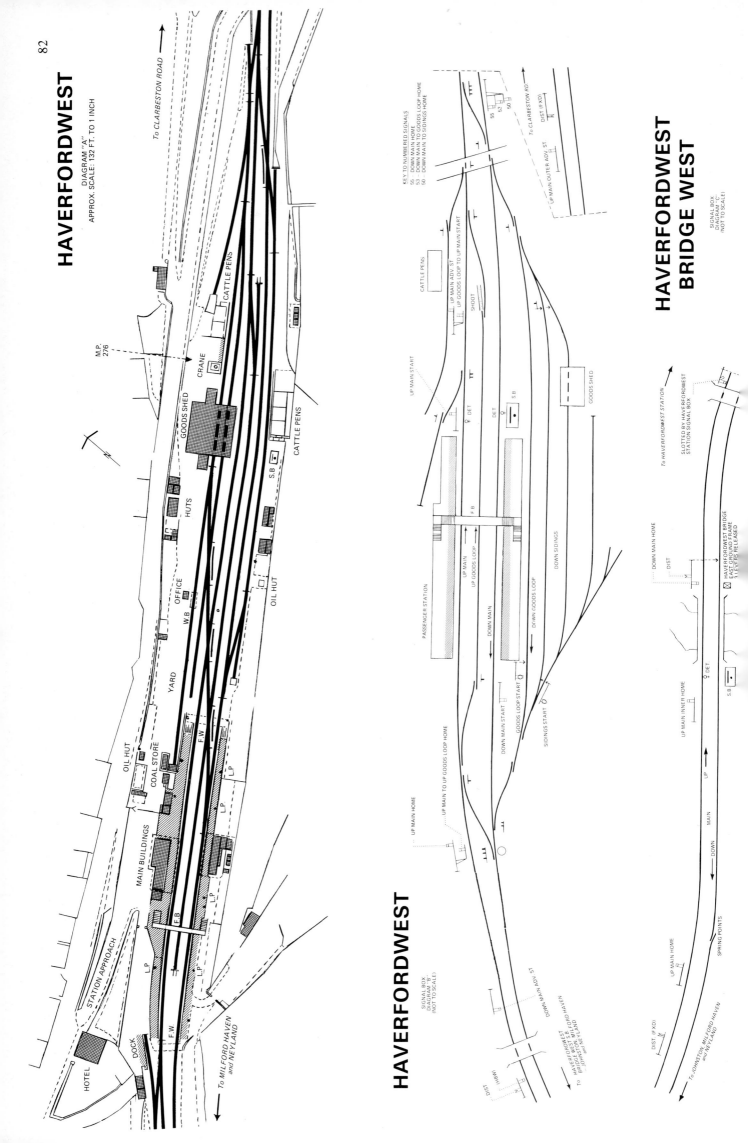

82

HAVERFORDWEST
DIAGRAM "A"
APPROX. SCALE: 132 FT. TO 1 INCH

To CLARBESTON ROAD

M.P.
276

CATTLE PENS

CRANE

GOODS SHED

HUTS

CATTLE PENS

S.B

OFFICE

OIL HUT

W.B

YARD

OIL HUT

OIL HUT

COAL STORE

F.W.

L.P

L.P

L.P

L.P

MAIN BUILDINGS

F.B

L.P

L.P

L.P

STATION APPROACH

HOTEL

DOCK

F.W

F.W

L.P

To MILFORD HAVEN
and NEYLAND

HAVERFORDWEST

SIGNAL BOX
DIAGRAM 'B'
(NOT TO SCALE)

UP MAIN HOME

UP MAIN TO UP GOODS LOOP HOME

CATTLE PENS

UP MAIN ADV ST

UP GOODS LOOP TO UP MAIN START

SHOOT

DET

DET

S.B

PASSENGER STATION

F.B

GOODS SHED

UP MAIN

UP GOODS LOOP

DOWN MAIN

DOWN GOODS LOOP

DOWN SIDINGS

DOWN MAIN START

GOODS LOOP START

SIDINGS START

UP MAIN HOME

DOWN MAIN ADV ST

HAVERFORDWEST S.B.
To HAVERFORDWEST MILFORD HAVEN
BRIDGESTON, MILFORD HAVEN
and NEYLAND

DIST
(HBW)

KEY TO NUMBERED SIGNALS
55 – DOWN MAIN HOME
53 – DOWN MAIN TO GOODS LOOP HOME
50 – DOWN MAIN TO SIDINGS HOME

55
53
52
50

To CLARBESTON RD.

DIST (FXD)

UP MAIN OUTER ADV ST

HAVERFORDWEST
BRIDGE WEST

SIGNAL BOX
DIAGRAM "C"
(NOT TO SCALE)

To HAVERFORDWEST STATION

SLOTTED BY HAVERFORDWEST
STATION SIGNAL BOX

DOWN MAIN HOME

DIST

HAVERFORDWEST BRIDGE
EAST GROUND FRAME
3 LEVERS RELEASED

UP MAIN INNER HOME

DET

S.B

UP

DOWN

MAIN

UP MAIN HOME

SPRING POINTS

DIST (FXD)

To JOHNSTON, MILFORD HAVEN
and NEYLAND

HAYLE

DIAGRAM "A"

APPROX. SCALE: 121½ FT TO 1 INCH

Origin: West Cornwall Railway (absorbing the Hayle Railway)
Leased by G.W., B. & E., and S.D.R. jointly from 1 July 1865 and
absorbed by those companies on 1 Jan. 1866.
Finally absorbed by G.W.R. on 1 Aug. 1878

Opened: 11 Mar. 1852 (2nd station on main line) (Public opening)
Closed: 8 June 1964 (G) Except for PS traffic, since withdrawn.
Plan date: c. 1905

The old terminus in Foundry Square, Hayle was closed on 16 Feb. 1852.

The single line from Truro to Penzance was laid as standard gauge, and it was over 14 years before the broad gauge rail was added (Nov. 1866) and broad gauge goods trains used the line as well as standard gauge. Broad gauge passenger trains started to run on 1 March 1867. The line was not converted back again to standard gauge until 20 May 1892. The track was doubled between Hayle and St. Erth on 10 Sept. 1899 and between Angarrack and Hayle on 19 Dec. 1909.

The signal box on the 'up' platform replaced an old "West" box, which was formerly off the end of the down platform, and ultimately the old East signal box which was closed in 1911. Before the end of the 1st. World War, a third siding was added, parallel to the curved two beside the Wharves branch. The engine shed was closed in 1906. Public goods traffic ceased on the Hayle Wharves branch on 1 May 1967. Further rationalisation both before and after this date disposed of the remaining sidings and connections leaving the main line and the Hayle Wharves branch (for private siding traffic) and a trailing crossover beyond the west access to the branch.

Hayle signal box was (1938) open from 5.40 a.m. to 9.40 p.m. weekdays and closed on Sundays, and was provided with a switch. The Wharf signal box (not shown in the above diagrams) was opened as required, and had no switch.

FURTHER READING

"The Hayle, West Cornwall and Helston Railways" by G. H. Anthony. Oakwood Press
"The Story of Cornwall's Railways" by A. Fairclough. Tor Mark Press, Truro
"The Railways of Cornwall, 1809–1963" by C. R. Clinker. David & Charles

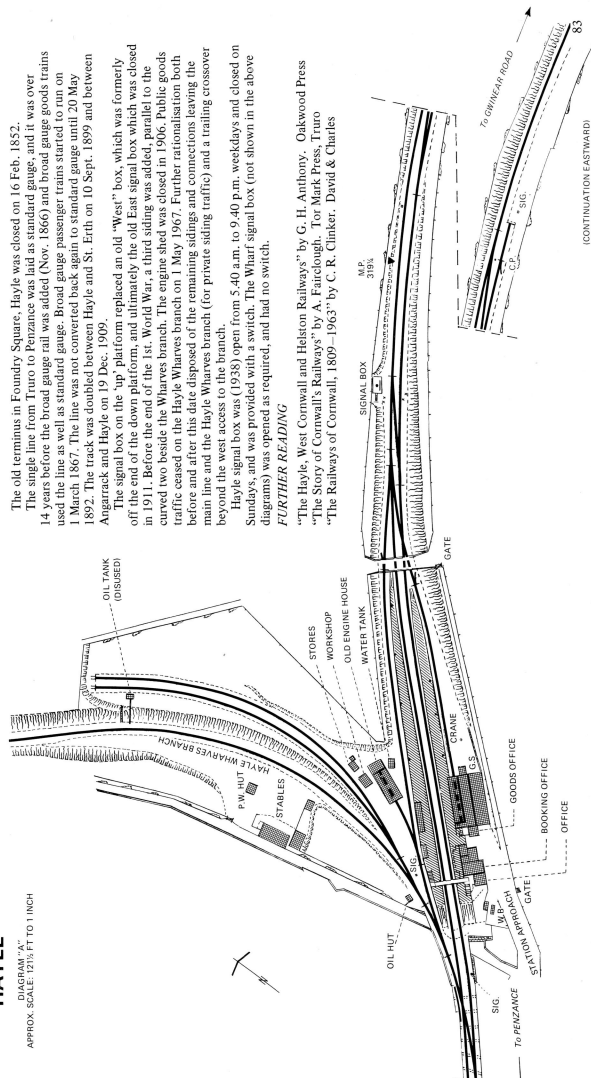

84

Hayle.   Looking towards Penzance. The engine shed can be seen behind the water tank.

H.C. Casserley

Hayle.   The signal box and waiting room on the up platform.

Lens of Sutton

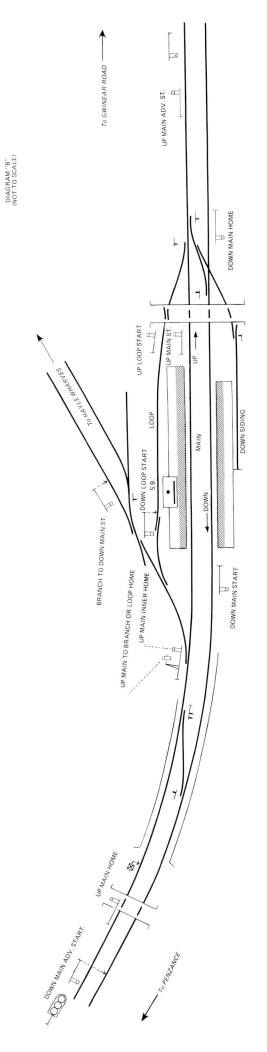

HAYLE

DIAGRAM "B"
(NOT TO SCALE)

To GWINEAR ROAD

UP MAIN ADV. ST.

DOWN MAIN HOME

To HAYLE WHARVES

UP LOOP START

UP MAIN ST.

UP

LOOP

DOWN LOOP START

S.B.

MAIN

DOWN SIDING

BRANCH TO DOWN MAIN ST.

DOWN

UP MAIN TO BRANCH OR LOOP HOME

UP MAIN INNER HOME

DOWN MAIN START

UP MAIN HOME

DOWN MAIN ADV. START.

To PENZANCE

HEATHFIELD

Origin: Moretonhampstead & South Devon Railway
Absorbed by the South Devon Railway in 1872, thence by G.W.R. in 1878

Opened: 4 July 1866 (as "Chudleigh Road", renamed "Heathfield" on 1 Oct. 1882)

Closed: 2 Mar. 1959 (P)
4 Dec. 1967 (G) (Open for coal traffic only from 14 June 1965)

Plan date: c. 1915

The station was 3m. 70c. up the broad gauge Moretonhampstead branch from Newton Abbot, on a ruling gradient of 1 in 70 (steepening to 1 in 53 and 1 in 66 as far as Bovey). By the date of Diagram "A" the station had achieved some importance by virtue of the development of private siding traffic, which further developed in later years.

On 9 Oct. 1882 the first part of the Teign Valley standard gauge line was opened for the first 6¼ miles as far as Ashton (a week after "Chudleigh Road" changed its name to "Heathfield") and the station became an interchange one for both broad and standard gauge trains, without any physical connection between the two branches. The Teign Valley branch was therefore completely isolated from the rest of the G.W. system for nearly 10 years—until the Moretonhampstead–Newton Abbot line was converted on 23 May 1892.

Certain track alterations were made and completed by 2 Oct. 1916 by taking out the connection from the 'up' (Moretonhampstead line) siding to the (Teign Valley line)

platform line, plus the following crossover to the back siding, and replacing the formation with a direct lead from the 'up' siding (referred to above) to the Teign Valley branch (in' effect, a reversal of the old connection), and the moving of the crossover (to the back siding) further down, to lead into the Teign Valley branch in the same direction.

This gave at least two new facilities. The back siding, parallel to the Teign Valley platform line, could now be used as a 'run-round' and Teign Valley trains could run direct to and from the Moretonhampstead line platform. Further alterations were completed by 9 June 1927, by the opening of a new crossing loop on the main line (making the station a double-road, two platform one). In 1943, there were again small revisions of the layout, and in 1961 a new private siding was added on the Teign Valley side of the station. Thereafter, and at long intervals, the layout dwindled into decline, to become no more than a small group of private sidings served direct from Newton Abbot.

In 1938, Heathfield signal box was opened for the first train and closed after the last train had cleared. On Sundays, the box was opened as required.

FURTHER READING

R.W.   1958 p. 47 H. Para. Pos.
R. Mod. 1970 p. 392 S.B. Diagram.
R.W.   1976 pp. 434–435 D.A.P.
"Reg. History of the Railways of Great Britain" Vol. 1. (The West Country) by D. St. J. Thomas. Phoenix

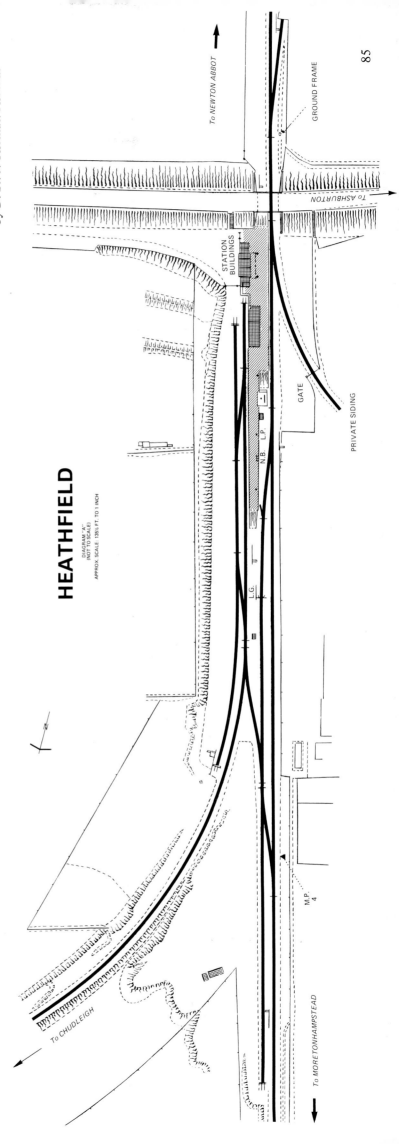

HEATHFIELD

DIAGRAM "A"
(NOT TO SCALE)
APPROX. SCALE 135⅓ FT. TO 1 INCH

To NEWTON ABBOT

To ASHBURTON

To CHUDLEIGH

To MORETONHAMPSTEAD

GROUND FRAME

STATION BUILDINGS

GATE

PRIVATE SIDING

M.P. 4

Heathfield. Looking towards Moretonhampstead. Note the oil lamps. *Lens of Sutton*
An old picture probably taken about 1920.

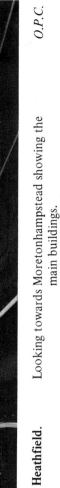

Heathfield. Looking towards Moretonhampstead showing the
main buildings. *O.P.C.*

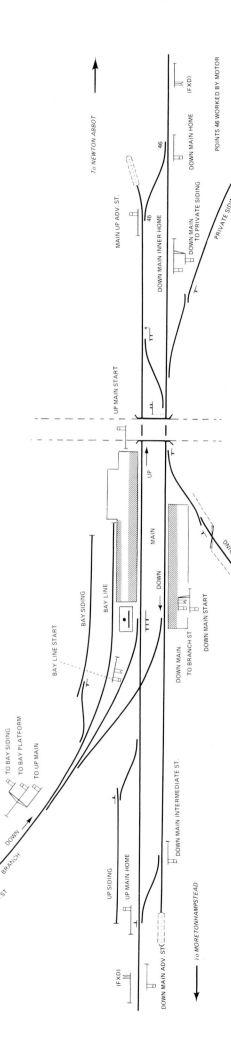

HEATHFIELD

DIAGRAM "B"
(NOT TO SCALE)

line were revised, including the removal (in 1899) of a trailing crossover which was formerly at the western end of the platforms. During the late war, on 30 Nov. 1943, a long upside loop was brought into use north of the station, and the trailing lead from the main goods yard into the up main line was discontinued on the same day. The 1960's rationalisation programme eventually reduced the layout (other than the main line) to the 'down' and 'up' loops, the short cattle pen siding, and part of the "loop" coal siding, which had been cut just beyond the goods shed.

In 1938 (summer period) the signal box was open continuously, and there was no switch.

FURTHER READING

R.W. 1957 p. 240 Pos.
"Reg. Hist. of the Railways of Great Britain" Vol. 1. (The West Country)
by D. St. J. Thomas. Phoenix

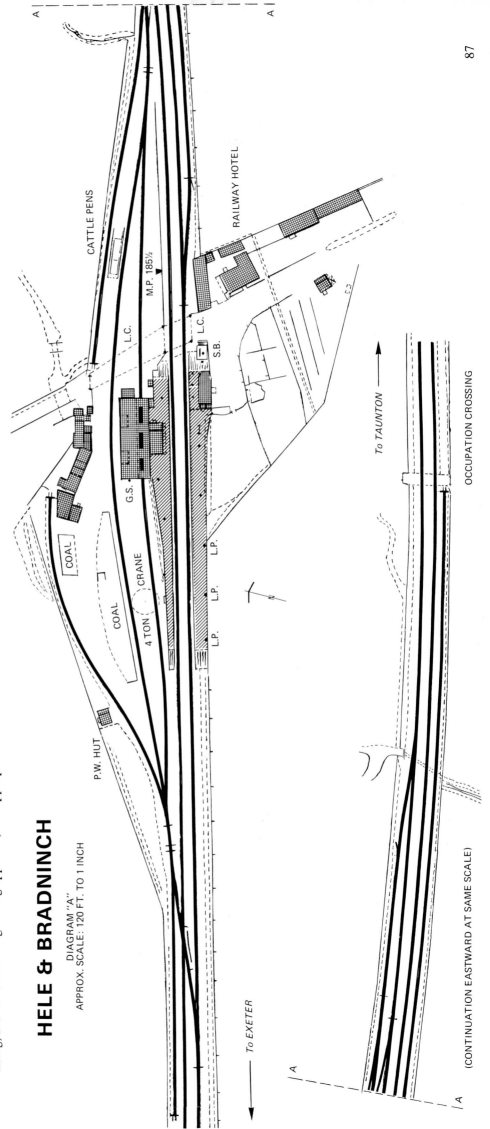

HELE & BRADNINCH

DIAGRAM "A"
APPROX. SCALE: 120 FT. TO 1 INCH

Origin: Bristol & Exeter
Amalgamated with the G.W.R. on 1 Aug. 1876
Opened: 1 May 1844
Closed: 5 Oct. 1964 (P)
17 May 1965 (G)
Plan date: c. 1913

Hele & Bradninch was opened (as "Hele") on the Bristol & Exeter's broad gauge main line 22m. 32ch. west of Taunton, and just over half way down the 20 mile long descent from Whiteball to Exeter (St. David's).

Between 1890 and 1898, there were track additions to the layout, which included the terminating coal siding (facing west), the up side shunting neck, and (in Feb. 1899) the single slip across the up main line. During the same period the terminating cattle pen siding, and the down refuge siding appeared, and appropriate connections to the main

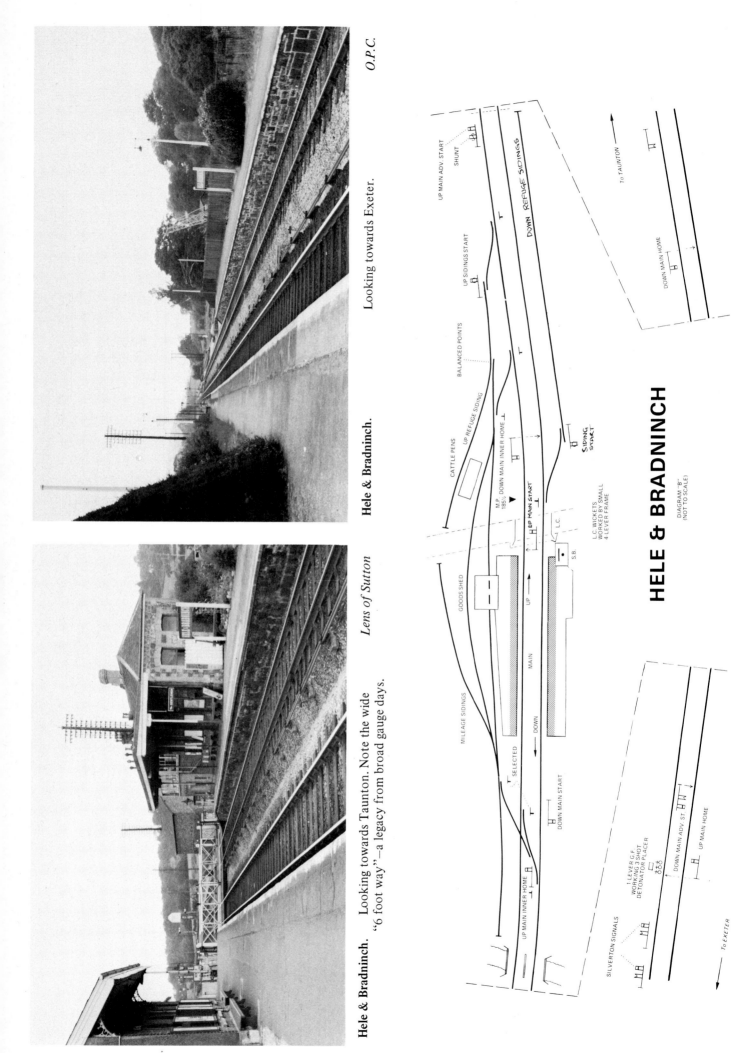

Hele & Bradninch.   Looking towards Exeter.   *O.P.C.*

Hele & Bradninch.   Looking towards Taunton. Note the wide "6 foot way"—a legacy from broad gauge days.   *Lens of Sutton*

HELE & BRADNINCH

DIAGRAM "B"
(NOT TO SCALE)

UP MAIN ADV. START

SHUNT

UP SIDINGS START

BALANCED POINTS

UP REFUGE SIDING

CATTLE PENS

M.P. 185¾

DOWN MAIN INNER HOME

UP MAIN START

GOODS SHED

MILEAGE SIDINGS

SELECTED

DOWN MAIN START

UP MAIN INNER HOME

DOWN REFUGE SIDINGS

SIDING START

L.C.

MAIN

UP

DOWN

S.B.

L.C. WICKETS
WORKED BY SMALL
4 LEVER FRAME

SILVERTON SIGNALS

1 LEVER G.F.
WORKING 3 SHOT
DETONATOR PLACER

DOWN MAIN ADV. ST

UP MAIN HOME

TO TAUNTON

DOWN MAIN HOME

To EXETER

HELSTON

Origin:	Helston Railway
	Absorbed by the Great Western Railway 1 July 1898
Opened:	9 May 1887
Closed:	3 Nov. 1962 (P)
	4 Oct. 1964 (G)
Plan date:	c. 1908

Literary coverage of this once attractive little terminus has been considerable, and comment here is confined mainly to the track layout. Only an occasional alteration was made to the original layout, the main one being that the access road to the engine shed was moved from the down loop to the platform road (just outside the signal box), and the cattle pen and dock road connection was moved from the goods shed road to the loop road nearer the road overbridge. The carriage shed at the extreme terminus of the line was demolished in the late 1950's.

The whole branch was (1938) worked by Electric Train Staff, with passing places at Helston, Nancegollan and Gwinear Road. The signal box was open on weekdays between 6.20 a.m. and 10.30 p.m. (or until the last train had cleared the section), and the box was not provided with a switch. There was no Sunday service on the branch (in 1938).

Helston. Close-up of station buildings.

Lens of Sutton

Helston. Looking towards Gwinear Road from the end of the platform.

O.P.C.

FURTHER READING

R. Mag. 1908 (Vol. 22) p. 301 Pos.
R. Mag. 1952 p. 644 H. Para.
T.I. 1952 pp. 203–207. D.A.P. Pos
R.W. 1964 pp. 424–428 H.A.P.M.
M.R.N. 1967 pp. 29, 31, 78–79, 128–129, 223, 251, 284–285, 344–345, 387–389, pp. 442–443, 444, 506–507. (Comprehensive series of articles with diagrams of station buildings on the branch.)
R. Mod. 1972 pp. 11, 89. S.B. Diagram, and letter (respectively.)
"The Hayle, West Cornwall, & Helston Railways" by G. H. Anthony. Oakwood Press
"Great Western Engine Sheds, 1947" by E. Lyons. Oxford Publishing Company
"The Railways of Cornwall, 1809–1963" by C. R. Clinker. David & Charles
"The Story of Cornwall's Railways" by A. Fairclough. Tor Mark Press
"The Great Western at the turn of the Century" (a fine Pos.) by A. R. Kingdom.
Oxford Publishing Co.

"Regional History of the Railways of G.B." Vol. 1. (The West Country)
by D. St. J. Thomas. Phoenix

HELSTON

DIAGRAM "A"
APPROX. SCALE: 106 FT. TO 1 INCH

CHURCH ROAD BRIDGE
SPAN 14' 0"

SLAUGHTER HOUSE

STABLES

LOADING PLATFORM

CATTLE PENS

OIL STORES

L.G.

• 4 TON CRANE

MAIN BUILDINGS

GOODS SHED

OFFICE

MOTOR SHED ⊠ W.B.

OFFICE

COAL

GATE

CHURCH F.P.

STATION APPROACH

GATE

CARRIAGE SHED

DISC.

L.P.

L.P.

L.P.

L.P.

L.P.

L.P.

L.P.

L.P.

YARD

P.W. HUT

▲ M.P. 8¾

OFFICE

ASH

COAL

COAL

E.S.

STORE

S.B.

DISC.

(ONE TRACK)

(ONE TRACK)

ACTUAL ARRANGEMENT OF RAIL TRAPS (ABOVE)

To GWINEAR ROAD

N

INDEX TO STATION ROOMS

1 – URINAL   5 – BOOKING OFFICE
2 – STORE   6 – OFFICES
3 – STORE   7 – STORE
4 – LADIES   8 – PARCELS
                  9 – REFRESHMENTS

4	5	6	7		9
1			8		
2					
3					

HELSTON

DIAGRAM "B"
(NOT TO SCALE)

CARRIAGE SHED

SPRING POINTS
SLOTTED BY LEVER 12.

GOODS SHED

LOADING BANK

DOWN

UP

MAIN

PASSENGER STATION

SIGNAL BOX

UP MAIN START

UP MAIN TO
LOCO START

UP MAIN TO
SIDINGS HOME

DOWN MAIN HOME

UP MAIN ADV. ST.
C.O.

DOWN MAIN TO
SIDINGS HOME

ENGINE SHED

To GWINEAR ROAD

HORRABRIDGE

Origin:	South Devon & Tavistock
	(Absorbed by South Devon Railway—July 1865
	Absorbed by G.W.R. 1878)
Opened:	22 June 1859 (P) (Formal opening 21 June 1859)
	1 Feb. 1860 (G)
Closed:	31 Dec. 1962 (P)
	31 Dec. 1962 (G)
Plan date:	c. 1910

It can be said that Dartmoor is completely ringed by attractive railway stations, and Horrabridge was one of them. The passenger part of it consisted of two platforms ('up' and 'down'), the up side containing a small building for booking and waiting purposes, and a canopy over its platform frontage to fit, a low signal box, a waiting shelter on the 'down' side, and a wide level crossing at the Yelverton end. Considering that the goods yard handled traffic for Yelverton in addition to its own, facilities seem to have been quite limited, for it is known that it was a busy station. There was a small goods shed and dock, and it did have a yard crane, whose capacity seemed to reduce as the years progressed. In 1877, it had a 5 ton crane, in 1891 it had a 4½ tonner, and by 1910 it had been reduced to a 3¾ ton crane (according to official records) but by 1938 the capacity had been increased to 3½ tons and the yard could accept "Horse Boxes and Prize Cattle Vans" which, apparently, it could not at the earlier periods mentioned! In the meantime, and down to post War years, the track layout had not altered at all although the gauge was mixed (broad and standard) in May 1876 and finally to standard gauge only in 1892.

In 1938, the line was worked by Electric Train Staff, and there was an overall speed restriction of 40 m.p.h.

Horrabridge signal box was open on weekdays from 6.15 a.m. until 12.20 (midnight), and from 11 a.m. to 9.45 p.m. on Sundays, with two breaks. The box was not provided with a switch.

FURTHER READING

R. Mag. 1908 (Vol. 23) pp. 473—479 H.D.A.P.M.
R. Mag. 1909 (Vol. 24) pp. 38—45 H.D.A.P.M.
"The Tavistock, Launceston & Princetown Railways" by G. H. Anthony. Oakwood Press
"Plymouth & Launceston" by T.W.E. Roche
"Reg. Hist. of the Railways of Great Britain" Vol. 1. (The West Country)
                                              by D. St.J. Thomas. Phoenix.

Horrabridge.   An early picture of a Tavistock-Plymouth train entering the station.

Lens of Sutton Collection

Horrabridge.   Looking towards Yelverton.

Lens of Sutton

HORRABRIDGE

DIAGRAM "A"
APPROX. SCALE: 120 FT. to 1 INCH

To YELVERTON

To PLYMOUTH

TO MAIN ROAD

To TAVISTOCK

To BUCKLAND MONACHORUM

SIG

To HORRABRIDGE

SIG

L.C.

W.C.

GATE

MAIN BUILDINGS

S.B

CRANE

G.S

LOADING BANK

W.C.

To ROBOROUGH DOWN

SIG

M.P. 9

L.G

W.B

TANK

W.C.

SIG

To TAVISTOCK

HORRABRIDGE

DIAGRAM "B"
(NOT TO SCALE)

To YELVERTON

(FXD)

SHUNT

UP MAIN START

SPRING POINTS
SLOTTED BY 5

DOWN MAIN HOME

SIGNAL BOX

DOCK

UP

MAIN

DOWN

DOWN MAIN START

UP MAIN HOME

UP SIDING

DOWN SIDING

(FXD)

To TAVISTOCK

IVYBRIDGE

Origin: South Devon Railway
(Absorbed by G.W.R. in 1878)

Opened: 1848

Closed: 2 Mar. 1959 (P)
29 Nov. 1965 (G)

Situated high above, and some distance from the small village from which it takes its name, Ivybridge station could not offer much encouragement for development in the district. It follows that the layout remained simple and compact down to the Beeching era. Although the date of Diagram "A" is not known it is reasonable to expect that it is at some time between the abolition of the broad gauge in May 1892 and the end of King Edward's reign. The building of the goods yard and shed were obviously anticipated as is evidenced by the position of the signal box and the short piece of track which was to form the connection of the yard to the main line and up siding.

Also, the crossover at the viaduct end of the station had been removed before 1910.

Rationalisation of the layout included the redundancy of the trailing connection to the up siding on 1 Sept. 1963, the lifting of the up siding *and* the up refuge siding in Sept. 1964, the down siding becoming a private siding (with revised main line connections) and the lifting of the remainder of the goods yard track, both events occurring on 14 Jan. 1968.

The signal box was open on weekdays continuously from 5.15 a.m. on Mondays to 6.0 a.m. Sundays, and opened again from 2.0 p.m. to 4.0 p.m. and from 7.45 p.m. to 10.0 p.m. (Sundays) and it was provided with a switch.

FURTHER READING

M.R.C. 1956 pp. 10, 33. Plans and elevations (scaled)
"The G.W.R. in the 19th Century" by O. S. Nock. Ian Allan (Includes an early P.O.S.)
"Reg. Hist. of the Railways of Great Britain" Vol. 1. (The West Country) by D. St. J. Thomas. Phoenix

Ivybridge. Showing the start of the viaduct immediately beyond the end of the platform ramps. *O.P.C.*

Ivybridge. Looking towards Totnes. General view. *O.P.C.*

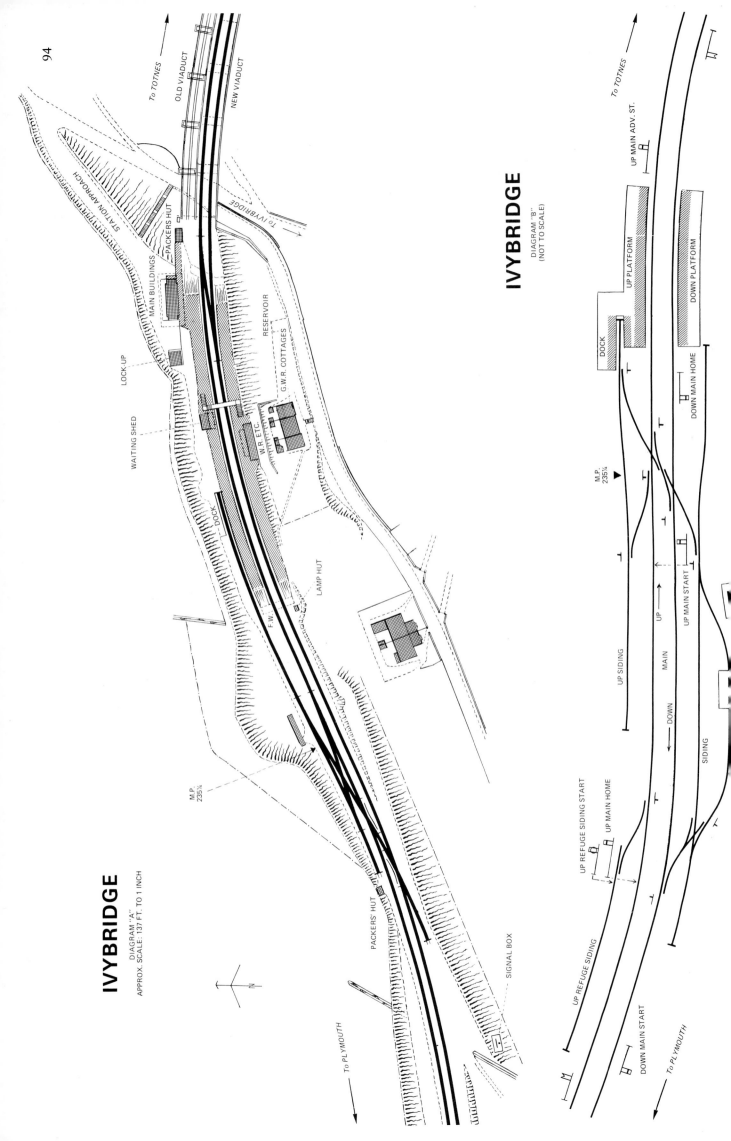

94

IVYBRIDGE
DIAGRAM "A"
APPROX. SCALE: 137 FT. TO 1 INCH

To TOTNES

OLD VIADUCT

NEW VIADUCT

TO IVYBRIDGE

STATION APPROACH

PACKERS HUT

MAIN BUILDINGS

LOCK-UP

RESERVOIR

WAITING SHED

G.W.R. COTTAGES

W.R. ETC.

DOCK

LAMP HUT

F.W.

M.P. 235¼

N

PACKERS' HUT

SIGNAL BOX

To PLYMOUTH

IVYBRIDGE
DIAGRAM "B"
(NOT TO SCALE)

To TOTNES

UP MAIN ADV. ST.

UP PLATFORM

DOWN PLATFORM

DOCK

DOWN MAIN HOME

M.P. 235¼

UP

UP MAIN START

UP SIDING

MAIN

SIDING

DOWN

UP REFUGE SIDING START

UP MAIN HOME

UP REFUGE SIDING

DOWN MAIN START

To PLYMOUTH

KINGSBRIDGE

DIAGRAM "A"
APPROX SCALE : 120FT. TO 1 INCH

OFFICE
W.M.

PRATTS
PETROL STORE

CRANE 21 CWT
3 TON SINGLE CHAIN
6 TON DOUBLE CHAIN

GARAGE

PETROL

OIL

GOODS OFFICE

CANOPY

GOODS SHED

SIGNAL BOX

P.W. HUT

STORE

BRICK ARCH BRIDGE
SPAN 15 FT

CULVERT
2' 0"

CULVERT
3' 6" DIA

FLOW

FLOW

To BRENT

1 IN 60   1 IN 660

1 IN 660

1 IN 300

FOOTPATH

SAND

OIL

G.P.O.
LETTER
BOX

L.P

MAIN BUILDINGS

FORECOURT

To SALCOMBE

GATE

L.P

CATTLE
PENS

ENGINE SHED

COAL   ASH   TANK

SIG   W.C.   L.P

L.P

DISC

COAL

SIG

SIG

To KINGSBRIDGE

KEY TO ROOMS IN MAIN BUILDINGS

1	2		4	5	6	7
	3					

1 STORES
2 GENTS
3 LAVS
4 LADIES W.R.
5 GENERAL W.R.
6 STATION MASTER'S OFFICE
7 PARCELS OFFICE

KINGSBRIDGE

Origin: Great Western Railway
Opened: 19 Dec. 1893
Closed: 16 Sept. 1963 (P. & G.)
Plan date: c. 1913

The dot in the middle of the goods shed is a 300 cwt. crane with a radius of 14'6". The 'flag' on the platform side of the parcels office is a small weighing machine.

By the nature of the terrain in Devon and Cornwall the railways therein abound in curves and twists, and there is barely a straight length of track in the whole of the Kingsbridge branch from its junction at Brent to the buffer stops at Kingsbridge. As can be seen from the diagrams and photos, Kingsbridge station itself is on a curve for the whole of its length.

Before the middle of August 1915, the platform line extended a short distance beyond the platform limit to the buffer stops, but it was foreshortened at that time.

The main station buildings, engine shed, goods shed and the lower part of the signal box were solidly built of stone, but the carriage shed (which is not shown on the official scaled diagram), located on the siding adjacent to the run-round loop, was a mere corrugated iron shelter painted black. It must have been added at a much later date than the opening of the branch. It sheltered two passenger coaches only.

Subsequent to the date of the main plan shown here, the siding which abuts on to the end of the platform ramp was removed and the platform considerably extended on both the main and bay faces, although it was rare for lengthy passenger trains to be operated on the branch except in the height of the summer seasons in the 'twenties and 'thirties.

Kingsbridge station, although handling a fair amount of freight and passenger traffic in its own right, also served the popular resort of Salcombe Regis, and local horse-drawn coach operators did brisk business in early days "meeting the trains". Horse traction eventually gave way, of course, to the internal combustion engine, which, in turn superseded the railway itself.

FURTHER READING

R. Mod. 1956 p. 114
T.I.   1958 pp. 94—97   H.A.P. Pos.
R. Mag. 1958 p. 661   H. Para.
M.R.C.   1964 pp. 10—12   D.A.P. Pos + layout plan
"Great Western Engine Sheds, 1947" by E. Lyons (1972) O.P.C.
"Great Western Branch Line Album" by Ian Krause (p. 42 Pos.) Ian Allan Ltd.
"Reg. Hist. of the Railways of Great Britain" Vol. 1. (The West Country) by D. St. J. Thomas. Phoenix

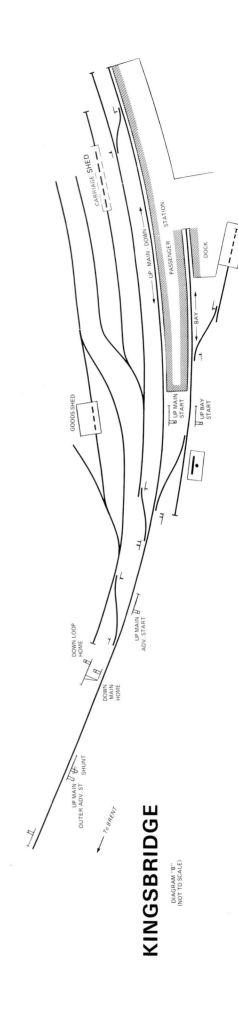

Kingsbridge. Before the motor car had reached these parts—probably not long after the line was opened.

Author's collection

Kingsbridge. General view into station with 2-6-2T No. 5533 taking water. August 1956.

R.H. Clark

KINGSBRIDGE

DIAGRAM "B"
(NOT TO SCALE)

KINGSWEAR

Origin: Dartmouth & Torbay Railway
Absorbed by the Great Western Railway in 1878.
Transferred from B.R. (W) to the Dart Valley Railway Co. on 1 Nov. 1972

Opened: 16 Aug. 1864 (P)
2 Apr. 1866 (G)

Closed: 4 May 1964 (G) Remained open for private siding traffic, but now withdrawn.

Plan date: c. Nov. 1915

The original scheme was to take the line across the river from near Greenway, to run down the opposite river bank into Dartmouth itself. In the event, Dartmouth Station was built without its railway, and Kingswear became the terminating point of the branch from Newton.

The whole broad gauge branch was worked by the South Devon Railway from the outset, and was leased to that Company from 1 Jan. 1866, who finally absorbed it in 1872, and S.D.R. itself being absorbed into the G.W.R. in 1878.

The character and general layout of the station will be widely familiar, but certain historical details are worthy of note.

With the exception of the turntable and its roads, Diagram "A" is exactly as the layout was at the turn of the century, the turntable, together with two additional carriage sidings being added between 1900 and 1905. After this, there were few alterations until the engine shed was closed on 14 July 1924. Further extensions of track accommodation, and revision of pointwork took place in the late 1920's, together with an extension of the platform, and the whole scheme was completed by May 1929, by which time the jetty tracks, and small turntables had disappeared. For the next 37 years, the layout remained much the same, when the major B.R. rationalisation programme began. By the time of transfer of the station and line to the Dart Valley Railway Preservation Society, the station had been stripped of its sidings and outer platform bay. All the sidings behind the signal box, and the goods shed road were lifted in Nov. 1966, the remaining sidings near the sea wall, and the No. 2 platform line becoming redundant, and disused on 20 Oct. 1968, as did the signal box.

In 1938 (summer period), the signal box was opened on weekdays at 4.20 a.m., and closed after the clearance of the 12.5 a.m. light engine (12.30 a.m. Friday nights) from Kingswear. The box was opened as required on Sundays, closing at 1.0 a.m. (night), and there was no switch provided.

FURTHER READING

R. Mag. 1930 (Vol. 66) pp. 253–265 H.D.A.P.M.; also p. 485 (notes on branch).
R. Mag. 1934 (Vol. 75) p. 120 (Picture of signal box and approach lines)
T.I. 1954 p. 5 Pos.
T.I. 1958 pp. 360–373 H.A.P. Pos. (and approach lines.)
R. Mag. 1958 p. 661 Historical paragraph.
"Reg. History of the Railways of Great Britain." Vol. 1 (The West Country) by D. St. J. Thomas. Phoenix

The publications of the Dart Valley Railway Preservation Society.

O.P.C.

Kingswear. General view of the station looking across the water to Dartmouth.

O.P.C.

Kingswear. Looking towards Churston.

KINGSWEAR

DIAGRAM "A"
APPROX. SCALE 120 FT. TO 1 INCH

98

To CHURSTON

MUD

110 FT. TO STOPS

110 FEET TO STOPS

To CHURSTON

MUD

GRIDIRON

FOOTPATH

SIGNAL BOX

TURNTABLE

L.P.

W.C.

L.P.

L.P.

CATTLE PENS BOARD

CATTLE PENS RAMP

GATE

PACKERS HUT

FOOTBRIDGE

OFFICE

L.P.

STEPS
(DOWN TO F.B.)

L.P.

L.G.

ENGINE SHED

COAL STAGE

TANK

T.P.

MP 228¾

T.P.

L.P.

RIVER DART

JETTY

LIGHTHOUSE

TRAVELLING CRANE

GOODS YARD

NAME BOARD

DISC

T.P.

T.P.

T.P.

T.P.

P.H.

2 TON CRANE

GOODS SHED

CANOPY

CANOPY

MAIN BUILDINGS

FOUNTAIN

PONTOON
LANDING STAGE
(G.W.R.)

KINGSWEAR
ROYAL DART
HOTEL

KINGSWEAR
SLIP FERRY

T.T.

KINGSWEAR

DIAGRAM "B"
(NOT TO SCALE)

UP SIDINGS

OUTER ADV. START

DOWN HOME

UP

MAIN

DOWN

DOWN SIDINGS

To CHURSTON

UP ADV. STARTS

DOWN
INNER HOMES

PLAT. 1 START

No. 2 PLATFORM
2ND. STARTER

S.B.

DOWN LOOP

To TURNTABLE

SIDINGS

FOOTBRIDGE

SIDING

UP LOOP

No. 1 PLATFORM

No. 2 PLATFORM

A

A

No. 2 PLATFORM
1 ST. STARTER

GOODS SHED

GROUND FRAME
WORKING POINTS "A"
INTERLOCKING LEVER 22

PASSENGER
STATION

LAPWORTH

Origin: Great Western Railway
(by absorption of the Birmingham & Oxford Junction Railway on
31 Aug. 1848)

Opened: 1855 ("Kingswood" until 1 May 1902)
Closed: 11 Nov. 1963 (G)
Plan date: c. 1925

Lapworth. Looking towards Birmingham. *O.P.C.*

Lapworth. Looking towards Birmingham, after rebuilding. *O.P.C.*

The mixed gauge line from Banbury to Birmingham was opened on 1 Oct. 1852.

The original station at Lapworth had long since been replaced by the time of the diagram, and was further improved and extended in the great "modernisation" process over the main line system, which took place at the turn of the century and after.

The station as shown in the layout plan, was partially "staggered" with about half of each platform opposite the other, and conveniently joined by a (roofed) standard steel footbridge.

Since the survey (illustrated), the platform canopies have been modernised and extended southward, as have the platforms, and the 'up' platform has been extended northward to finish opposite the end of the 'down' platform.

Parallel with the 'down' bay line, a further siding has been added to extend beside the 'down' main line for a considerable distance, connected to the 'down' main (with a single slip for the bay) just to the north of the signal box.

In the summer of 1938, the signal box was open from 5 a.m. on Monday mornings, until 11.15 p.m. the following Sunday evening, and *was* provided with a switch.

FURTHER READING

R. Mag. 1968 p. 382 Pos. (Article on G.W.R. in the Shakespeare Country)
"Reg. Hist. of the Railways of Great Britain" Vol. 7. (The West Midlands)
by R. Christiansen. David & Charles

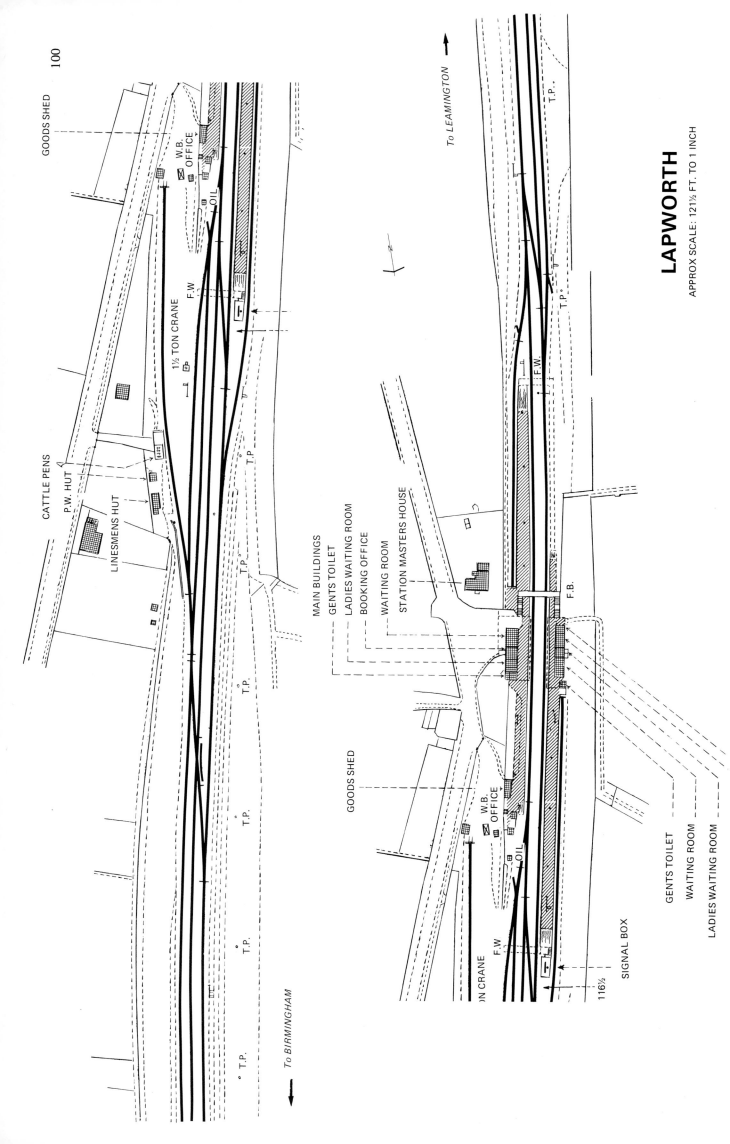

100

GOODS SHED

W.B.
OFFICE

OIL

1½ TON CRANE

F.W

To BIRMINGHAM

CATTLE PENS

P.W. HUT

LINESMENS HUT

T.P.

T.P.

T.P.

T.P.

T.P.

T.P.

T.P.

MAIN BUILDINGS
GENTS TOILET
LADIES WAITING ROOM
BOOKING OFFICE
WAITING ROOM
STATION MASTERS HOUSE

To LEAMINGTON

N

T.P.

T.P.

F.W.

F.B.

GOODS SHED

W.B.
OFFICE

OIL

F.W

N CRANE

SIGNAL BOX

116½

GENTS TOILET

WAITING ROOM

LADIES WAITING ROOM

LAPWORTH

APPROX SCALE: 121½ FT. TO 1 INCH

Leominster. General view looking towards Ludlow. *O.P.C.*

Leominster. Close-up of part of signal box support. *Lens of Sutton*

Leominster. Signal box and main-line platforms. *Lens of Sutton*

LEOMINSTER

Origin: Shrewsbury & Hereford Railway
Leased to the L.N.W.R., G.W.R., and West Midland Railway jointly from
1 July 1862

Opened: 6 Dec. 1853 (Through goods traffic over the line to Hereford from
30 July 1852

Closed: 2 Jan. 1967 (G) Except for private siding traffic.
Plan date: c. 1914

Considering the line's strategic importance, with a large city at each end, and two sizeable stations and goods depots intermediately, as well as being shared by so many different companies for most of its life, the Shrewsbury & Hereford line has attracted surprisingly little attention in railway literature.

Leominster was one of those two intermediate stations (the other being Ludlow—also dealt with in this book). In addition to its rural and agricultural importance, Leominster did have direct rail communication with Worcester, via Bromyard, and a branch which pointed optimistically westward towards Aberystwyth, which finally petered out short of the remote village of New Radnor.

Although Leominster passenger station itself was rather plain, with long, low main buildings, and a plain steel or iron footbridge, it had 4 platform faces (latterly reduced to 3, when the No. 2 branch platform on the eastern side was discontinued as a passenger platform), and much of the ample platform accommodation was under shelter.

The outstanding feature of the station, however, is the large signal box standing high on a single line of supports, with horizontal girders attached to another line of uprights on the island (branch) platform. Its style is reminiscent of the old ex-L.N.W.R. signal box which used to adorn Atherstone on the L.M. main line near Nuneaton.

With the arrival of the Beeching era, and the vast increase in roadborne passenger and freight traffic, wholesale rationalisation was inevitable, and today, barely a shadow of the station's former busy glory remains.

FURTHER READING

R. Mag. 1908 (Vol. 22) pp. 55–63 H.A.P.M., + grade profile.
R.W. 1965 p. 180 Pos. (a fine view of the signal box.)
"Great Western Engine Sheds, 1947" by E. Lyons. O.P.C.

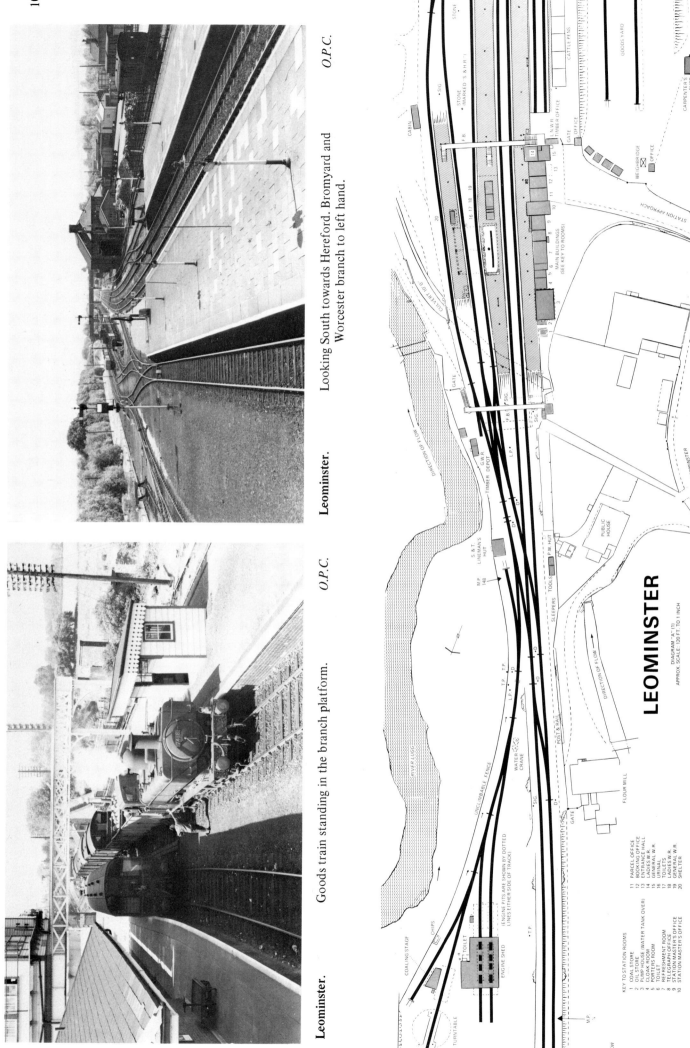

Leominster. Goods train standing in the branch platform. *O.P.C.*

Leominster. Looking South towards Hereford. Bromyard and Worcester branch to left hand. *O.P.C.*

LEOMINSTER

DIAGRAM "A" 11
APPROX. SCALE: 120 FT. TO 1 INCH

KEY TO STATION ROOMS
1 COAL STORE
2 OIL STORE
3 PUMP HOUSE (WATER TANK OVER)
4 CLOAK ROOM
5 PORTERS ROOM
6 TOILET
7 REFRESHMENT ROOM
8 TELEGRAPH OFFICE
9 STATION MASTERS OFFICE
10 STATION MASTERS OFFICE
11 PARCEL OFFICE
12 BOOKING OFFICE
13 ENTRANCE HALL
14 LADIES W.R.
15 GENERAL W.R.
16 URINAL
17 TOILETS
18 LADIES W.R.
19 GENERAL W.R.
20 SHELTER

(ENGINE PITS ARE SHOWN BY DOTTED
LINES EITHER SIDE OF TRACK)

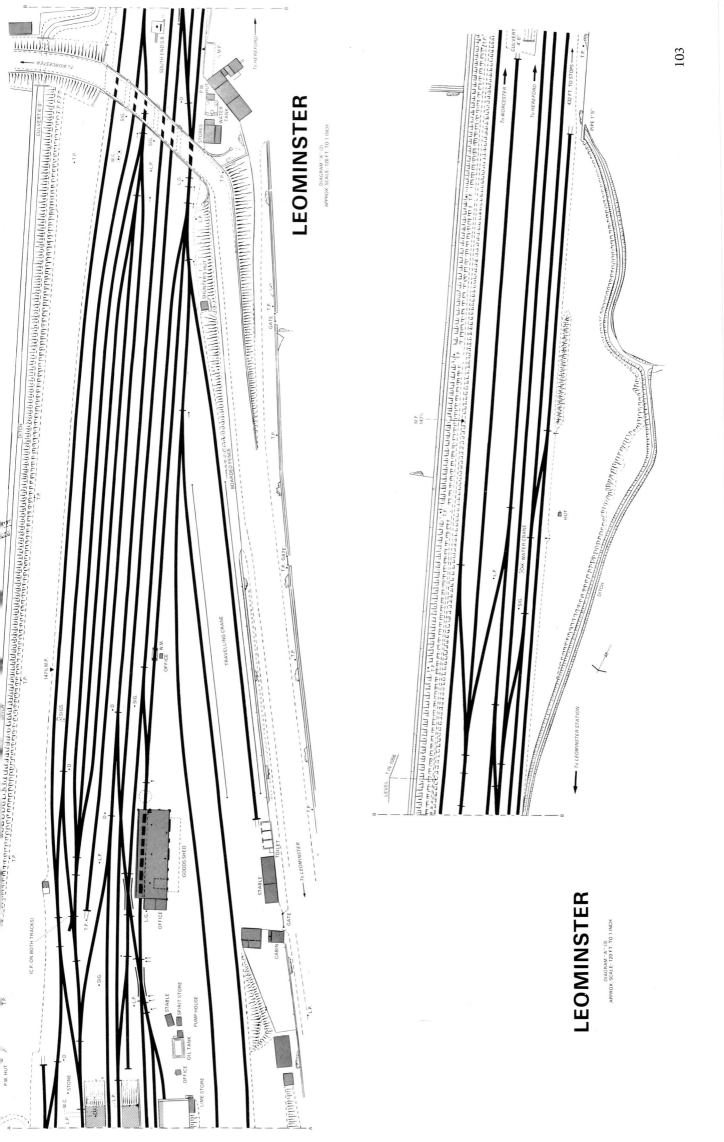

LEOMINSTER

DIAGRAM "A" (2)
APPROX SCALE 120 FT TO 1 INCH

LEOMINSTER

DIAGRAM "A" (3)
APPROX SCALE 120 FT TO 1 INCH

103

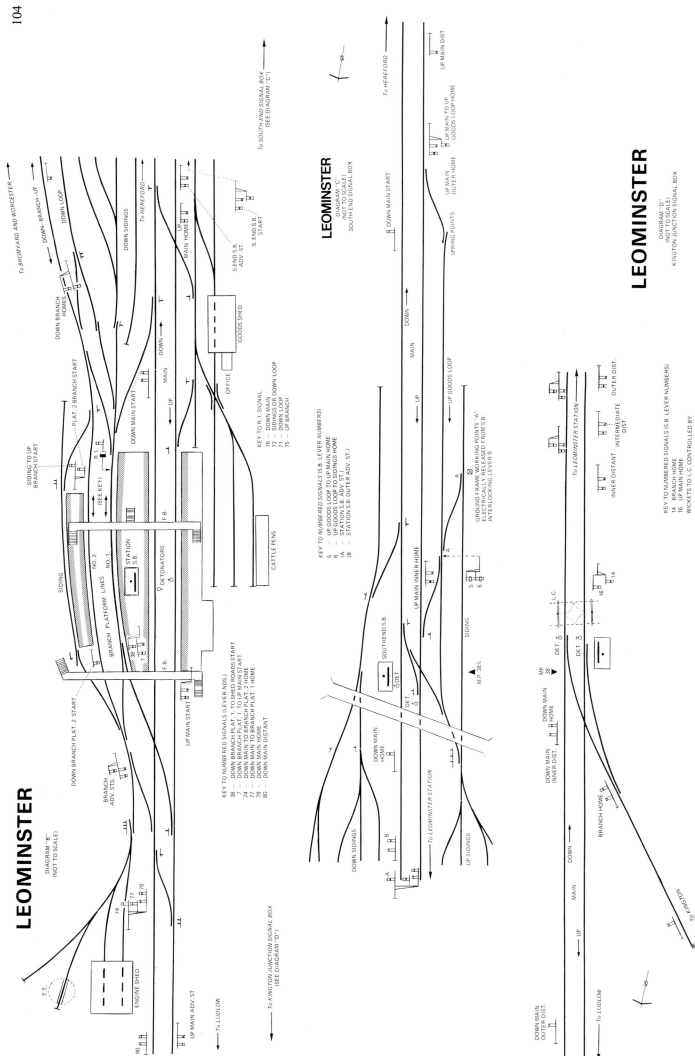

LEOMINSTER

DIAGRAM "B"
(NOT TO SCALE)

To BROMYARD AND WORCESTER →

DOWN-BRANCH-UP

DOWN LOOP

DOWN SIDINGS

To HEREFORD →

DOWN BRANCH HOMES

PLAT. 2 BRANCH START

SIDING TO UP
BRANCH START

SIDING

NO. 2.

NO. 1.

BRANCH PLATFORM LINES

STATION
S.B.

DETONATORS

F.B.

UP
MAIN HOME

DOWN MAIN START

MAIN

DOWN →

UP →

R.1.
(SEE KEY)

S. END S.B.
ADV. ST.

S. END S.B.
START

GOODS SHED

OFFICE

CATTLE PENS

To SOUTH END SIGNAL BOX
(SEE DIAGRAM "C")

KEY TO R.1. SIGNAL

76 — DOWN BRANCH
72 — SIDINGS OR DOWN LOOP
71 — DOWN LOOP
75 — UP BRANCH

DOWN BRANCH PLAT. 2 START

BRANCH
ADV. STS.

KEY TO NUMBERED SIGNALS (LEVER NOS.)

38 — DOWN BRANCH PLAT. 1. TO SHED ROADS START
7 — DOWN BRANCH PLAT. 1. TO UP MAIN START
74 — DOWN MAIN TO BRANCH PLAT. 2 HOME
77 — DOWN MAIN TO BRANCH PLAT. 1 HOME
79 — DOWN MAIN HOME
80 — DOWN MAIN DISTANT

F.B.

38

7

F.B.

UP MAIN START

T.T.

80

ENGINE SHED

74

77

79

UP MAIN ADV. ST.

← To LUDLOW

UP MAIN ADV. ST.

← To KINGTON JUNCTION SIGNAL BOX
(SEE DIAGRAM "D")

LEOMINSTER

DIAGRAM "C"
(NOT TO SCALE)
SOUTH END SIGNAL BOX

N

DOWN MAIN START

To HEREFORD →

UP MAIN TO UP
GOODS LOOP HOME

UP MAIN
OUTER HOME

UP MAIN DIST.

SPRING POINTS

DOWN →

MAIN

UP →

UP GOODS LOOP

A

A

GROUND FRAME WORKING POINTS "A"
ELECTRICALLY RELEASED FROM S.B.
INTERLOCKING LEVER 9.

KEY TO NUMBERED SIGNALS (S.B. LEVER NUMBERS)

5 — UP GOODS LOOP TO UP MAIN HOME
6 — UP GOODS LOOP TO SIDINGS HOME
1A — STATION S.B. ADV. ST.
1B — STATION S.B. OUTER ADV. ST.

SOUTHEND S.B.

DET.

UP MAIN INNER HOME

5
6

SIDING

DET.

M.P. 38¾

DET.

DOWN MAIN
HOME

To LEOMINSTER STATION →

DOWN SIDINGS

A
B

B

A

UP SIDINGS

← To LEOMINSTER STATION

LEOMINSTER

DIAGRAM "D"
(NOT TO SCALE)
KINGTON JUNCTION SIGNAL BOX

To LEOMINSTER STATION →

OUTER DIST.

INNER DISTANT

INTERMEDIATE
DIST.

L.C.

14

16

DET.

DET.

MP
38

DOWN MAIN
HOME

DOWN MAIN
INNER DIST.

BRANCH HOME

UP →

MAIN

DOWN →

To KINGTON →

KEY TO NUMBERED SIGNALS (S.B. LEVER NUMBERS)

14 — BRANCH HOME
16 — UP MAIN HOME

WICKETS TO L.C. CONTROLLED BY

DOWN MAIN
OUTER DIST.

← To LUDLOW

Limpley Stoke.   Looking towards Freshford.   *Lens of Sutton*

LIMPLEY STOKE

Origin: Great Western Railway
Opened: 2 Feb. 1857
Closed: 3 Oct. 1966 (P)
             4 Jan. 1960 (G)

Plan date: c. 1913

Limpley Stoke was built on the broad gauge single line from Bathampton (a new station on the main Paddington—Bristol line, and opened at the same time as Limpley Stoke), and Bradford-on-Avon. In the course of building the track bed was made wide enough to take a double line, but this did not come about until 17 May 1885. By then the line had been converted to standard gauge (on 18/22 July 1874).

The small station buildings were of timber construction, and were located at the extreme southern end of the 'down' platform. At the other end of the same platform was the short bay used by the Camerton and Hallatrow branch passenger trains, and the unusual connecting formation with the main line will be noted.

The connection into the 'up' main line was lifted in Sept. 1927, and in the same month the signal box (the "North" box) on the 'down' platform was reduced in status to that of "Ground Frame". Both the North and South signal boxes had been opened on 25 Apr. 1910. The South box was eventually closed on 24 Aug. 1969. The branch to the bay platform became redundant on 7 Dec. 1958, and the remaining connection (into the down main line) was lifted in Dec. 1960.

There were extensive sidings and running loops to the south of the station, for the handling of coal trains from the Cam Valley branch, and these lasted (for other purposes) well beyond the closure of both the mines and the branch, surviving down to the 1960's rationalisation programme. Between 1963 and 1969, all had become redundant.

Limpley Stoke signal box was (1938) open from 6.0 a.m. until 10.0 p.m. on weekdays, and was closed all day on Sundays. The box was provided with a switch.

Limpley Stoke.   Showing the old signal box between the water tank and the station buildings.   *B.R. (O.P.C.)*

Limpley Stoke.   Looking towards Bathampton. c.1962.   *Lens of Sutton*

FURTHER READING

R. Mag. 1911 (Vol. 29) p. 33   H.A.P.
R. Mag. 1961 pp. 597–603   H.A.P.M.
"Reg. History of the Railways of Great Britain." Vol. 1. (The West Country)
                                                        by D. St. J. Thomas. Phoenix

LIMPLEY STOKE

DIAGRAM "A"
APPROX. SCALE: 106 FT. TO 1 INCH

N

To FRESHFORD

FOOT CROSSING

GOODS SHED

CRANE

SAW MILLS

GATE

RIVER AVON

SIG.
F.W.
L.P.
F.B.
W.R.
TANK
MAIN BUILDINGS
S.B.
L.P.
L.P.
M.P. 4
L.P.
L.P.
L.P.
GATE
GATE
F.W.
SIG.

MAIN LINES TO BATHAMPTON

W.C. CO'S.

SIG.
SIG.
SIG.

BRANCH TO CAMERTON

To BATH

LIMPLEY STOKE

DIAGRAM "B"
(NOT TO SCALE)

KEY TO SIGNALS (NUMBERED)

4 — UP MAIN INNER HOME
7 — UP MAIN TO UP G.R.L. INNER HOME
8 — UP MAIN TO UP SIDING INNER HOME

A   A

8 7 4

SIGNAL BOX

UP MAIN INTERMEDIATE HOME

DOWN MAIN START

UP

MAIN

DOWN

GROUND FRAME
WORKING SIGNALS, POINTS
(& F.P.L's) MARKED "X"
ELECTRICALLY RELEASED
FROM S.B.
INTERLOCKING LEVER 15

UP MAIN HOME

DOWN MAIN ADV. ST.

UP BRANCH HOME

DOWN MAIN TO BRANCH ADV. START

BAY

UP MAIN START

To FRESHFORD

To BATHAMPTON

To CAMERTON

UP SIDING

UP GOODS RUNNING LOOP

UP

MAIN

DOWN

DOWN GOODS RUNNING LOOP

DOWN SIDING

DOWN MAIN HOME

A   A

LISKEARD

Origin: Cornwall Railway
         Leased from opening to the G.W.R., B. & E., & S.D.R.
         Absorbed by G.W.R. in 1889

Opened: 4 May 1859 (P)
         10 Oct. 1859 (G)

Closed: 16 Dec. 1963 (G)

With its "right-angled" station, and high elevation, the layout at Liskeard was about the most unusual to be found on the system—and the most difficult to emulate by the modeller, unless he put it in the garden. The station did not attain this shape, however, until the connecting loop from Coombe Junction wound its way on a steep curve from the valley below to the new station on a level with the main line in 1901.

The old signal box on the upside platform was closed on 3 June 1915 and a new box was opened at the Plymouth end of the 'down' platform (see Diagram "B"). The branch signal box off the 'country' end of the platform was closed on 15 Mar. 1964, the ground frame replacing it (further out, and on the other side of the line) having been operational from a week earlier. Rationalisation took its toll of most of the sidings opposite the branch platform between 1965 and 1971, but the goods shed, loading dock (with tracks), and the 'up' refuge siding escaped similar treatment.

In 1938 (summer period), the main line signal box was opened at 5.0 a.m. on Mondays, and closed at 4.50 p.m. on Sundays and the box was provided with a switch. The branch box was opened at 6.45 a.m. (Mondays to Fridays), 5.30 a.m. on Saturdays and in each case closed upon completion of the service. On Sundays, the branch box was open from 8.20 a.m. until 10.15 p.m. This box was not provided with a switch.

Between Liskeard and Coombe Junction, there was a maximum speed restriction of 15 m.p.h. for all trains in each direction, and an overall maximum of 25 m.p.h. over the entire branch to Looe. The branch was worked by Electric Train Token, the only crossing place being at Coombe Junction.

On the main line, there was a 50 m.p.h. speed restriction for all down trains west of Liskeard station.

FURTHER READING

R. Mag. 1902 (Vol. 11)   p. 441–447, 536–541   H.A.P. + Grade profile.
R. Mag. 1917 (Vol. 41) p. 316   H.A.P.M.
R. Mag. 1950 (Vol. 96) p. 215 H. Paragraph
R. Mag. 1970 p. 270 Pos. (Branch platform.)
R.W.   1971 p. 123 Pos.

"Railways of Looe & Caradon" (1974) Published by Forge Books, Bracknell
"The Story of Cornwall's Railways" by A. Fairclough. Tor Mark Press, Truro
"The Railways of Cornwall, 1809—1963" by C. R. Clinker.   David & Charles
"The Great Western at the turn of the Century", Pos. by A. R. Kingdom.   O.P.C.
"Reg. History of the Railways of Great Britain." Vol. 1. (The West Country)
                            by D. St. J. Thomas. Phoenix

Liskeard.   Looking towards Plymouth. Note connection to the Looe branch in centre of picture.   *O.P.C.*

Liskeard.   Towards Bodmin Road showing the goods shed and yard.   *O.P.C.*

108

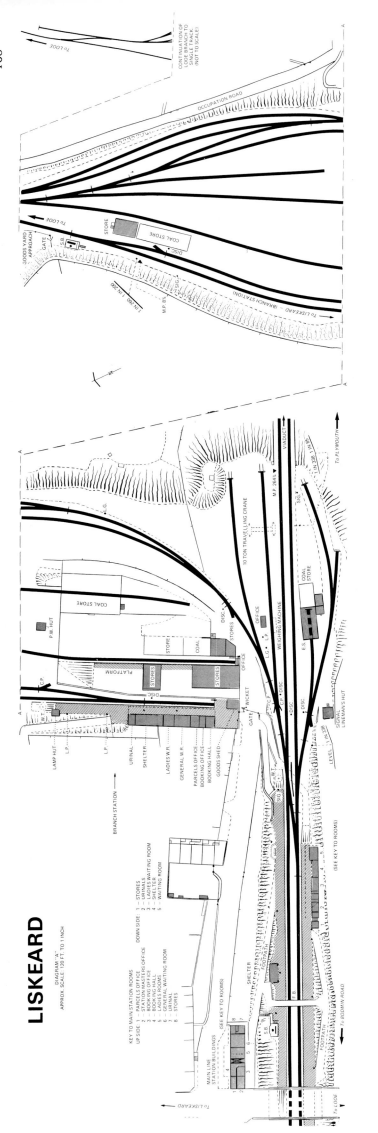

LISKEARD

DIAGRAM "A"
APPROX. SCALE 120 FT. TO 1 INCH

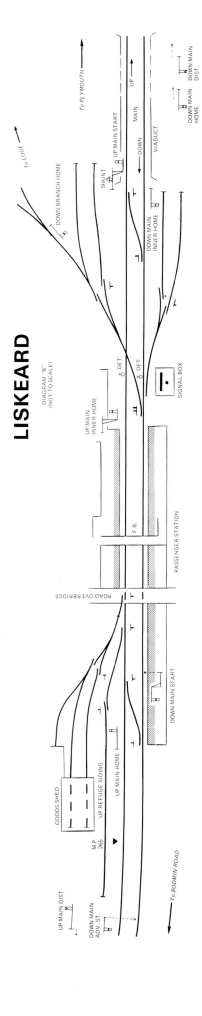

LISKEARD

DIAGRAM "B"
(NOT TO SCALE)

Origin: Manchester & Milford Railway
(Absorbed by G.W.R. in 1911)

Opened: 12 Aug. 1867

Closed: 14 Dec. 1964 (P) (Premature closure due to floods)
2 Dec. 1963 (G)

Plan date: Diagram "A" 1908

The station was on the northern section of the M. & M. nearly 6 miles from Aberystwyth and on the long 25 mile climb from the coast to Llangybi, the ruling gradient from Llanrhystyd Road just over 3 miles away towards the coast, being 1 in 90, and thence down into Aberystwyth at 1 in 42, the steepest ruling gradient on the entire line. It was rather bleak in its appearance and location, being on the hillside above the Ystwyth Valley, and serving not much more than the local pub and a handful of houses on the main road, a few hundred yards above.

In 1908, the station consisted of a single platform with small plain buildings thereon and, in common with nearly all the stations between Aberystwyth and Carmarthen, was devoid of any platform weather protection, the exceptions being Pencader and Lampeter.

The passing loop, which eventually became the 'up' main line was equipped with catch points at each end, and a curious feature is that it was found necessary to have points platforms (one on each side of the line) at the coast end of the station when there would appear to be an adequate signal box the other end. An 'up' platform was put beside this loop, and catch points abolished in more recent years.

The box was (1938) open on weekdays from 6.35 a.m. until clearance of the last train, and no switch was provided. There was a 10 m.p.h. speed restriction for all trains passing through the station.

Llanilar.   Looking towards Aberystwyth. 6 June 1963.   *M. Hale*

FURTHER READING

"The Teifi Valley Railway" by Roger Padfield & Barrie Burgess
Laidlaw-Burgess, Haverfordwest

LLANILAR

DIAGRAM "A"
APPROX. SCALE: 120 FT. TO 1 INCH

□ TOOL BOX

To LAMPETER

RIVER   YSTWYTH

BREAKWATER

CP

SIG.

S.B.

LEVEL 1 IN 220

P.W. DEPT

LAVS.

G.S.

W.R.

B.O.

POINTS PLAT

GATE

CP

SIG

POINTS PLAT

GOODS STORE

WEIGH OFFICE
WEIGH BRIDGE

COAL OFFICE

GATE

To ABERYSTWYTH

LLANILAR

DIAGRAM "B"
(NOT TO SCALE)

To LAMPETER

UP ADV START

UP MAIN START

PASSENGER STATION

UP

UP MAIN HOME

MAIN

DOWN MAIN HOME

DOWN

DOWN
MAIN
START

TO SIDINGS
START

S.B.

To ABERYSTWYTH

SIDINGS

Looking towards Carmarthen, 15 June 1962.　*M. Hale*

LLANPUMPSAINT

Origin: Carmarthen & Cardigan Railway
(Absorbed by G.W.R. in 1881)
Opened: 28 Mar. 1864
Closed: 22 Feb. 1965 (P)
2 Dec. 1963 (G)
Plan date: Diagram "A" 17 July 1912

Three miles down the line from Conwil (towards Pencader) was Llanpumpsaint, sharing the same valley, and in as delightful a setting as its more southern neighbour. The track layout was similar to that at Conwil, except that the siding came off the down main at the northern end of the station instead of the southern end. Furthermore there was a short 'neck' trailing into the down main line a few yards beyond the under-bridge southward. The station was much nearer to its village than was the case with Conwil, being only about ¼ mile therefrom.

From Llanpumpsaint station, all the way down to Pencader (some 5 miles northward) the line fell away steeply at a ruling gradient of 1 in 55 and there were two "Stop" boards intermediately.

The signal-box opening times were similar to those of Conwil except that it opened 10 minutes later. There was no switch provided.

Llanpumpsaint.

FURTHER READING

T.I.　1959 pp. 39–42; 44–45　H.A.P.M.
R.W.　1973 pp. 76–77　H.A.P.M. (Short historical article on Carmarthen & Cardigan Railway)

"The Teifi Valley Railway" by Roger Padfield & Barrie Burgess
Laidlaw-Burgess, Haverfordwest

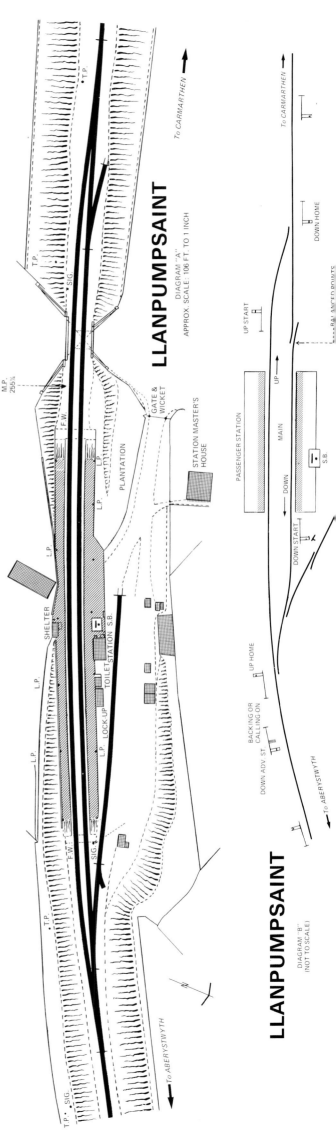

LLANPUMPSAINT

DIAGRAM "A"
APPROX. SCALE: 106 FT. TO 1 INCH

LLANPUMPSAINT

DIAGRAM "B"
(NOT TO SCALE)

LODDISWELL

Origin: Great Western Railway
Opened: 19 Dec. 1893 (P)
Closed: 16 Sept. 1963 (P)
4 Sept. 1961 (G)

Plan date: 3 Dec. 1914

The layout at this station was almost identical to that at Avonwick, even to the north and south ground frames and being on a curve in the line. The station buildings, too were similarly arranged with the goods sheds against the platforms, slightly to the north of the main buildings.

The ruling gradient from Gara Bridge is 1 in 110 (falling). South of the station, the gradient rises at a rule of 1 in 50 for nearly 2 miles, thence at the same grade down to Kingsbridge.

FURTHER READING

T.I. 1958 pp. 94–97 H.A.P. Pos.
"Reg. Hist. of the Railways of Great Britain" Vol. 1. (The West Country)
by D. St. J. Thomas. Phoenix

Loddiswell. View towards Brent showing surrounding approaches. *R.H. Clark*

LODDISWELL

APPROX SCALE: 120 FT. TO 1 INCH

To KINGSBRIDGE

STATION MASTER'S HOUSE

PUMP HOUSE

OFFICE

S.M.O.

G.S.

BOOKING HALL
LADIES W.R.
GENTS TOILETS

1 IN 50

1 IN 300

111

P.W. HUT

LODDISWELL SOUTH G.F.

CRANE 3 TON SINGLE CHAIN
6 TON DOUBLE CHAIN
RADIUS 21 FT

L.G.

CATTLE PENS

1 IN 300

1 IN 182

LODDISWELL NORTH G.F.

To BRENT

LOOE

Origin: Liskeard & Caradon Railway
Leased from the Liskeard & Looe Union Canal Co. and vested in the
Great Western Railway from 1 July 1909.
The Liskeard & Looe Railway remained independent until Grouping.

Opened: 11 Sept. 1879 (P)
27 Dec. 1860 (G)—Date of opening to the Quay, not the passenger station.

Closed: 4 Nov. 1963 (G)

Plan date: c. 1912

NOTE. The opening dates referred to above, relate to the opening of the line from Moorswater.

Much has been written about the Liskeard & Looe Railway which, although worked by the Great Western Railway since 1 Jan. 1909, retained its independence right down to the 1923 Grouping. Even to this day (1978) the little 8¾ mile branch manages to keep going its 2-car d.m.u. (strengthened at "peak" times to 4-cars), and the service is not infrequent. Looe station will be too familiar to need further description here except for drawing attention to the "half-platform" canopy with its unadorned supports lined up along the edge of the roof, rather than the more usual 'set-in' style. The small engine shed at the seaward end of the platform was closed on 2 Apr. 1917. The date of closure of the carriage shed is not known, but the platform was extended southward by 96 feet in 1928.

It was not until well after the 2nd. World War, however, that major rationalisation of the track layout took place, and all track beyond the "zero" mile post (near to the loading gauge) were tarmacked over in 1954. The remaining track to the end of the platform became redundant in Nov. 1963 (when freight services were withdrawn) and lifted in 1964, the signal box being closed on 15 March of that year. Finally, the track in the platform itself was shortened on the 28 Apr. 1968.

FURTHER READING

R. Mag. 1917 (Vol. 41) p. 316   H.A.P.M. Pos.
R. Mag. 1935 (Vol. 77) pp. 413—421   H.A.P.M. Pos.
R. Mag. 1959 p. 219 Para. on proposed new branch from St. Germans to Looe.
"Railways of Looe and Caradon" by Forge Books, Bracknell
"Great Western Branch Line Album" by Ian Krause.   Ian Allan
"The Story of Cornwall's Railways" by A. Fairclough.   Tor Mark Press, Truro
"The Railways of Cornwall, 1809—1963" by C.R. Clinker.   David & Charles
"Reg. History of the Railways of Great Britain." Vol. 1. (The West Country)
by D. St. J. Thomas. Phoenix

Branch train in the station. 23 May 1935.

H.C. Casserley

Looe.

Looking towards the quay.

O.P.C.

Looe.

DIAGRAM "A" (1)
APPROX. SCALE: 120 FT. TO 1 INCH

To POLPERRO

ROAD BRIDGE

STEPS

OFFICE

CARRIAGE SHOOT

3 TON CRANE

L.G.

GATE

ROADWAY

T.P.

L.P.

T.P.

T.P.

P.W. HUT

CARRIAGE SHED

ENGINE SHED

SIG.

LOOE COAL HUT

C.P.

RAMP

T.P.

GATE

To LISKEARD

SIG.

SIG.

ROADWAY

LOADING BANK

WATER TANK

TANK

OIL HUT

GATE

CATTLE MARKET

AUCTION RING

ROADWAY

(CONTINUATION AT SAME SCALE)

RAMP

GOODS OFFICE

G.S.

STABLES

(SEE KEY)

T.P.

T.P.

GATE

KEY TO STATION ROOMS
1. LAVATORIES
2. LADIES WAITING ROOM
3. BOOKING HALL
4. BOOKING OFFICE
5. GOODS LOCK UP

HARBOUR

M.P.

M.P.

T.P.

To QUAY

M.P.

ROADWAY

HARBOUR

LOOE

(QUAY)
DIAGRAM "A" (2)
CONTINUATION AT SAME SCALE.
"A"..."A"

To LOOE STATION

M.R.
M.R.
M.P.
M.R.
M.P.
M.R.
M.P.
M.R.
M.P.
M.R.
M.P.

LAMP

BULLER QUAY

T.P.

URINAL

GUILDHALL

LOOE HOTEL

T.P.

LAMP

STONE

T.P.

TRAVELLING CRANE (OVERHEAD)

CRANE

O.M.R.

M.R.

M.P.

M.R.

O.M.R.

O. M.R.

M.P.

M.P.

O.M.R.

O.M.R.

M.R.

O. M.R.

T.P.

M.P.

T.P.

M.P.

STEPS

M.R.

O. M.R.

STEPS

M.R.

M.P.

T.P.

LOSTWITHIEL

Origin: Cornwall Railway
Leased from opening to the G.W.R., B. & E. and S.D.R.
Absorbed by the G.W.R. in 1889.

Opened: 4 May 1859 (P)
3 Oct. 1859 (G)

Closed: 1 June 1964 (G) Remained open for private siding traffic

Plan date: c. 1910

Ten years after the main line station was opened, a broad gauge branch was built by the Lostwithiel & Fowey Railway and opened to Carne Point, just short of Fowey, for goods traffic (which was mainly china clay), and Lostwithiel developed its layout accordingly to deal with the resulting interchange traffic. For nearly 11 years, the branch continued thus, trying to undercut its competing rival, the Cornwall Minerals line from St. Blazey to such an extent that it virtually brought about its own closure on 1 Jan. 1880.

The branch was eventually revived (as a standard gauge line) to make an end-on junction with the Cornwall Minerals line at Fowey itself, and re-opened to carry passengers as well as goods on 16 Sept. 1895.

Such were the origins of Lostwithiel's own branch line, but looking at the main line station itself, one can only describe it as having a typical "West Country" character. There was nothing spectacular about its simple low buildings, or its signal box (which remained at the Plymouth end of the 'down' platform—presumably to operate the level crossing

gates—or the corrugated iron footbridge, but the whole station with its shrubbed "palms" told the passenger that he was well down into Cornwall, and if he happened to be a modeller, that here was a worthwhile station to model.

Before Dec. 1923, the station had two signal boxes, the main line one referred to above, and the branch signal box (as in Diagram "A"), but the latter was dispensed with, and the former took control of most of the layout thereafter.

The trailing point into the 'down' main line just to the east of the level crossing, led to a 'down' refuge siding (and an adjacent one) (Diagram "A"). This refuge siding was converted to a 'down' loop on 28 June 1936. The 'up' loop was brought into regular use in mid 1943.

In Sept. 1946, two additional sidings were installed parallel to the Fowey branch. During the B.R. rationalisation programme and right down to 1973, the layout suffered several modifications, and even before this started, the lifting shop and neighbouring workshops had gone.

In 1938, Lostwithiel signal box was open continuously, and was not provided with a switch.

FURTHER READING

R. Mag. 1956 p. 676 (Picture of east end of layout with level crossing.)
"The Railways of Cornwall, 1809–1963" by C. R. Clinker. David & Charles
"Reg. History of the Railways of Great Britain." Vol. 1. (The West Country)
by D. St. J. Thomas. Phoenix
O.P.C.

Lostwithiel.   Looking towards Bodmin Road, showing alterations.

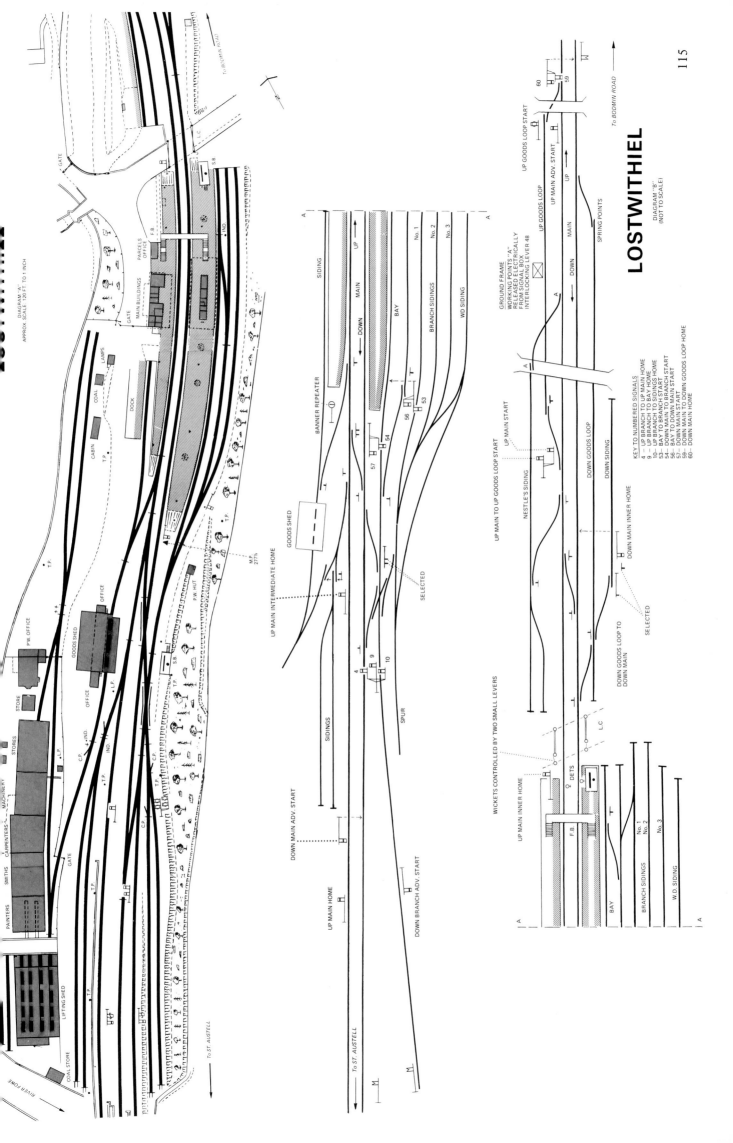

LOSTWITHIEL

DIAGRAM "B"
(NOT TO SCALE)

115

DIAGRAM "A"
APPROX SCALE 120 FT TO 1 INCH

To BODMIN ROAD →

To ST. AUSTELL →

RIVER FOWE

GROUND FRAME
WORKING POINTS "A"
RELEASED ELECTRICALLY
FROM SIGNAL BOX
INTERLOCKING LEVER 48

KEY TO NUMBERED SIGNALS

4 — UP BRANCH TO UP MAIN HOME
9 — UP BRANCH TO BAY HOME
10 — UP BRANCH TO SIDINGS HOME
53 — BAY TO BRANCH START
54 — DOWN MAIN TO BRANCH START
56 — BAY TO DOWN MAIN START
57 — DOWN MAIN START
59 — DOWN MAIN TO DOWN GOODS LOOP HOME
60 — DOWN MAIN HOME

UP GOODS LOOP START

UP GOODS LOOP

UP MAIN ADV. START

UP

MAIN

DOWN

SPRING POINTS

UP MAIN TO UP GOODS LOOP START

UP MAIN START

NESTLE'S SIDING

DOWN GOODS LOOP

DOWN SIDING

DOWN GOODS LOOP TO
DOWN MAIN

DOWN MAIN INNER HOME

SELECTED

WICKETS CONTROLLED BY TWO SMALL LEVERS

UP MAIN INNER HOME

L.C

DETS

F.B

BAY

BRANCH SIDINGS

No. 1
No. 2
No. 3

W.D. SIDING

UP MAIN INTERMEDIATE HOME

BANNER REPEATER

GOODS SHED

DOWN MAIN ADV. START

UP MAIN HOME

DOWN BRANCH ADV. START

SIDINGS

SPUR

SELECTED

4
9
10
57
54
56
53

UP

DOWN

MAIN

BAY

SIDING

No. 1
No. 2
No. 3

BRANCH SIDINGS

WD SIDING

To ST. AUSTELL

M.P.
277¾

Ludlow.   North end of station towards Shrewsbury.   O.P.C.

LUDLOW

Origin: Shrewsbury & Hereford Railway Co.
              (Leased to the L.N.W.R., G.W.R., & West Midland jointly from
                                                                    1 July 1862)

Opened: 21 April 1852 (Line opened as a single line from Shrewsbury)
Closed: 6 May 1968 (G)
Plan date: Diagram "A" c. 1930   Diagram "B" c. 1955

The 'flag' on the platform side of the ticket office is a weighing machine, and the erection to the right is a ticket collector's kiosk. The dots beneath the platform awning indicate the positions of the awning supports, while those near to the footbridge on both platforms are lamp posts. The two dots in the goods shed are cranes.

In the 'continuation' plan, I have made an enlargement of the two rail-traps to show the actual arrangement of the rails as indicated on the official plan. This gives the impression that the original draughtsman may have been in error, as close examination will reveal.

During the 25 years or so between the two diagrams there seems to have been very little alteration to the track layout, except that by the middle 'fifties or thereabout the

Ludlow.   Looking towards Hereford.

third "loop" siding on the eastern side of the complex had been severed to make two 'stop' sidings with an additional one to the left hand. Also, the short terminating siding to the north of the goods shed had been taken out.

The passenger station (as well as the goods yard) was well appointed, and ample platform accommodation provided. The main buildings on the up side were large, with a substantial platform canopy, the supports of which fanned out in four directions beneath its cover. The down side buildings were less ambitious, and there was no canopy.

Beyond Ludlow, to the south, the line proceeded to Hereford (Barr's Court) and goods trains started to use it from 30 July 1852. It was not until 6 Dec. 1853 that through passenger trains ran between Shrewsbury and Hereford. The line was laid as standard gauge throughout.

The signal box was open from 6.0 a.m. Mondays to 5.30 a.m. Sunday mornings, and was provided with a switch.

FURTHER READING

R. Mag. 1908 (Vol. 22) pp. 55—63   H.A.P.M. + Grade profile
"Great Western Branch Lines, 1955—1965" by C. J. Gammell. Oxford Publishing Co.

LUDLOW

DIAGRAM "B"
(NOT TO SCALE)

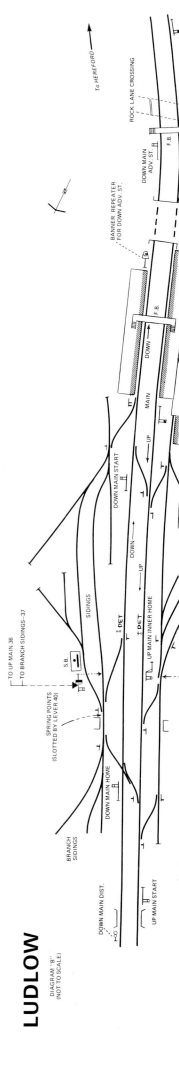

LUDLOW

DIAGRAM "A" (1)
APPROX SCALE: 120 FT TO 1 INCH

To HEREFORD

TUNNEL

PUBLIC FOOTPATH

LADIES W.R.   GENERAL W.R.

MAIN BUILDINGS
(SEE KEY TO ROOMS BELOW)

M.P. 27¾

N.B.

F.B.

GATE

STATION APPROACH

To LUDLOW

GATE   GATE

HUT

GATE

GATES

CATTLE PENS

KEY TO ROOMS IN MAIN BUILDINGS

1. PORTERS ROOM
2. LAVATORY
3. LADIES W.R.
4. GENERAL W.R.
5. STATION MASTER
6. PARCELS OFFICE
7. TICKET OFFICE
8. HALL

DISC.

SIG.

LINESMAN'S HUT

P.W. HUT

OIL

L.P.

T.P.

CHIPS

DISC.

SIG.

DISC.

L.P.

COAL

LAV.   MESS ROOM

OFFICE

WEIGH BRIDGE

L.G.

OFFICE

CANOPY   GOODS SHED

OFFICE

CHIPS

PETROL PUMP

TRAVELLING GANTRY

T.P.

L.P.

[FOR CONTINUATION OF LAYOUT NORTHWARDS
SEE DIAGRAM "A" (2).]

To SHREWSBURY

LUDLOW

DIAGRAM "A" (2)
CONTINUATION NORTHWARDS
AT SAME SCALE (120 FT. TO 1 INCH)

To LUDLOW STATION

T.P.

WATER CRANE

LAV.

LUDLOW SIGNAL BOX

W.C.

L.P.

SIG.

DISC.

WATER TANK

M.P. 27¾

DISC.

L.P.

T.P.

CHIPS

ENLARGEMENT (NOT TO SCALE) OF INDICATED RAIL TRAPS

ALSO SEE NOTES

C.P.

DISC.   CHIPS

DISC.

T.P.

L.P.   C.P.

DISC.

P.W. HUT

T.P.

L.P.

DISC.

SIG.

RIVER CORVE
(DIRECTION OF FLOW)

COVER

T.P.

CHIPS

To SHREWSBURY

RESERVOIR

117

MAES-Y-CRUGIAU

Origin: Manchester & Milford Railway
(Leased by G.W.R. and absorbed in 1911)

Opened: ?
Closed: 22 Feb. 1965 (P)
6 Sept. 1965 (G)

Plan date: 12 July 1907

Although it appears that this station retained its title from the outset, it is also apparent that it took its name from the nearby estate. The actual village which it served was Llanllwni, hard by the station.

Basically, the track layout was almost identical to that of Llanpumpsaint, 9 miles to the south on the former Carmarthen & Cardigan section except that there was a catch point (which was spring operated) on the up line at the southern end of the platform, and each had balanced points on the down line 'traps'. Also, Maes-y-Crugiau's signal box was off the northern end of the down platform instead of on it. The box was (1938) open on weekdays only from 6.0 a.m. until clearance of the last train, and was not provided with a switch.

FURTHER READING

T.I. 1959 pp. 39—42; 44—45 H.A.P.M.
"The Teifi Valley Railway" by Roger Padfield & Barrie Burgess

Laidlaw Burgess, Haverfordwest

Lens of Sutton

Maes-y-Crugiau. Towards Pencader from the main platform.

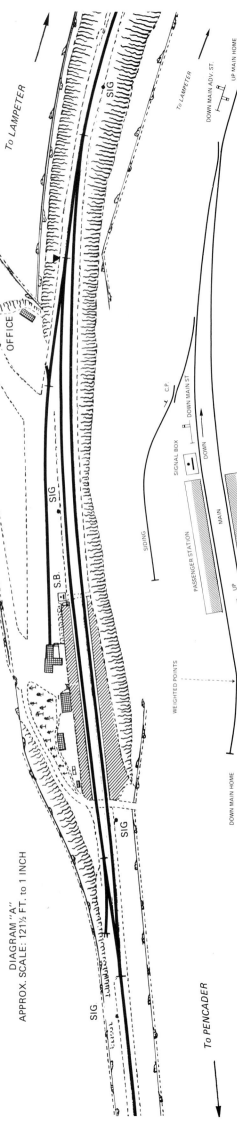

MAES-Y-CRUGIAU

DIAGRAM "A"
APPROX. SCALE: 121½ FT. to 1 INCH

MAES-Y-CRUGIAU

DIAGRAM "B"
(NOT TO SCALE)

MAIDEN NEWTON

Origin:	Great Western Railway
	(by absorption of the Wilts, Somerset & Weymouth Railway in 1851)
Opened:	20 Jan 1857
Closed:	5 Apr. 1965 (G) Remained open for P.S. traffic, since withdrawn
Plan date:	c. 1911

Like Evershot, Maiden Newton was built on the same broad gauge single line between Yeovil and Dorchester, and was opened on the same day, 154 miles 7 chains (via Chippenham) from Paddington.

The passenger station was of unusual design with a long canopy over the up platform extending beyond the main buildings and attached to the small, overall roof portion covering part of the Bridport bay line, and a lattice footbridge, which seemed out of character over a G.W. line. The large goods shed contained an 'island' platform with a single track one side, and covered road access the other.

By 1925, the old signal box in the 'down' platform had been replaced by a new box off the end of the same platform. From then on, nothing much altered down to the Beeching rationalisation period in the 1960's, starting with the lifting of the 'down' siding adjacent to the main line on 20 Dec. 1963. In Sept. 1967, the other 'down' siding became redundant, and in the following two years, the layout was trimmed until only the main line (which had been singled on 26 May 1968) and the branch remained. The Bridport branch was closed on 5 May 1975.

In 1938 (summer period) the box opening hours were from 6.0 a.m. (Mondays), 5.30 a.m. on other days until 6.0 a.m. the following Sunday, re-opening the same morning at 9.30 a.m. and closing at 10.30 p.m. The box was provided with a switch.

FURTHER READING

R. Mag. 1970 p. 620 Pos.

"Railways of Dorset" by J. H. Lucking   R.C. & T.S.

"Reg. Hist. of the Railways of Great Britain" Vol. 1. (The West Country)
                     by D. St. J. Thomas. Phoenix

"The Bridport Branch" by B. L. Jackson & M. J. Tattershall. Oxford Publishing Co.
                                      O.P.C.

Maiden Newton.　Looking towards Yeovil. 29 Aug. 1961.　*M. Hale*

Maiden Newton.　Looking towards Dorchester. Bridport branch on the right hand side.

MAIDEN NEWTON

DIAGRAM "A"
APPROX. SCALE: 120 FT. TO 1 INCH

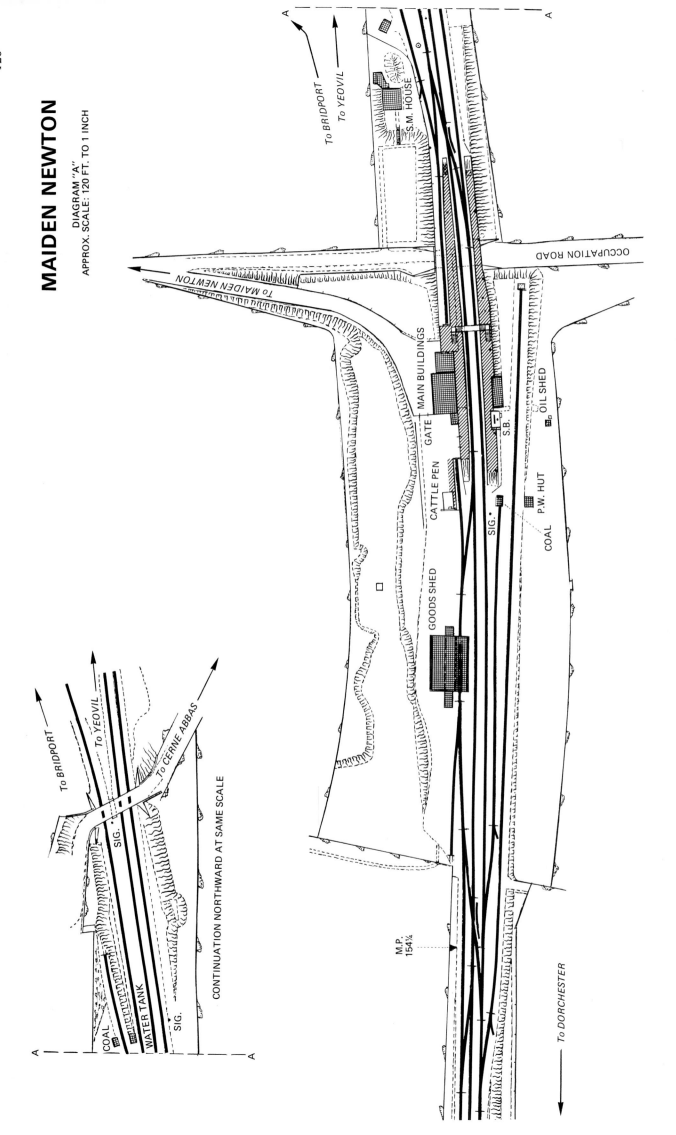

To BRIDPORT

To YEOVIL

S.M. HOUSE

OCCUPATION ROAD

To MAIDEN NEWTON

MAIN BUILDINGS

GATE

CATTLE PEN

S.B.

OIL SHED

SIG.

COAL

P.W. HUT

GOODS SHED

M.P. 154¼

To DORCHESTER

To BRIDPORT

To YEOVIL

To CERNE ABBAS

COAL

WATER TANK

SIG.

SIG.

CONTINUATION NORTHWARD AT SAME SCALE

A

A

A

A

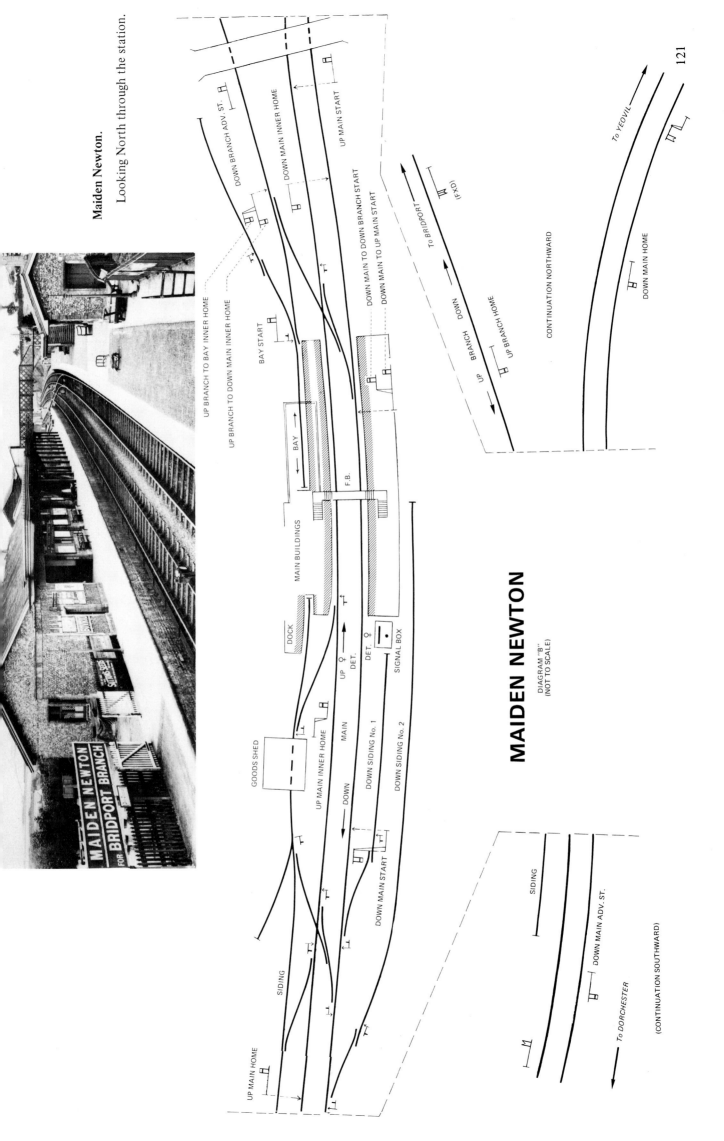

Maiden Newton.

Looking North through the station.

121

MAIDEN NEWTON

DIAGRAM "B"
(NOT TO SCALE)

To YEOVIL

CONTINUATION NORTHWARD

DOWN MAIN HOME

To BRIDPORT

(FXD)

UP   BRANCH   DOWN

DOWN MAIN TO DOWN BRANCH START

DOWN MAIN TO UP MAIN START

UP BRANCH HOME

UP MAIN START

DOWN MAIN INNER HOME

DOWN BRANCH ADV. ST.

UP BRANCH TO BAY INNER HOME

UP BRANCH TO DOWN MAIN INNER HOME

BAY START

BAY

F.B.

MAIN BUILDINGS

DOCK

GOODS SHED

UP MAIN INNER HOME

UP   DET.

DET.

SIGNAL BOX

DOWN   MAIN

DOWN SIDING No. 1

DOWN SIDING No. 2

DOWN MAIN START

UP MAIN HOME

SIDING

SIDING

DOWN MAIN ADV. ST.

To DORCHESTER

(CONTINUATION SOUTHWARD)

M

MARLOW

Origin: Great Marlow Railway
Absorbed by the Great Western Railway in 1897

Opened: 28 June 1873 (1st. station)
10 July 1967 (2nd. station—a new platform adjacent)

Closed: 10 July 1967 (1st. station)
18 July 1966 (1st. station) (G)—except for private siding traffic

Plan date: c. 1910

These notes refer to the first station as the "2nd" one was built merely as a new platform, adjacent to the former.

The station was opened as "Great Marlow" and renamed "Marlow" on 14 Feb. 1899. Considering that the station was well within the London 'commuter' belt, and the growth of this traffic down through the years, it is surprising that the layout remained much as it was for so long.

The signal box was closed from 26 Sept. 1954, and its track functions transferred to two new ground frames. The engine shed was closed in July 1962 and was demolished in June 1964. In 1966, considerable revision of the layout was undertaken, and in the following year, the old station was closed when the new platform was opened, utilising one of the sidings opposite to the goods shed.

On the official plan, the dip in the platform (old station) is not indicated, nor is the loading gauge, but the latter has been inserted in its correct position. Also omitted from the scaled plan is the small goods 'lock-up' on the platform side of the goods shed.

Before the 2nd. War, the single line branch from Bourne End was worked by Electric Train Token, and the box hours at Marlow were—Weekdays, open from 5.20 a.m. until 11.30 p.m. except Wednesday and Saturday nights when it stayed open until 1.0 a.m. (night). On Sundays, the box was open from 8.30 a.m. until 10.10 p.m. with a break from 10 a.m. to 2.30 p.m. It was not provided with a switch.

Lens of Sutton

Marlow. 0-4-2T and trailer standing at platform.

FURTHER READING

R. Mag. 1933 (Sept.) pp. 157–164 H.A.P.M. Pos and pp. 321–326 (Nov.)
M.R.C. 1955 p. 178 Pos. (4) p. 201 Pos. (3) p. 202—Layout plan.
R. Mag. 1957 pp. 655–657 H.A.P.
M.R.C. 1966 pp. 39–42 D.A.P.M. Pos. (10)
"Great Western Branch Lines, 1955–1965" by C. J. Gammell. O.P.C.
"Victorian & Edwardian Railways" (plate 26) by J. G. Spence. Batsford.
"Great Western Engine Sheds, 1947" by E. Lyons. Oxford Publishing Co.
"Great Western Branch Line Album" by Ian Krause. Ian Allan.

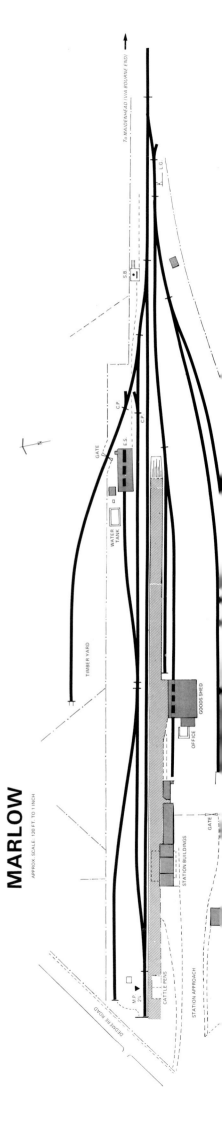

MARLOW

APPROX. SCALE 120 FT. TO 1 INCH

MILFORD HAVEN

Origin: Milford Railway
             (But see notes)

Opened: 7 Sept. 1863

Closed:

Plan date: 1912

In the matter of "looks", there was little to choose between Milford Haven and its neighbour the other side of the town—Neyland, although the former might score more points on account of its more robust construction, whereas the latter was little more than a timber shed—albeit it had a form of crude shelter in front of it.

Milford Haven, like so many other of the Great Western branch termini, was built on a sharp curve with the dock lines at the seaward end, and (ultimately), considerable marshalling and storage sidings opposite.

Although the Milford Railway Company constructed the 4 mile branch from Johnston, it was the Great Western Company which opened it, but the former Company was not absorbed by the latter until 1896.

The short branch was (1938) worked by Electric Train Token, and there were no intermediate crossing places. The signal box was open from 5.45 a.m. on Mondays, (5.0 a.m. Tues.–Fridays) and closed at 12.45 a.m. (but ½ hour later on Weds., Fridays and Sundays). The normal opening time on Sundays was 12.20 p.m. to 6.10 p.m. with a break between 1.20 p.m. and 5.10 p.m. (Summer Season only).

The branch was converted from broad gauge to standard gauge on 11–13 May 1872.

FURTHER READING

R. Mag. 1939 (Vol. 85) pp. 197–202   H.D.A.P.

R. Mag. 1972 p. 28 Pos. (part)

"Great Western Engine Sheds, 1947" by E. Lyons (1972)   O.P.C.

Milford Haven.   Towards terminus.   O.P.C.

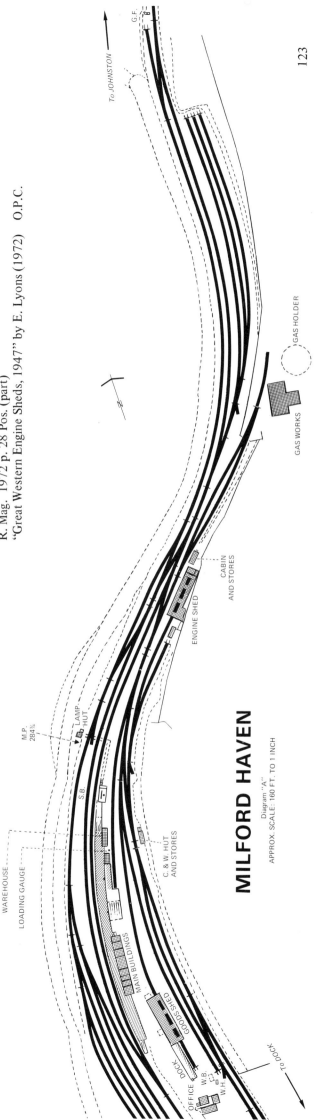

MILFORD HAVEN

Diagram "A"

APPROX. SCALE: 160 FT. TO 1 INCH

123

MILFORD HAVEN

DIAGRAM "B"
(NOT TO SCALE)

SIDINGS

GAS WORKS SIDING

LOOP SIDING START

ENGINE SHED

MILFORD DOCK Co.
DOWN HOME SIGNAL
OPERATED BY HAND LEVER

14 SELECTED

8 SELECTED

To DOCKS

DOCK Co's. SIDINGS

LOOP   UP

DOWN   MAIN

STATION

FOULING BAR

DOWN MAIN
TO DOCKS START

FROM DOCKS HOME

GOODS SHED

S.B.

To DOCKS

MILFORD HAVEN (DIAGRAM "B")

```
3 – MAIN
22 – GOODS LOOP
23 – SIDINGS
```

To DOCKS

KEY TO NUMBERED SIGNALS (S.B. LEVER NUMBERS)

```
2  – FROM DOCKS TO MAIN STARTING
3  – UP MAIN STARTING
4  – UP MAIN INTERMEDIATE STARTING
7  – FROM DOCKS TO LOOP STARTING
8  – LOOP TO LOOP SIDING OR MAIN STARTING (SELECTED)
14 – SIDINGS TO LOOP SIDING OR MAIN STARTING (SELECTED)
15 – DOWN SIDINGS TO UP & DOWN GOODS LOOP STARTING
16 – DOWN SIDINGS TO DOWN MAIN STARTING
17 – UP MAIN TO UP & DOWN GOODS LOOP STARTING
22 – UP MAIN TO UP & DOWN GOODS LOOP STARTING
23 – UP MAIN TO DOWN SIDINGS STARTING
26 – UP & DOWN GOODS LOOP INNER HOME
27 – UP & DOWN LOOP TO DOWN SIDINGS INNER HOME
30 – UP & DOWN GOODS LOOP TO DOWN MAIN INTERMEDIATE HOME
31 – UP & DOWN GOODS LOOP INTERMEDIATE HOME
34 – DOWN SIDINGS TO UP & DOWN GOODS LOOP STARTING
35 – DOWN SIDINGS STARTING
46 – DOWN MAIN TO DOWN SIDINGS INTERMEDIATE HOME
47 – DOWN MAIN TO UP SIDINGS INNER HOME
49 – DOWN MAIN INNER HOME
50 – DOWN MAIN INNER INTERMEDIATE HOME
```

MILFORD HAVEN

DIAGRAM "B" (CONTINUATION)
(NOT TO SCALE)

To JOHNSTON

SPUR

DOWN MAIN HOME

DOWN MAIN TO UP & DOWN
GOODS LOOP HOME

SPUR TO UP & DOWN GOODS LOOP START

SPUR TO UP & DOWN GOODS LOOP TO UP MAIN ADV. START

SPRING POINTS SLOTTED BY 39

SPRING POINTS SLOTTED BY 41

W.F.B.

UP & DOWN GOODS LOOP TO UP MAIN ADV. START
UP & DOWN GOODS LOOP TO SPUR ADV. START

DOWN MAIN TO LOOP
SIDING INTERMEDIATE HOME

DOWN MAIN INTERMEDIATE HOME

UP MAIN OUTER ADV. START

LOOP SIDING TO MAIN START

UP MAIN ADV. START

REPEATER
TO 32

KLAXON HORNS

MILFORD HAVEN GROUND FRAME
1 LEVER WORKING POINTS "X"
RELEASED ELECTRICALLY
FROM S.B. INTERLOCKING
LEVER 36.

OPERATING BUTTON
FOR KLAXON HORNS

UP & DOWN GOODS LOOP HOME

UP & DOWN GOODS LOOP START

LOOP SIDING

DOWN MAIN UP

DOWN GOODS LOOP UP

SIDINGS

MORETONHAMPSTEAD

Origin: Moretonhampstead & South Devon Railway
Worked by the South Devon Railway and absorbed by that Company
in 1872

Opened: 4 July 1866
Closed: 2 Mar. 1959 (P)
6 Apr. 1964 (G) (Except for roadborne traffic until 1 Jan. 1965)

Plan date: c. 1913

The Moretonhampstead branch from Newton Abbot was built as a broad gauge single line, and in its 12½ miles, climbed 550 feet above sea level, onto the eastern slopes of Dartmoor. From the outset, and for the following 30 years or so, the train service on the branch was sparse and lightly loaded, but with the rapid growth of holidays for the masses, which originated in the later 1890's, traffic improved, and in 1906 when the G.W.R. started its own bus service to and from Chagford to connect with the trains, passenger traffic on the line was further enhanced.

The station at Moretonhampstead is a familiar memory in the minds of most Great Western enthusiasts who have passed the age of consent. Its outstanding features were the overall roof covering the terminal end of the station and run-round loop, the fair-sized goods shed butting onto the passenger platform, and an unusual arrangement of the signal box sharing part of the wall of the engine shed.

The layout remained unaltered down to rationalisation times except for the closure of the engine shed in 1947, and the similar fate of the little signal box on 2 Mar. 1959. The track as far as Bovey Tracy was lifted in June 1965.

In 1938, the signal box was open for the day's train service on weekdays, and "as required" on Sundays. There was no switch provided.

Moretonhampstead. Exterior of station buildings.

FURTHER READING

R. Mag.   1913 (Vol. 32) pp. 46–50   H.A.P.
R. Mag.   1953 p. 313 Pos.
R. Mag.   1959 p. 252 Pos.
R.W.   1976 pp. 434–435   D.A.P. Pos.
"Great Western Engine Sheds, 1947" by E. Lyons.   Oxford Publishing Co.

O.P.C.

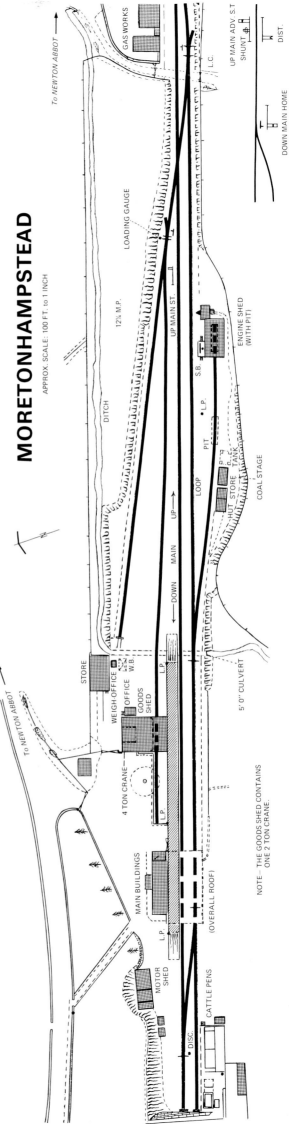

MORETONHAMPSTEAD

APPROX. SCALE: 100 FT. to 1 INCH

NANCEGOLLAN

Origin: Helston Railway (worked by the G.W.R. from opening and absorbed by that Company on 1 July 1898).

Opened: 9 May 1887 (old station)
19 Sept. 1937 (new station on same site)

Closed: 5 Nov. 1962 (P)
5 Oct. 1964 (G)

Plan date: c. 1911

The old station consisted of one passenger platform with the usual offices, a passing loop (for goods) which served a small loading dock, and a short siding behind the passenger platform. The layout was controlled by a ground frame on the station.

The main layout alterations which occurred were the diversion of the siding lead trailing into the 'down' main to a facing lead direct into the 'up' main in 1915, and the addition of dock accommodation between 1928 and 1929.

By 19 Sept. 1937, the station had been almost completely rebuilt to take the form shown in Diagram "B" with additional sidings on the south-west side, with a goods shed beside the nearest of the four, and a new signal box to take the place of the old ground frame. The station then became a crossing place—the only one on the Helston branch.

The maximum permitted speed for all up and down trains from mile post 5, through the station and nearly into Helston station was 25 m.p.h., thence into the terminus at 15 m.p.h.

The signal box was (1938) open from 6.20 a.m. to 10.20 p.m. (or as soon as the last train had cleared the section) on weekdays, and the box was not provided with a switch.

FURTHER READING

R.W.   1964 pp. 424–428   H.A.P.M.

M.R.N.   1967 pp. 29, 31, 78/9, 128/9, 223, 251, 284/5, 344/5, 387–389, 442/3, 444, 566/7.

(A comprehensive series of articles on the Helston branch. Illustrated.)

"The Hayle, West Cornwall, & Helston Railways" by G. H. Anthony. Oakwood Press

"The Story of Cornwall's Railways" by A. Fairclough. Tor Mark Press

"Reg. History of the Railways of Great Britain." Vol. 1. (The West Country) by D. St. J. Thomas. Phoenix

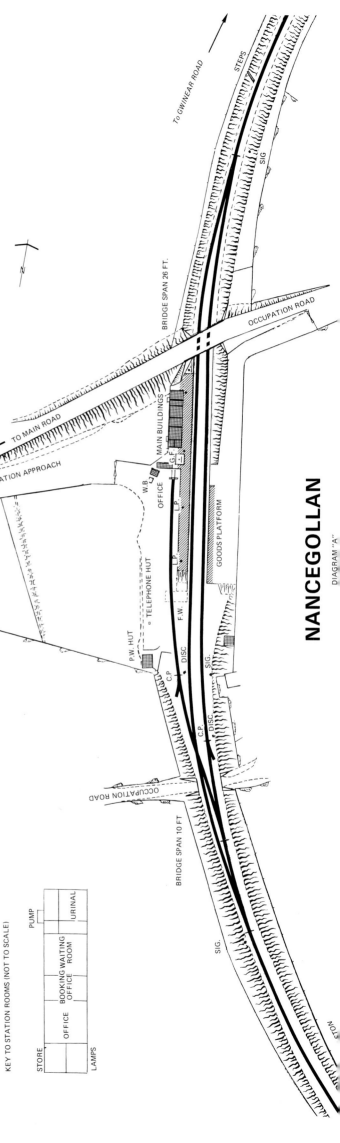

NANCEGOLLAN

DIAGRAM "A"

NANCEGOLLAN

DIAGRAM "B"
(NOT TO SCALE)

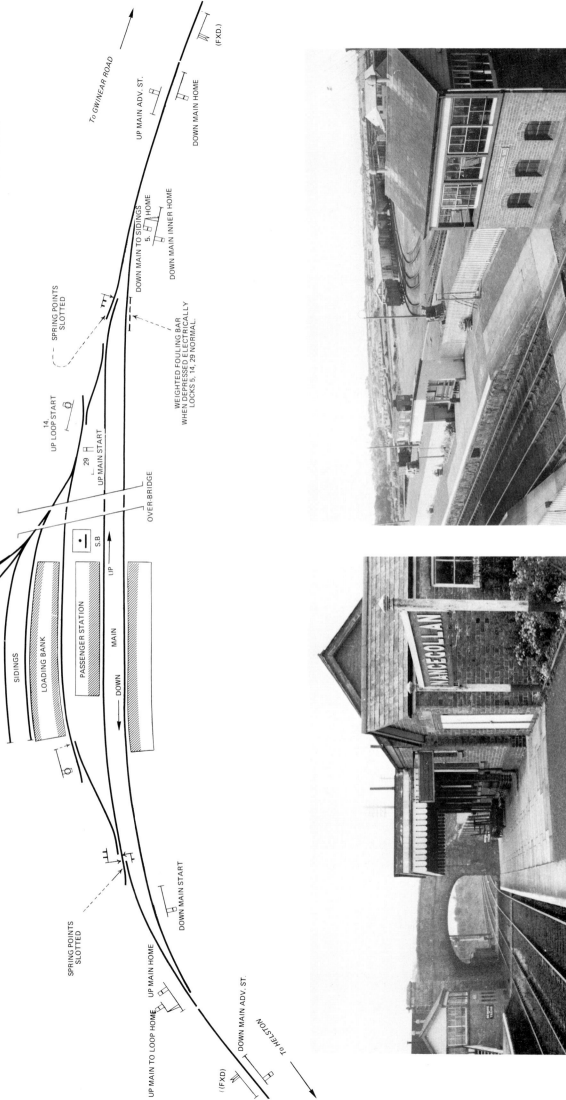

To GWINEAR ROAD

UP MAIN ADV. ST.

DOWN MAIN HOME

(FXD.)

SPRING POINTS SLOTTED

DOWN MAIN TO SIDINGS

5. HOME

DOWN MAIN INNER HOME

WEIGHTED FOULING BAR
WHEN DEPRESSED ELECTRICALLY
LOCKS 5, 14, 29 NORMAL.

14.
UP LOOP START

29

UP MAIN START

OVER-BRIDGE

S.B

UP

SIDINGS

LOADING BANK

PASSENGER STATION

MAIN

DOWN

SPRING POINTS
SLOTTED

DOWN MAIN START

UP MAIN HOME

UP MAIN TO LOOP HOME

DOWN MAIN ADV. ST.

((FXD)

To HELSTON

Nancegollan. Looking towards Gwinear Road. *Lens of Sutton*

Nancegollan. Showing the additional sidings. Aug. 1957.

H.C. Casserley Collection

127

128

NEATH GENERAL

Origin:	South Wales Railway
	Amalgamated with the G.W.R. and West Midland on 1 Aug. 1863
Opened:	18 June 1850 (1st. station)
	c. 1865 (2nd. station)
	1877 (3rd. station—present one)
Closed:	1st. station (on site of goods depot) c. 1865, on opening of 2nd. station on the west bank of the river
	2nd. station 1877, on opening of 3rd. station
Plan date:	c. 1912

The first station at Neath was opened on the South Wales Company's broad gauge double line from Chepstow to Swansea (High St.) when the line was opened on 18 June 1850, and the line was worked with Great Western locomotives and rolling stock. The signalling was of the disc and crossbar type, and the track was constructed with 'bridge' rails on longitudinal timbers. The 163¼ miles from Grange Court to New Milford was converted to standard gauge on 11–12 May 1872.

Although the three subsequent arrivals, the Neath & Brecon, the Vale of Neath, and the Rhondda & Swansea Bay companies each had their own stations at Neath, the

Great Western station (later "Neath General") was the principal station, and is the subject illustrated here.

The buildings on both platforms were long, and contained all the usual 'classified' establishments of the period, including 1st. and 3rd. class Ladies' and General Waiting rooms, and 1st. and 3rd. class Refreshment Rooms on both the 'up' and 'down' platforms. Verandah roofing extended the entire length of the buildings on all platforms, and on the 'up' side, the main roof was further characterised by three ornate 'turret' structures of rectangular shape, surmounted by decorative ironwork.

The opening hours of the three signal boxes during the summer period of 1938 were:—

Neath Engine Shed:	4.15 a.m. Mondays until 6.0 a.m. the following Sunday.
	A switch was provided.
Neath East:	Open continuously. No switch provided.
Neath (General) West:	3.30 a.m. Mondays until 6.0 a.m. the following Sunday, re-opening from 8.50 a.m. to 9.15 p.m. with one break. A switch was provided.

FURTHER READING

R. Mag. 1914 (Vol. 35) pp. 377–378. H.D.A.P. Pos.
R. Mag. 1956 pp. 429–435, 481, 517–523. H.A.P.M. Pos. (western approach)

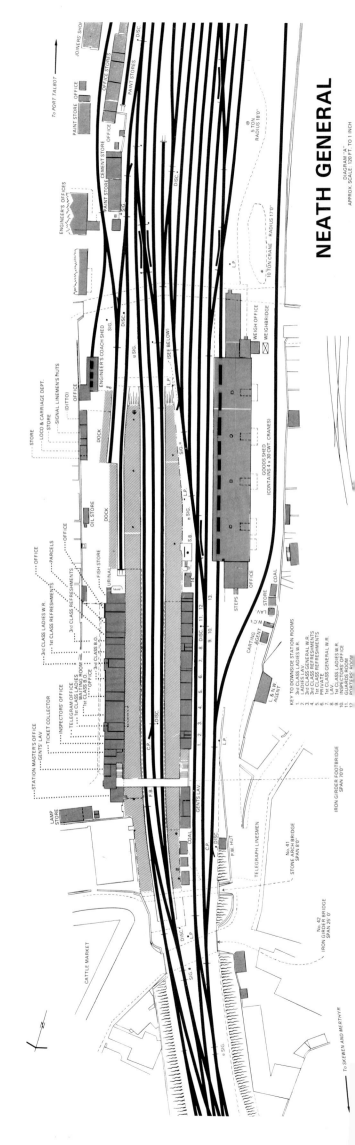

NEATH GENERAL

DIAGRAM "A"
APPROX. SCALE 120 FT. TO 1 INCH

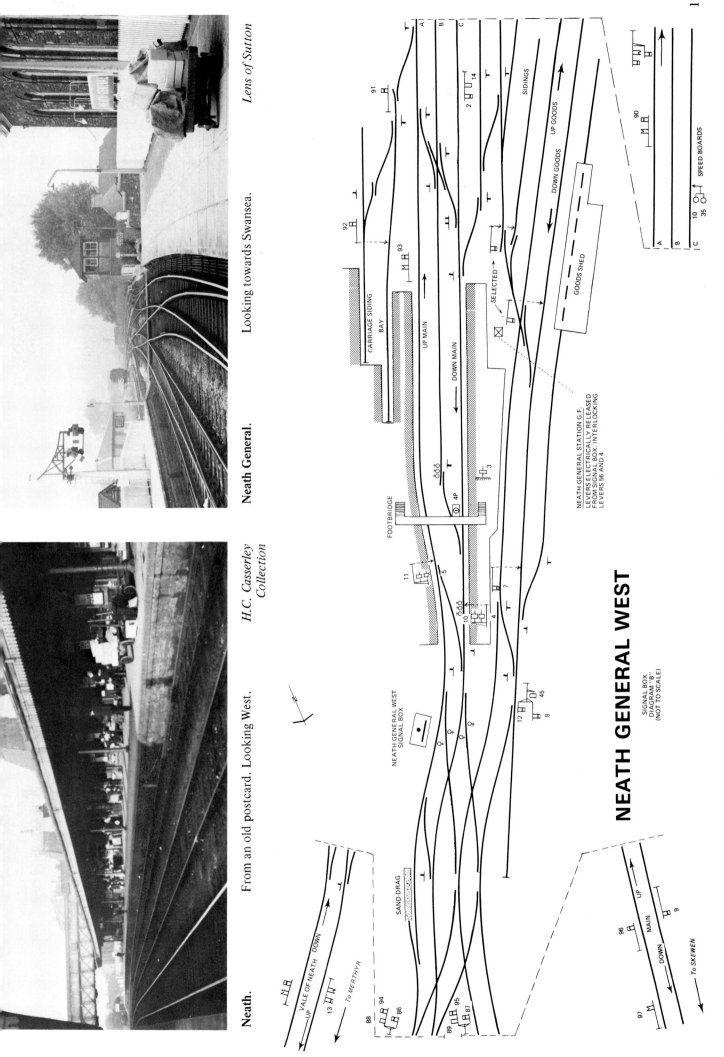

Neath. From an old postcard. Looking West.

Neath General. Looking towards Swansea.

Lens of Sutton

H.C. Casserley Collection

NEATH GENERAL WEST

SIGNAL BOX.
DIAGRAM 'B'.
(NOT TO SCALE)

NEATH GENERAL STATION G.F.
LEVERS ELECTRICALLY RELEASED
FROM SIGNAL BOX. INTERLOCKING
LEVERS 56 AND 4

NEATH GENERAL WEST
SIGNAL BOX

FOOTBRIDGE

CARRIAGE SIDING

BAY

UP MAIN

DOWN MAIN

SIDINGS

UP GOODS

DOWN GOODS

GOODS SHED

SELECTED

SPEED BOARDS

SAND-DRAG

VALE OF NEATH

UP DOWN

TO MERTHYR

DOWN MAIN UP

To SKEWEN

R.C. Riley

Newcastle Emlyn. 0-4-2T No. 1472 on the branch train in platform.

NEWCASTLE EMLYN

Origin:	Great Western Railway
Opened:	1 July 1895
Closed:	15 Sept. 1952 (P)
	22 Sept. 1973 (G)—but see notes
Plan date:	c. 1911

As its title implies, the original aim of the erstwhile Carmarthen & Cardigan Railway was to link those two places via Newcastle Emlyn. In the event, as is well known, the line never went beyond that town, although the building of it would not have proved difficult. As with so many railway projects of the 1860's, financial difficulties prevented the original proposal from coming to fruition, and, in later years the poor prospect of viability after the Cardigan branch from Whitland had been opened in 1886.

The Carmarthen & Cardigan line reached Llandyssul in 1864, and this was the terminus of the branch for the next 31 years, when the 7 mile extension to Newcastle Emlyn was built by the G.W.R.

The station was well laid out with ample siding accommodation and separate road accesses for passengers, cattle and ordinary goods. There was a small engine shed, pit and turntable, and a well-spaced coal yard.

The signal box was open on weekdays from 5.15 a.m. until the clearance of the last train, and was closed on Sundays. There was no switch provided. The branch was single line with crossing places at Llandyssul, Henllan, and the terminus, and was worked by Electric Train Staff.

In spite of the much earlier withdrawal of passenger services than of goods, the branch attracted sufficient interest for attempts to be made for its continued existence in more recent years by preservation enthusiasts, but promises of support were not fulfilled in sufficient measure. This, coupled with the advent of inflation, finally drowned any prospect of revival of the branch.

FURTHER READING

R. Mag. 1939 (Vol. 85) p. 198 (included in article "G.W.R. in West Wales".)
R. Mag. 1959 p. 509 H. Para.
"The Teifi Valley Railway" by R. Padfield and B. Burgess

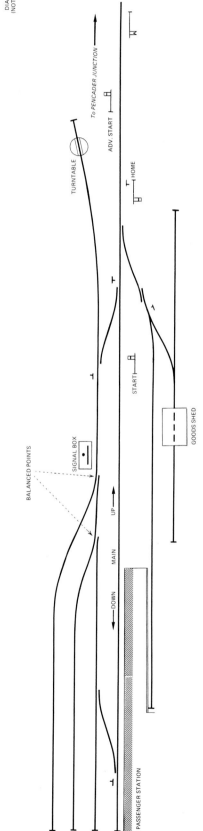

NEWCASTLE EMLYN

DIAGRAM "A"
APPROX. SCALE: 160 FT. TO 1 INCH

To PENCADER JUNCTION

To LLANDYSS UL

E.S.

CULVERT 8' 0"

T.T.

WATER CRANE

WATER TANK

GOODS SHED

L.P.

S.B.

OFFICE

M.P. 270¾

OIL TANK

L.P. CATTLE PENS

COAL WHARVES

CRANE

MAIN BUILDINGS

HUTS

L.P.

To NEWCASTLE EMLYN

N

NEWCASTLE EMLYN

DIAGRAM "B"
(NOT TO SCALE)

To PENCADER JUNCTION

TURNTABLE

ADV. START

HOME

START

SIGNAL BOX

BALANCED POINTS

UP

MAIN

DOWN

GOODS SHED

PASSENGER STATION

NEWQUAY

Origin: Cornwall Minerals Railway
(Leased to the G.W.R. in 1877 and absorbed by that Company in 1896)

Opened: 20 June 1876 (P) (from Fowey)
1 June 1874 (G) (from Fowey)

Closed: 7 Sept. 1964 (G) (Newquay Harbour closed in 1926)

Plan date: 1912

When the railway finally reached Newquay (from Fowey) by various and devious routes and means, and rail passengers were admitted for the first time, they little knew that they were the pioneers of a great boom in the prosperity of the town, and that it was to become one of the principal seaside "resorts" of the far west. The original route was supplemented by further passenger services, this time from Chacewater on 2 Jan. 1905 via St. Agnes and Perranporth, and Newquay's future as a holiday resort was firmly established right down to the present day, even though it has lost the last mentioned rail access, and a large number of rail-borne passengers from Par.

The station itself is on a curve, and the buildings are unpretentious. By virtue of the resort's popularity, extensive carriage sidings were added to the original layout for stabling the many passenger trains, both timetabled and special workings, and the platforms were considerably lengthened, necessitating a complete revision of the layout at the 'country' end of the station. The 1960's rationalisation programme, however, took its toll of these sidings and the goods yard, the latter being lifted the year following withdrawal of freight services. By 1970, three of the seven carriage sidings had gone.

In 1938, the signal box was open Mondays to Fridays from 6.25 a.m. to 10.20 p.m. (or when the last train had cleared section) and to 10.45 p.m. on Saturdays, and on Sundays it was open from 9.45 a.m. to 11.10 p.m. with a 2-hour break in the afternoon from 1.50 p.m. to 3.50 p.m. The box was not provided with a switch.

The new signal box beyond the extended platform dates from 20 Mar. 1946.

FURTHER READING

R. Mag. 1925 (Vol. 57) pp. 193–203 H.A.P.M. Pos.
T.I. 1953 pp. 416–421 H.A.P.M.
"The Railways of Cornwall, 1809–1963" by C. R. Clinker. David & Charles
"The Story of Cornwall's Railways" by A. Fairclough. Tor Mark Press, Truro
"Reg. Hist. of the Railways of Great Britain" Vol. 1. (The West Country)
by D. St. J. Thomas. Phoenix

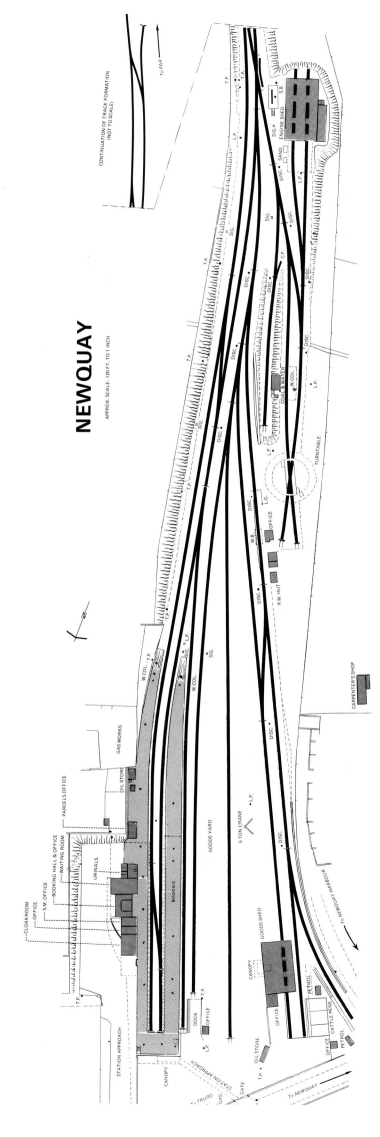

NEWQUAY

APPROX. SCALE: 120 FT. TO 1 INCH

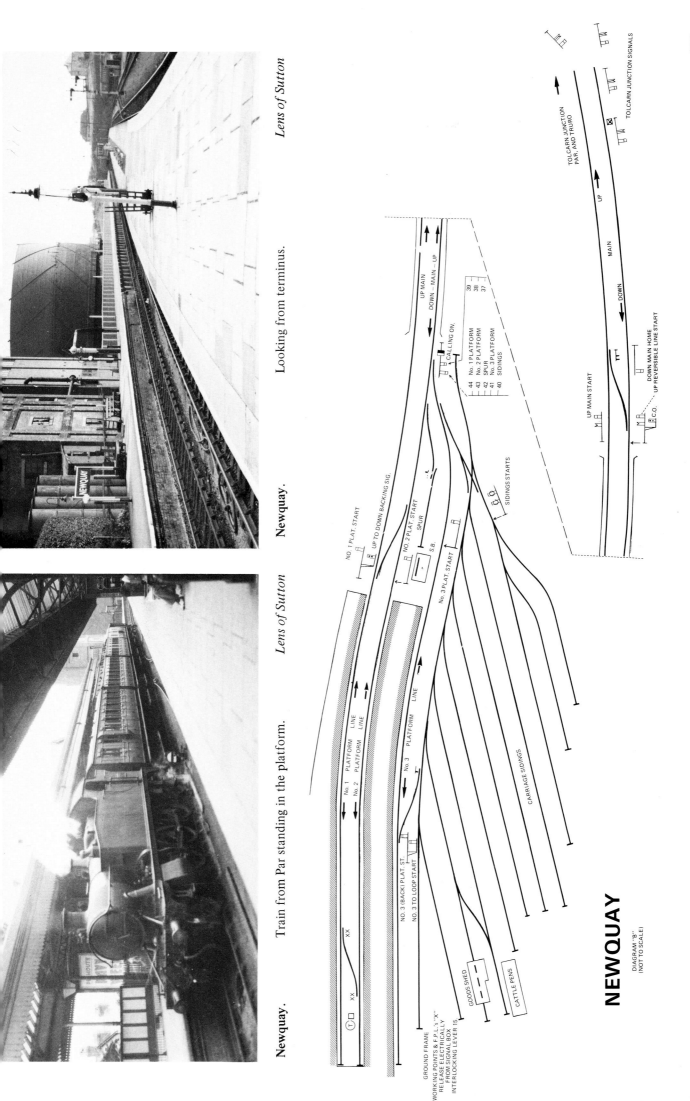

Lens of Sutton

Looking from terminus.

Lens of Sutton

Train from Par standing in the platform.

Newquay.

Newquay.

TOLCARN JUNCTION SIGNALS

TOLCARN JUNCTION
PAR. AND TRURO

UP

DOWN

MAIN

DOWN MAIN HOME
UP REVERSIBLE LINE START

UP MAIN START

C.O.

UP MAIN

DOWN — MAIN — UP

CALLING ON.

No. 1 PLATFORM
No. 2 PLATFORM
SPUR
No. 3 PLATFORM
SIDINGS

44
43
42
41
40

39
38
37

SIDINGS STARTS

NO. 1 PLAT. START

UP TO DOWN BACKING SIG.

NO. 2 PLAT. START

SPUR

S.B.

No. 3 PLAT. START

No. 1   PLATFORM   LINE

No. 2   PLATFORM   LINE

No. 3   PLATFORM   LINE

CARRIAGE SIDINGS

NO. 3 (BACK) PLAT. ST.
NO. 3 TO LOOP START

XX

XX

GROUND FRAME

WORKING POINTS & F.P.L.'s "X"
RELEASE ELECTRICALLY
FROM SIGNAL BOX
INTERLOCKING LEVER 15.

GOODS SHED

CATTLE PENS

NEWQUAY

DIAGRAM "B"
(NOT TO SCALE)

133

NEYLAND

Origin: South Wales Railway
Absorbed by the G.W.R. in 1863.

Opened: 15 Apr. 1856 (as "Milford Haven")

Renamings: "Neyland" from Feb. 1859; "New Milford" from Nov. 1859;
"Neyland" from 30 Aug. 1906

Closed: 15 June 1964 (P)
2 Dec. 1963 (G)

Plan date: c. 1930 (Diagram "B" 1932)

Neyland (to use its final title) was opened as the terminus of the broad gauge single line from Haverfordwest, and which was doubled on 1 July 1857. Before this, Fishguard had already been considered for being the port for Southern Ireland, but Neyland ("Milford Haven") was chosen as being more sheltered, with deep water channels, and with more space to develop than was the case with the former scheme. A temporary terminus was provided at opening, before the final passenger station was built.

The station could not be described as "attractive" at any time in its history, but it very soon became a busy one, bearing in mind that before the railway came, there was no trade at all. The harbour was dredged to allow coal shipping to berth at the new staithes which were erected, and a fixed pier built to reach water deep enough to berth the vessels which were to provide a thrice-weekly service to Waterford, and an additional service to Cork.

As can be seen from the diagrams, the layout was extensive, and remained fully utilised even when Milford Haven station and sidings were built 7 years later, on the other side of the hill. Neyland even retained its sleeping car service from Paddington down to well within the memory of the writer, in spite of later competition from the Fishguard service.

It was inevitable, however, that Fishguard should become more in favour as THE port for Ireland (and, for a period, Ocean-going traffic), and passenger traffic declined at Neyland, although the yard continued for a time to handle industrial freight.

In 1938 (summer period), the signal box was open on weekdays from 5.45 a.m. to 12.35 a.m. (next morning), and on Sundays from 5.25 a.m. to 7.45 a.m. and from 5.0 p.m. to 6.40 p.m. The box was not provided with a switch.

FURTHER READING

R. Mag. 1939 (Vol. 85) pp. 197–202 H.A.P. Pos.
R. Mag. 1956 pp. 628–632 H.A.P.
"Great Western Engine Sheds, 1947" by E. Lyons. Oxford Publishing Company. (includes whole-page picture of station from above)

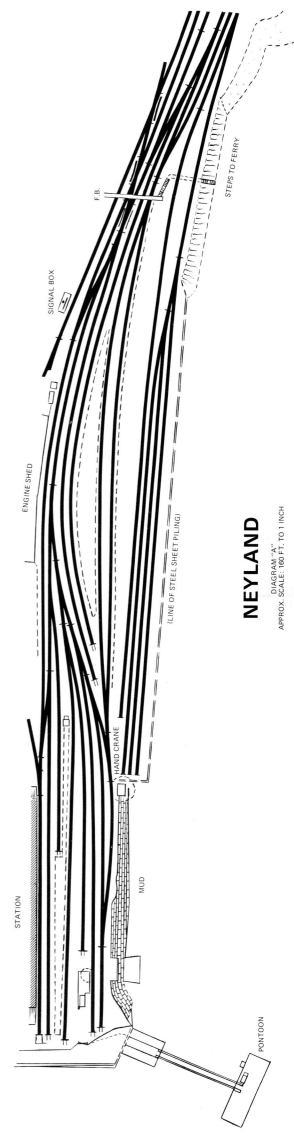

NEYLAND

DIAGRAM "A"
APPROX. SCALE: 160 FT. TO 1 INCH

Neyland.   Looking towards buffers. Main buildings on right.   *M. Hale*

Neyland.   Engine shed. View towards Haverfordwest.   *O.P.C.*

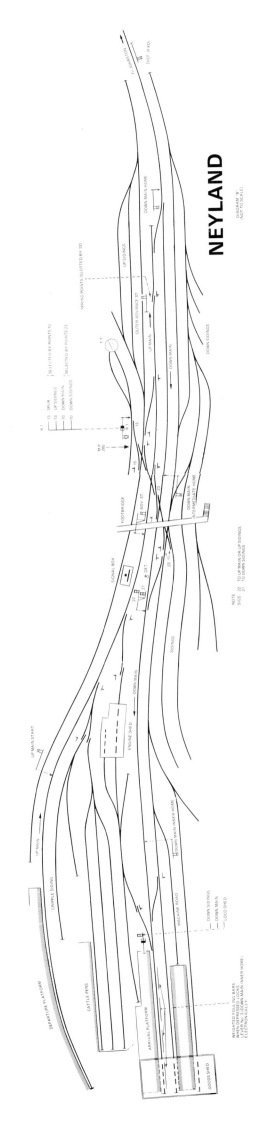

NEYLAND

DIAGRAM 'B'
(NOT TO SCALE)

To JOHNSTON

DIST. (FXD)

DOWN MAIN HOME

UP SIDINGS

OUTER ADVANCE ST.

SPRING POINTS (SLOTTED BY 12)

UP MAIN

DOWN MAIN

DOWN SIDINGS

R 1
13   SPUR
13   UP SIDINGS   SLOTTED BY POINTS 15
10   DOWN MAIN
10   DOWN SIDINGS   SELECTED BY POINTS 23

15

M.P.
295½

FOOTBRIDGE

ADV ST.

DOWN MAIN
INTERMEDIATE HOME

SIGNAL BOX

3 DET

23

23

SIDINGS

NOTE
SIGS.   22   TO UP MAIN OR UP SIDINGS
       27   TO DOWN SIDINGS

UP MAIN START

ENGINE SHED

DOWN MAIN

DEPARTURE PLATFORM

CRIPPLE SIDING

CATTLE PENS

UP MAIN

DOWN MAIN INNER HOME

ARRIVAL PLATFORM

MACHINE ROAD

DOWN SIDINGS

DOWN MAIN

LOCO SHED

GOODS SHED

WEIGHTED FOULING BARS
WHEN DEPRESSED LOCKS
LEVER No. 3 (DOWN MAIN INNER HOME)
ELECTRONICALLY

135

NORTON FITZWARREN

Origin: Bristol & Exeter Railway
          Absorbed by the Great Western Railway in 1878.
Opened: 1873
Closed: 30 Oct. 1961 (P)
          6 July 1964 (G)—except for private siding traffic
Plan date: c. 1913

Although diminutive in size as a passenger station, Norton Fitzwarren was, neverthe-less, 'overseer and caretaker' of a major Great Western junction where the Barnstaple and Minehead branches diverged from the main West of England line, 2 miles west of Taunton. It is doubtful if more than a handful of passengers ever used it as an exchange station, for all branch trains ran to and from Taunton.

The yard used to handle train-loads of cider apples from the vast orchards abounding in the district, and a fair amount of other agricultural traffic, considering the limitations of the sidings layout.

Space does not permit of a detailed description of the rise and fall of this station, for it would run into many pages, but it might be true to say that few such small layouts developed into such proportions, only to disappear so completely that, today, it would be difficult to ascertain for certain where the original station and its tracks once stood.

Although there were certain minor modifications to the layout prior to 1930, revision of the yard layout, and connections to the main line began in earnest in Sept. 1931, followed a month later by the redundancy of the down refuge siding, south of the main line. From then on, the engineers were busy at both ends of the station, starting with the building of two entirely new platforms at the Taunton end of the old ones. These were opened on 2 Dec. 1931. By the outbreak of the 2nd. War, the layout had reached its zenith.

It was not until 1959 that the decline set in, and in March 1970 (when the signal box was closed), the demise of Norton Fitzwarren station was virtually complete.

In the summer of 1938, the signal box opening hours were—Weekdays: 4.0 a.m. until 5.0 a.m. (Sunday mornings) and on Sundays from 9.20 a.m. until 10.0 p.m. with a break between 4.0 p.m. and 6.0 p.m. Switch provided.

FURTHER READING

R. Mag. 1934 (Vol. 75) pp. 263–270   H.A.P.M. (Taunton–Minehead) Pos.
T.I.   1951 pp. 272–274   H.D.A.P.
R. Mag. 1957 pp. 371–376   H.A.P.M. (Taunton–Barnstaple)
"Regional History of the Railways of Great Britain." (Vol. 1) The West Country
                              by D. St. J. Thomas. Phoenix

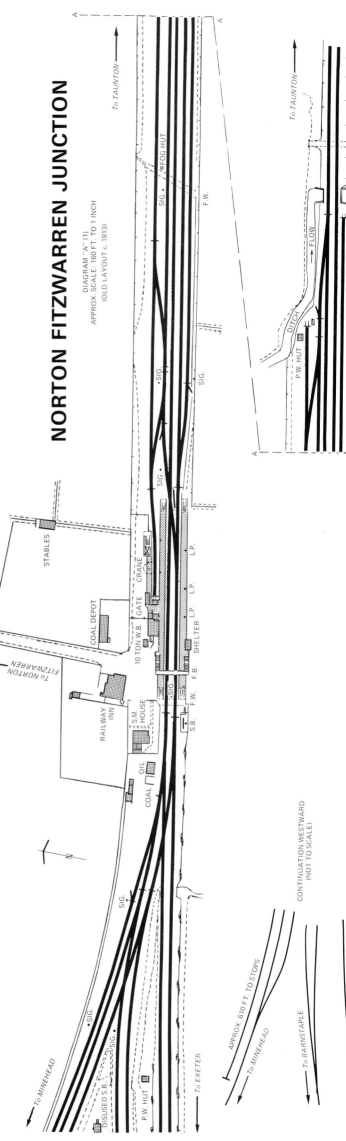

NORTON FITZWARREN JUNCTION

DIAGRAM "A" (1)
APPROX. SCALE: 160 FT. TO 1 INCH
(OLD LAYOUT c. 1913)

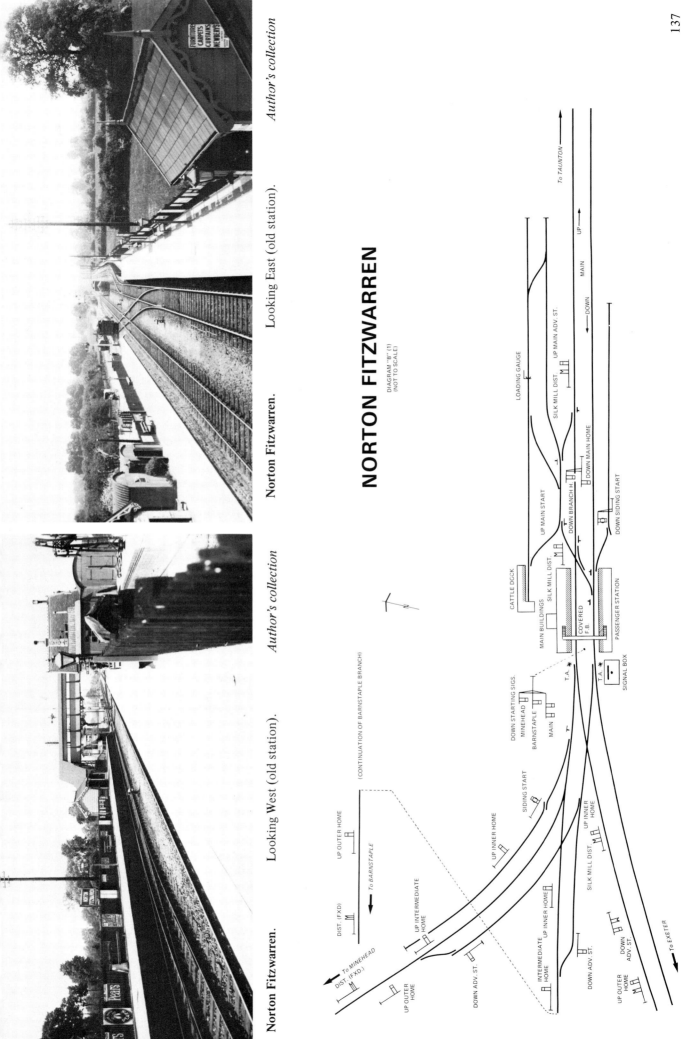

Looking West (old station).   *Author's collection*

Norton Fitzwarren.   Looking East (old station).   *Author's collection*

Norton Fitzwarren.

NORTON FITZWARREN

DIAGRAM "B" (1)
(NOT TO SCALE)

Norton Fitzwarren.　　　Looking East towards Taunton. 1961.　　　*R.H. Clark*

Showing the junction layout. c.1961.　　　*O.P.C.*

Norton Fitzwarren.

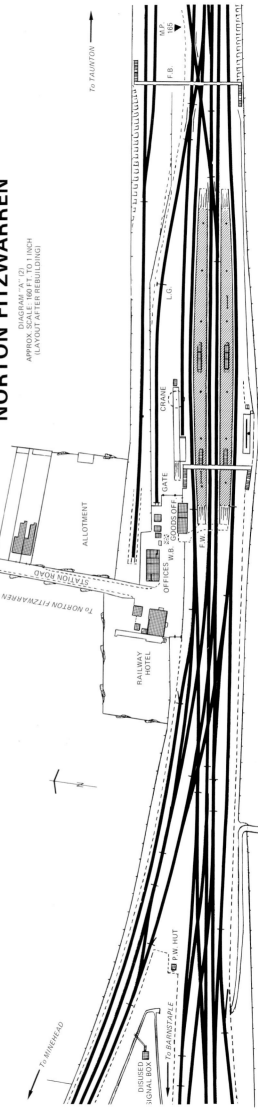

NORTON FITZWARREN

DIAGRAM "A" (2)
APPROX. SCALE: 160 FT. TO 1 INCH
(LAYOUT AFTER REBUILDING)

To TAUNTON

M.P.
165

F.B.

L.G.

CRANE

GATE

ALLOTMENT

OFFICES W.B. GOODS OFF.

F.W.

F.B.

STATION ROAD

To NORTON FITZWARREN

RAILWAY HOTEL

N

P.W. HUT

To BARNSTAPLE

To MINEHEAD

DISUSED
SIGNAL BOX

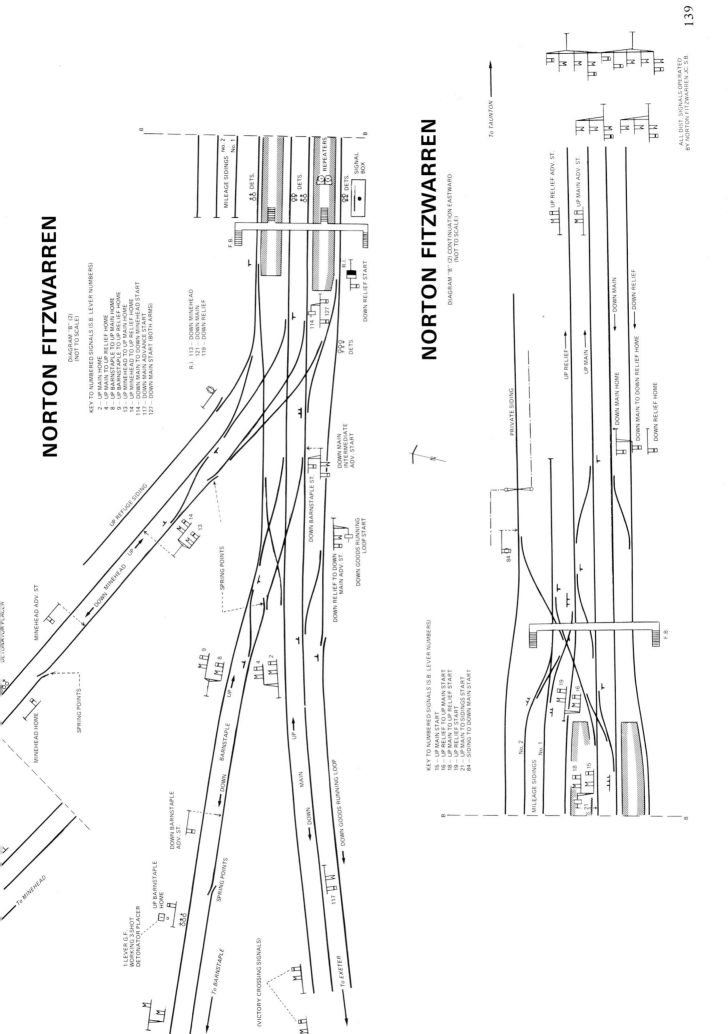

NORTON FITZWARREN

DIAGRAM "B" (2)
(NOT TO SCALE)

KEY TO NUMBERED SIGNALS (S.B. LEVER NUMBERS)
2 – UP MAIN HOME
4 – UP MAIN TO UP RELIEF HOME
8 – UP BARNSTAPLE TO UP MAIN HOME
9 – UP BARNSTAPLE TO UP RELIEF HOME
13 – UP MINEHEAD TO UP MAIN HOME
14 – UP MINEHEAD TO UP RELIEF HOME
114 – DOWN MAIN TO DOWN MINEHEAD START
117 – DOWN MAIN ADVANCE START
127 – DOWN MAIN START (BOTH ARMS)

R.I. 113 – DOWN MINEHEAD
121 – DOWN MAIN
119 – DOWN RELIEF

NORTON FITZWARREN

DIAGRAM "B" (2) CONTINUATION EASTWARD
(NOT TO SCALE)

KEY TO NUMBERED SIGNALS (S.B. LEVER NUMBERS)
15 – UP MAIN START
16 – UP RELIEF TO UP MAIN START
18 – UP MAIN TO UP RELIEF START
19 – UP RELIEF START
21 – UP MAIN TO SIDINGS START
84 – SIDING TO DOWN MAIN START

ALL DIST. SIGNALS OPERATED
BY NORTON FITZWARREN JC. S.B.

139

140

PAR

Origin: Cornwall Railway
Leased from opening to the G.W.R., B. & E., and S.D.R.
Absorbed by the Great Western Railway in 1889

Opened: 4 May 1859
Closed: 1 June 1964 (G)—Remained open for private siding traffic
Plan date: c. 1908

The loop line used by the Newquay trains from Par which joins the former Cornwall Minerals Railway at St. Blazey, was opened on 1 Jan. 1879. Up to this date St. Blazey was entitled "Par (St. Blazey)". The line from Milltown Viaduct to Par was doubled and brought into use on 19 Dec. 1894, the section beyond, as far as St. Austell having been doubled on 15 Oct. 1893.

The basic layout at Par did not alter between Edwardian times and the 1960's, except that a carriage siding came and went (it was lifted in August 1965), the trailing crossover at the northern end of the station was abolished and replaced by another beyond the yard leads. This was removed in May 1926, and replaced by a facing crossover to give direct access to the yard, and 'down' to 'up' main, as well as other minor alterations. The 'down' goods refuge siding was made into a loop in April 1943.

The whole layout was drastically rationalised in 1974, and by 1975 had been reduced to mere basic necessities.

Right down to the 1950's, Par was a busy station for both freight and passenger traffic, the latter mostly being generated by the Newquay branch, and to a small extent by the proximity of Fowey.

The station buildings were not ambitious, but the layout at any period offers possibilities to the modeller.

Today, Par is a mere skeleton of its former shape, but most main line trains stop there, mainly to provide rail communication between Newquay and the outside world. Par signal box was provided with a switch.

FURTHER READING

R. Mag. 1911 (Vol. 29) pp. 181–188; 382–388   H.A.P.M. Pos. + Grade profile
R. Mag. 1925 (Vol. 57) pp. 193–203   H.A.P.M. Pos.
T.I.   1953 pp. 416–421   H.A.P.M. Pos.
"Great Western Branch Lines, 1955–1965" by C. J. Gammell.   O.P.C.
"Railway History in Pictures—The West Country" by R. C. Riley.   David & Charles
"The Story of Cornwall's Railways" by A. Fairclough.   Tor Mark Press.
"The Railways of Cornwall, 1809–1963" by C. R. Clinker.   David & Charles
"Reg. History of the Railways of Great Britain." (Vol. 1.) The West Country by D. St. J. Thomas. Phoenix

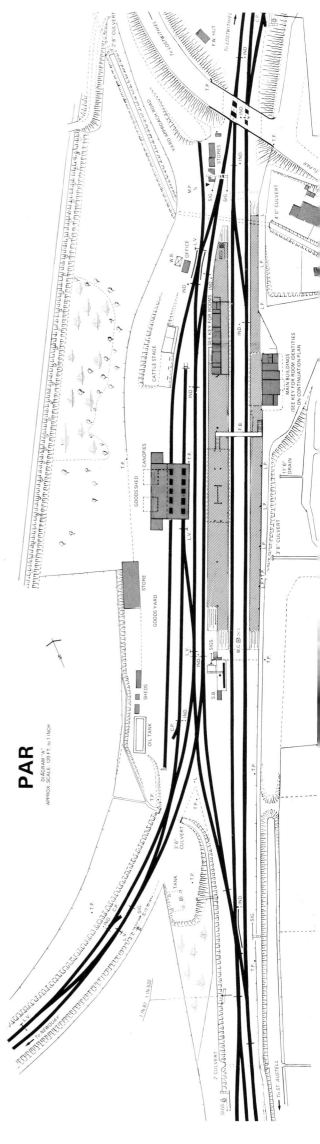

PAR
DIAGRAM "A"
APPROX. SCALE: 120 FT. to 1 INCH

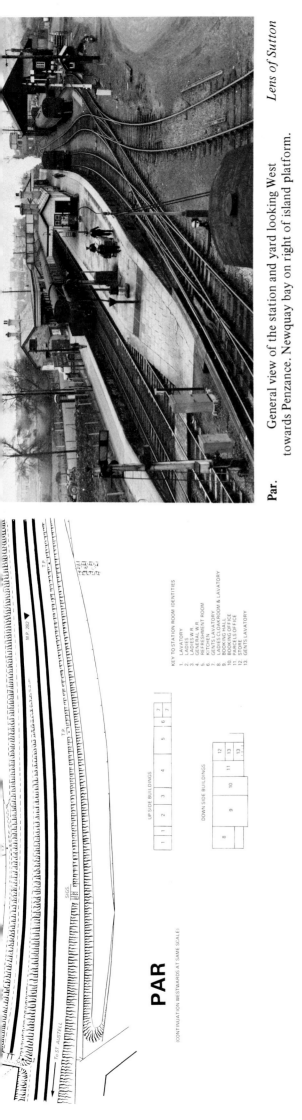

Par. General view of the station and yard looking West towards Penzance. Newquay bay on right of island platform.

Lens of Sutton

PAR

(CONTINUATION WESTWARDS AT SAME SCALE)

M.P. 282

To ST. AUSTELL

SIGS.

UP SIDE BUILDINGS

| 1 | 2 | 3 | 4 | 5 | 6 | 7 |
| | | | | | | 7 |

DOWN SIDE BUILDINGS

| 8 | 9 | 10 | 11 | 12 |
| | | | 13 | 13 |

KEY TO STATION ROOM IDENTITIES

1. LAVATORY
2. LADIES
3. LADIES W.R.
4. GENERAL W.R.
5. REFRESHMENT ROOM
6. KITCHEN
7. GENTS LAVATORY
8. LADIES CLOAKROOM & LAVATORY
9. BOOKING HALL
10. BOOKING OFFICE
11. PARCELS OFFICE
12. STORE
13. GENTS LAVATORY

PAR

DIAGRAM "B"
(NOT TO SCALE)

N

To NEWQUAY

UP

DOWN

To TRURO

UP MAIN DIST.

UP MAIN
INNER DIST.

DOWN MAIN
ADV. ST.

UP BRANCH TO SIDINGS
HOME

UP BRANCH
CALLING ON

UP BRANCH HOME

42 39
38 36

BOTH FPL'S BOLTED FOR 36

9

UP REFUGE SIDING

49

UP MAIN HOME

DOWN MAIN START

UP BRANCH No. 1
SPUR START

UP BRANCH
CALLING ON

UP BRANCH
TO MAIN START

No. 2 SPUR

No. 1 SPUR

25

22

LOOP

DOWN — BRANCH — UP

F.B.

MAIN

DOWN

DET.

DET.

S.B.

8

5

50

54

16 31

15 SELECTED

UP

PASSENGER STATION

DETONATORS WORKED BY
SMALL 2 LEVER FRAME.

KEY TO NUMBERED SIGNALS (S.B. LEVER NUMBERS)

5 – DOWN BRANCH TO DOWN MAIN START
8 – DOWN BRANCH START
9 – DOWN BRANCH ADV. START
49 – UP REFUGE TO UP MAIN START
50 – UP MAIN CALLING ON
54 – UP MAIN START
POINTS 18 WORKED BY MOTOR

D.M. INNER HOME

D.M. TO DOWN
BRANCH INNER HOME

To LOSTWITHIEL

UP MAIN ADV. ST.

18

SPRING
POINTS

DOWN GOODS LOOP

D.G.L. TO DOWN
MAIN START

D.M. HOME

D.M. TO DOWN GOODS
LOOP HOME

DOWN MAIN
DISTANT

141

PEMBROKE

Origin: Pembroke & Tenby
           (Absorbed by G.W.R. in 1897)
Opened: 30 July 1863
Closed:
Plan date: Diagram "A" 1908   Diagram "B" 1960

The tracks on the extreme right hand of the plan converge to single line beyond the plan's limit.

Considering the size of the town of Pembroke, its station seems to be rather small, being merely a single line platform with small buildings and a goods lock up. Apart from a single coal siding, an end-loading dock, a crane, a cattle pen on another (shorter) siding, and a weigh bridge with office, the small yard was otherwise devoid of a goods shed or similar ancillary buildings. The passing loop was clear of the station at the eastern end. This was the arrangement of things in late Edwardian times. In later years, two additional sidings were added on the down side, and a revision of the layout near the cattle pens resulted in the abolition of the loading dock (at the end of the cattle pen road) and continuation of this road to a private siding, as in Diagram "B".

Pembroke Dock signal box was (1938) opened at 6.20 a.m. and closed after the clearance of the last train on weekdays, and (in the summer period) on Sundays from 12.0 noon to 10.40 p.m. with a break from 6.25 p.m. to 8.35 p.m. The box was not provided with a switch.

(See Pembroke Dock notes for details of Train Staff and Token arrangements.)

FURTHER READING

R. Mag. 1914 (Vol. 35) pp. 65–68; 139–142   D.A.P.
R. Mag. 1957 p. 441 H. Para.
R. Mag. 1959 pp. 663–669; 724   H.A.P.M. Pos.
R. Mag. 1962 pp. 737–745   H.D.A.P.M.

Pembroke.   View towards Pembroke Dock. c.1961.   *Lens of Sutton*

Pembroke.   Looking towards Tenby.   *O.P.C.*

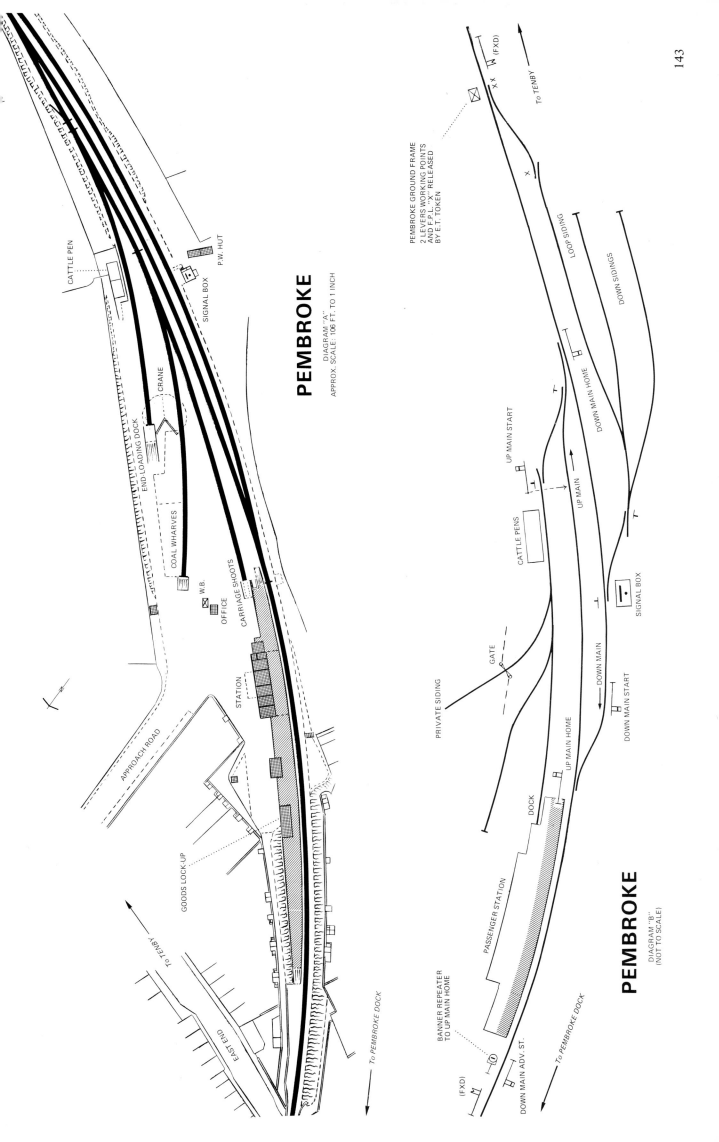

PEMBROKE

DIAGRAM "A"
APPROX. SCALE: 106 FT. TO 1 INCH

CATTLE PEN

P.W. HUT

SIGNAL BOX

CRANE

END-LOADING DOCK

COAL WHARVES

W.B.

OFFICE

CARRIAGE SHOOTS

STATION

APPROACH ROAD

GOODS LOCK-UP

EAST END

To TENBY

To PEMBROKE DOCK

PEMBROKE

DIAGRAM "B"
(NOT TO SCALE)

PEMBROKE GROUND FRAME
2 LEVERS WORKING POINTS
AND F.P.L. "X" RELEASED
BY E.T. TOKEN

(FXD)

X X

To TENBY

X

LOOP SIDING

DOWN MAIN HOME

DOWN SIDINGS

UP MAIN START

UP MAIN

CATTLE PENS

SIGNAL BOX

DOWN MAIN

DOWN MAIN START

PRIVATE SIDING

GATE

UP MAIN HOME

DOCK

PASSENGER STATION

BANNER REPEATER
TO UP MAIN HOME

(FXD)

DOWN MAIN ADV. ST.

To PEMBROKE DOCK

143

Pembroke Dock.   Looking towards terminus.   *Lens of Sutton*

Pembroke Dock.   An old picture of the station exterior.

H.C. Casserley Collection

PEMBROKE DOCK

Origin: Pembroke & Tenby
           (Absorbed by G.W.R. in 1897)
Opened: 9 Aug. 1864 (H. A. Vallance states "8th Aug. 1864")
Closed:
Plan date: 4 May 1910

Hobbs Point Pier was closed on and from 1 Jan. 1969.

The branch opened in two sections as a standard gauge single line, Pembroke–Tenby on 31 July 1863; Tenby–Whitland 4 Sept. 1866 (to a station adjoining that of the S.W. line at Whitland). The extension from Pembroke to Pembroke Dock was opened on 9 Aug. 1864.

Nearly 27½ miles from Whitland, the station is an ordinary 2-road passenger terminal, with long platforms and main buildings at the far end of the down platforms and main buildings at the far end of the down platform, the tracks converging beyond the footway into a reversing neck. Immediately opposite the main buildings and edging on to the 'up' platform is a through road goods shed. The stone-built engine shed was closed in Sept. 1963.

The single line branch was (1938) worked by Electric Train Staff between Whitland and Manorbier, and between Pembroke and Pembroke Dock, the intervening section being worked by Electric Train Token.

Starting at 11.0 a.m. each weekday, 5½ hours per day were allowed for passenger and goods shunting plus trips to Hobbs Point and the Dockyard. Mixed and goods trains were restricted to a maximum speed of 25 m.p.h. over the whole branch.

The weekday signal box hours were from 6.30 a.m. to the clearance of the last train, and there was no switch provided.

FURTHER READING

R. Mag. 1914 (Vol. 35) pp. 65–68; 139–142   D.A.P.
R. Mag. 1957 p. 441   H. Para.
R. Mag. 1959 pp. 663–669; 724   H.A.P.M.
R. Mag. 1962 pp. 737–745   H.D.A.P.M. Pos.
"Great Western Engine Sheds–1947" by E. Lyons   O.P.C.

PEMBROKE DOCK

DIAGRAM "A"
APPROX. SCALE: 120 FT. TO 1 INCH

To HOBBS POINT PIER

To WHITLAND

L.C. (OCCUPATION)

ENGINE SHED

GAS HOLDERS

GAS WORKS

WATER CRANE

T.T.

HUTS

S.B.

C.P.

SIG.

SIG.

M.P.
286¾

GOODS SHED

MAIN BUILDINGS

APLEY TERRACE

OFFICE

W.B.

C.P.

(To DOCK)

145

Penzance. Looking East showing approach layout. *O.P.C.*

Penzance. General view into station showing the harbour line off to the left. *O.P.C.*

PENZANCE

Origin: West Cornwall Railway
Leased from opening to G.W.R., B. & E., and S.D.R.
Absorbed by the Great Western Railway in 1878.

Opened: 11 Mar. 1852 (Standard gauge)
6 Nov. 1866 (for broad gauge goods trains)
1 Mar. 1867 (for broad gauge passenger trains)

Closed:

Plan date: c. 1911

The G.W.R., B. & E., & S.D.R. became absolute owners of the West Cornwall Railway from 1 Jan. 1866, and laid the broad gauge.

The 2-road engine shed just outside the station was closed in 1914 being replaced by a new 5-road shed at Long Rock, short of Marazion. Seven years later the old single-line viaduct was abolished in favour of a double-track embankment, suitably protected from the sea by rocks. The line was opened as double-track from Penzance to Ponsandine on 24 July 1921. By the outbreak of the 2nd War, goods facilities for Penzance had been transferred from the old shed to Ponsandine and the track-layout there considerably
altered

The station signal box was replaced by a new one on 24 Apr. 1938, and in the station itself, tracks and platforms had been re-arranged to serve each of the four lines (compare Diagrams "A" and "B"). The line down to Albert Quay lost its trains in Sept. 1967.

In 1938, the signal box was open from 5.50 a.m. until 12.00 (midnight) Mondays to Fridays, and on Saturdays until 12.25 a.m. (night). On Sundays it was open from 6.30 a.m. until 10.55 p.m. with an intermediate break between 2.45 p.m. and 4.45 p.m. The box was not provided with a switch.

FURTHER READING

R. Mag. 1925 (Vol. 57) pp. 193–203 H.A.P.M. Pos.
R. Mag. 1974 p. 2 Pos.
"Great Western Engine Sheds, 1947" by E. Lyons. Oxford Publishing Company.
"The Hayle, West Cornwall, & Helston Railways" by G. H. Anthony. Oakwood Press
"The Railways of Cornwall, 1809–1963" by C. R. Clinker. David & Charles
"Reg. History of the Railways of Great Britain." Vol. 1. (The West Country)
by D. St. J. Thomas. Phoenix

PENZANCE

Diagram "A"
APPROX. SCALE 120 FT TO 1 INCH

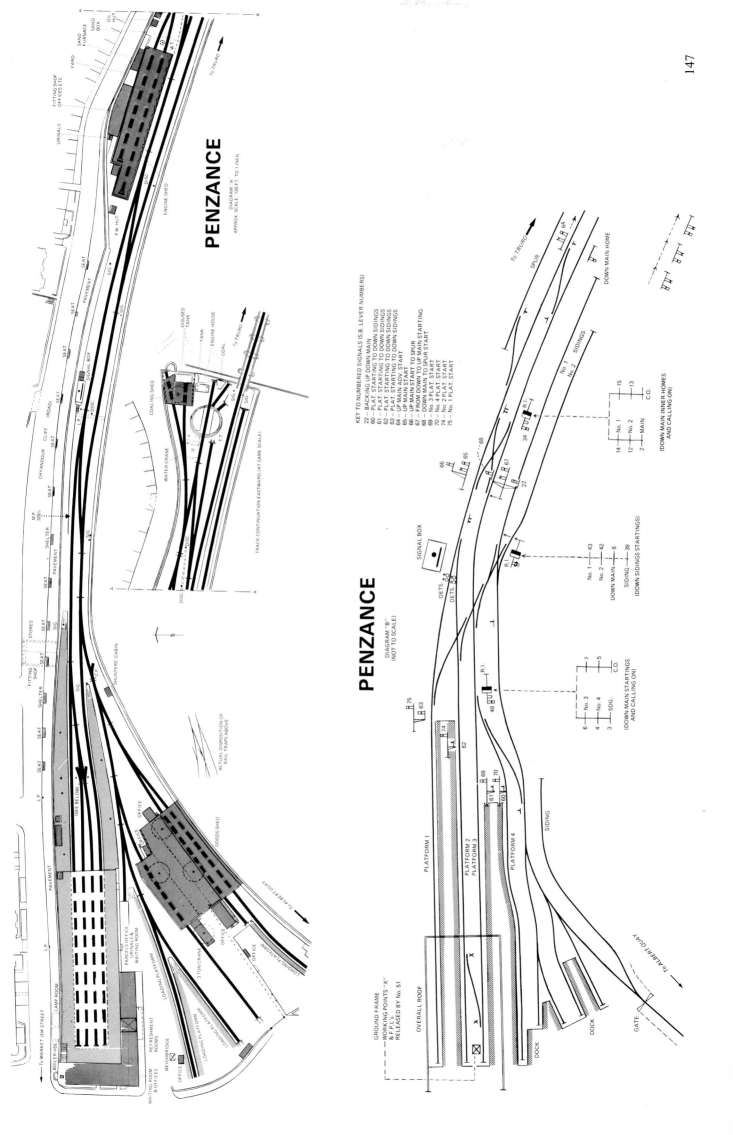

SAND BOX
OIL HUT
SAND FURNACE
YARD
FITTING SHOP OFFICES ETC.
URINALS
W.T.
To TRURO
DISC.
ENGINE SHED
SIG.
SIG.
SEAT
SEAT
PAVEMENT
SEAT
P W HUT
SIG.
SIGNAL BOX
SEAT
SEAT
SEAT (ROAD)
L.P. DISC.
DISUSED TANK
TANK
ENGINE HOUSE
COAL
COALING SHED
WATER CRANE
T.T.
SIG.
DISC.
SIG.
To TRURO
CHYANDOUR CLIFF
MP 326¾
SEAT
SEAT
PAVEMENT
SHELTER
SIG.
STORES
SEAT
SEAT
SHELTER
SEAT
SIG.
L.P.
SHUNTERS CABIN
FITTING SHOP
SEAT
SIG.
L.P.
N
ACTUAL DISPOSITION OF RAIL TRAPS ABOVE
TRACK CONTINUATION EASTWARD (AT SAME SCALE)
A
A
DISC.
A
A

To MARKET JEW STREET
BOILER HSE.
LAMP ROOM
L.P.
SEAT
L.P.
PAVEMENT
(SEE BELOW)
L.P.
OFFICE
OFFICE
OFFICE
GOODS SHED
OFFICE
To ALBERT QUAY
PARCELS OFFICE
URINALS & WAITING ROOM
LOADING PLATFORM
3 TON CRANE
OFFICE
LOADING PLATFORM
LOADING PLATFORM
WAITING ROOM & OFFICES
REFRESHMENT ROOMS
WEIGHBRIDGE
OFFICE

PENZANCE

Diagram "B"
(NOT TO SCALE)

KEY TO NUMBERED SIGNALS (I.S.B. LEVER NUMBERS)

22 — BACKING UP DOWN MAIN
60 — PLAT. STARTING TO DOWN SIDINGS
61 — PLAT. STARTING TO DOWN SIDINGS
62 — PLAT. STARTING TO DOWN SIDINGS
63 — PLAT. STARTING TO DOWN SIDINGS
64 — UP MAIN ADV. START
65 — UP MAIN ADV. START
66 — UP MAIN START TO SPUR
67 — FROM DOWN TO UP MAIN STARTING
68 — DOWN MAIN TO UP MAIN STARTING
69 — No. 3 PLAT. START
70 — No. 4 PLAT. START
74 — No. 2 PLAT. START
75 — No. 1 PLAT. START

To TRURO
SPUR
6A
T
DOWN MAIN HOME
No. 1 SIDINGS
No. 2 SIDINGS
R.I.
34
68
66
65
67
22
(DOWN MAIN INNER HOMES AND CALLING ON)
15
13
14   No. 1   C.O.
12   No. 2
2   MAIN

SIGNAL BOX
DETS.
DETS. 30
R.I.
No. 1   43
No. 2   42
DOWN MAIN   8
SIDING   39
(DOWN SIDINGS STARTINGS)

75
63
74
62
69
70
61
60
PLATFORM 1
PLATFORM 2
PLATFORM 3
PLATFORM 4
SIDING
R.I.
49
No. 3   7
No. 4   5
SDG.   C.O.
6   No. 3
4   No. 4
3   SDG.
(DOWN MAIN STARTINGS AND CALLING ON)

GROUND FRAME
——— WORKING POINTS "X"
& F.P.L.'s.
RELEASED BY No. 51

OVERALL ROOF
X
X
DOCK
DOCK
GATE
To ALBERT QUAY

147

PERSHORE

Origin: Oxford, Worcester & Wolverhampton Railway
Became part of West Midland Railway in 1860
(Absorbed by G.W.R. in 1863)

Opened: 1 May 1852
Closed: 2 Nov. 1964 (G)
Plan date: 1912

Situated on a fast stretch of the main line from Paddington to Worcester, in the Vale of Evesham, Pershore still (just about) survives, mainly for the convenience of commuting passengers for both Evesham and Worcester.

As originally built, the station offices were contained in a small chalet type timber structure with the large overhanging eave the whole way round, which was the typical "standard" pattern adopted by the O.W. & W.R. in the mid-Victorian period. This gave way, in the latter part of the 19th century, to the equally 'standard' pattern of brick building with tall chimneys and full length (and width) platform canopy, which was such a familiar sight right down to the recent "bus shelter" era. The buildings were on the 'down' side and the station is about 1¼ miles from the small town of Pershore itself.

When the station was opened, the section of the main line from Norton Junction to Evesham was standard gauge single track, but was doubled throughout by the end of July.

The 1960's rationalisation programme disposed of all tracks and sidings, except the main line, and this was reduced from double to single line on 25 Oct. 1971, using the down platform.

In 1938, the signal box opening hours were from 6.0 a.m. Mondays to 6.0 a.m. the following Sunday morning, re-opening at 9.0 a.m. (Sunday) until 11.0 p.m. with two intermediate breaks. The box was provided with a switch.

FURTHER READING

R. Mag. 1907 (Vol. 21) pp. 128–133; 251–255   H.A.P.M.
"Great Western Echo" Summer 1972 p. 4 Pos.
"The Oxford, Worcester, & Wolverhampton Railway" by S. C. Jenkins & H. I. Quayle
Oakwood Press

Pershore. Looking towards Worcester. Main buildings on the left.   *Lens of Sutton*

Pershore. Looking towards Evesham through the station.   *O.P.C.*

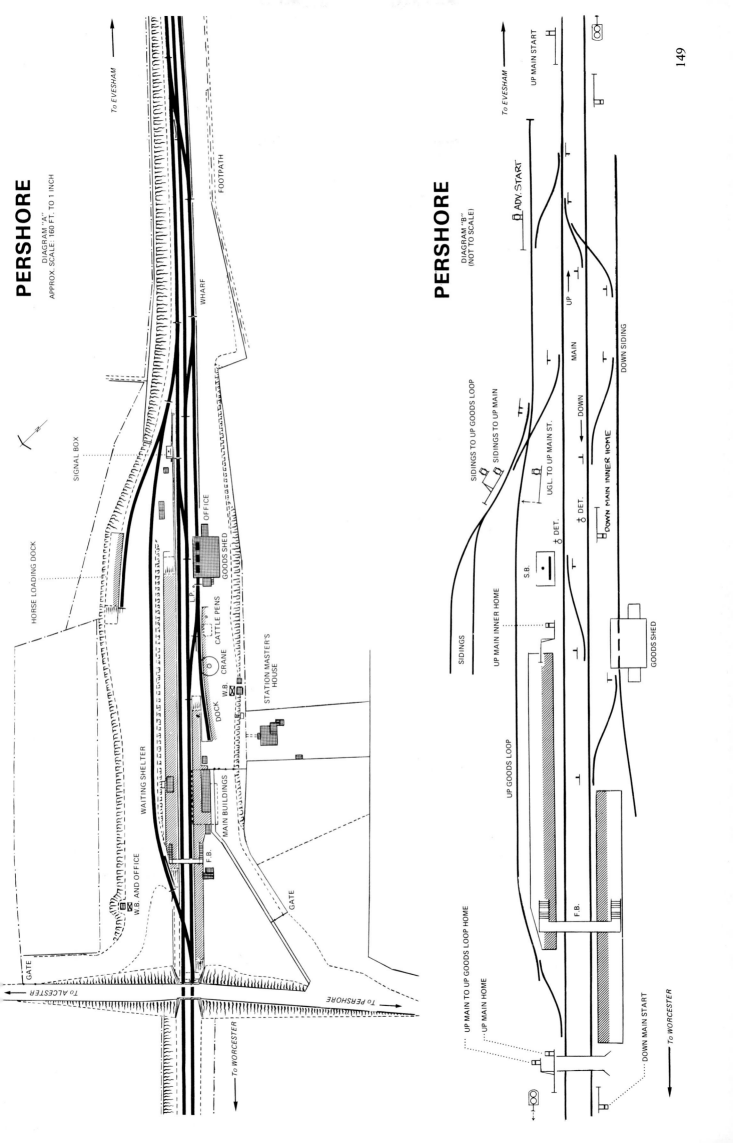

PERSHORE

DIAGRAM "A"
APPROX. SCALE: 160 FT. TO 1 INCH

To EVESHAM

HORSE LOADING DOCK

SIGNAL BOX

WHARF

FOOTPATH

OFFICE

GOODS SHED

L.P.

CATTLE PENS

CRANE

DOCK

W.B.

STATION MASTER'S HOUSE

WAITING SHELTER

W.B. AND OFFICE

F.B.

MAIN BUILDINGS

GATE

GATE

To ALCESTER

To PERSHORE

To WORCESTER

PERSHORE

DIAGRAM "B"
(NOT TO SCALE)

To EVESHAM

UP MAIN START

ADV. START

SIDINGS TO UP GOODS LOOP

SIDINGS TO UP MAIN

UGL. TO UP MAIN ST.

DET.

DET.

DET.

UP

MAIN

DOWN

DOWN SIDING

DOWN MAIN INNER HOME

SIDINGS

S.B.

UP MAIN INNER HOME

GOODS SHED

UP GOODS LOOP

F.B.

UP MAIN TO UP GOODS LOOP HOME

UP MAIN HOME

DOWN MAIN START

To WORCESTER

149

PONT LLANIO

Origin: Manchester & Milford Railway
(Leased by the G.W.R. in 1906 and absorbed by that Company in 1911)

Opened: 22 Feb. 1965 (P)

Closed: 16 Mar. 1964 (G) Except for P.S. traffic—since withdrawn

Plan date: c. 1908

There is always something 'romantic' about small isolated stations on remote railways in wild mountainous country, and Pont Llanio station can invoke a nostalgia consonant with the line upon which it was situated. No train was allowed to 'dash' through it, for there was a permanent speed restriction of 10 m.p.h. through the station in either direction, and the whole atmosphere of it was one of leisured tranquillity. For all that, the signal box was left open from 6.50 a.m. to the clearance of the last train (weekdays), and (1938) the box was closed on Sundays. As already stated elsewhere, the line was worked by Electric Train Token between Carmarthen Goods signal box and Aberystwyth. Although two passenger trains were not allowed to cross each other on the loops at the Tregaron end of Pont Llanio station, a passenger train and a goods train could do so provided the goods train was drawn to a stand in the up loop siding before the passenger train was allowed to pass on the 'main' line. The box was not provided with a switch.

Except for the later addition of the milk depot (on the terminal siding), the basic layout at the station, including the 'etceteras', remained unaltered from early times right down to closure, and even then the main line was kept open from Carmarthen for a time to serve the milk depot's private siding, but this itself has since been closed, of course.

View towards Aberystwyth. 15 June 1962. *M. Hale*

Pont Llanio.

FURTHER READING

T.I. 1959 pp. 39—42; 44—45 H.A.P.M.
"The Teifi Valley Railway" by Roger Padfield & Barrie Burgess
Laidlaw-Burgess, Haverfordwest

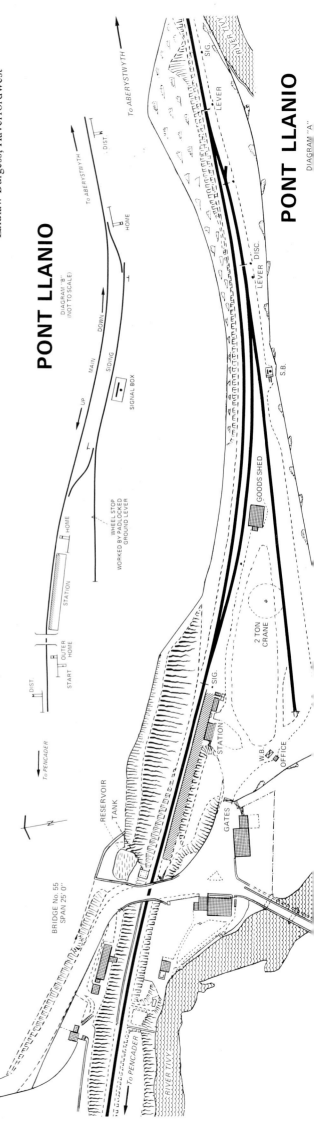

PONT LLANIO
DIAGRAM "B"
(NOT TO SCALE)

PONT LLANIO
DIAGRAM "A"

PRAZE

Origin: Helston Railway (worked by G.W.R.)
           (Absorbed by G.W.R. 1 July 1898)

Opened: 9 May 1887
Closed: 5 Nov. 1962   (P)
          5 Oct. 1964   (G)

Plan date: c. 1906

     The station consisted of a single platform of not very ample proportions—a small stone built structure containing the essential offices (including a ground frame) with a circular water tower at the northern end, and a goods siding/loop which protected the 'main' line with a catch point at each end thereof. The connection at the Helston end was discontinued and lifted a few years after the 2nd World War, thus reducing the "loop" to a plain siding. It was on a ruling gradient of 1 in 60, rising from Gwinear Road, and ordinary freight trains down the branch were (1938) allowed a point to point time of 8 minutes from the Junction, up trains being allowed 6 minutes for the run down the grade. In spite of its minor importance, the little station enjoyed the same passenger services as its bigger neighbour down the line (Nancegollan), and apart from the amendment to its layout referred to above, remained much as it ever was right down to final closure.

FURTHER READING   *O.P.C.*

R. Mag. 1963 opp. p. 76 Pos. (1904)
R.W.   1964 pp. 424–428   H.A.P.M.
"The Hayle, West Cornwall & Helston Railways" by G. H. Anthony. Oakwood Press
"The Railways of Cornwall, 1809–1963" by C. R. Clinker. David & Charles

Praze.   Looking towards Helston. 2-6-2T No. 4563 heading a passenger train from Helston to Gwinear Road.

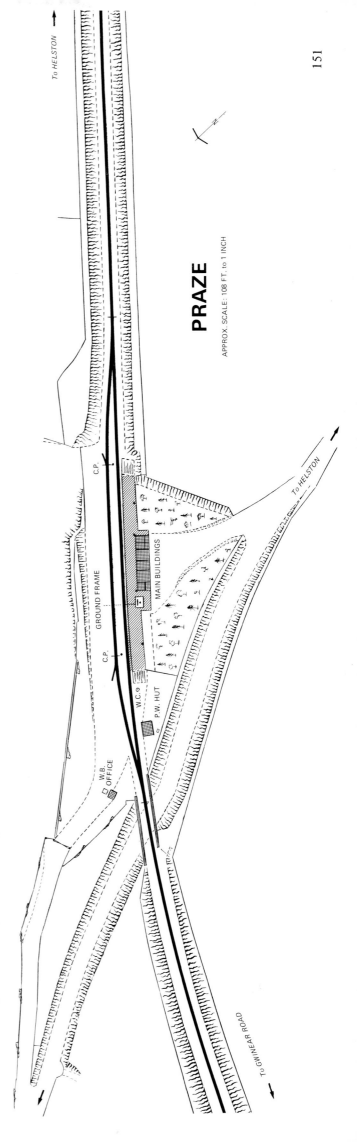

PRAZE

APPROX. SCALE: 108 FT. to 1 INCH

RHAYADER

Origin: Mid Wales Railway
Absorbed by the Cambrian Railways in 1904, thence by G.W.R. in 1922.

Opened: 21 Sept. 1864 (P)
1 Sept. 1864 (G)

Closed: 31 Dec. 1962 (P)
31 Dec. 1962 (G)—NRCD for coal until 5 Apr. 1965 (Final closure)

Plan date: c. 1914

Although no signalled diagram was available at the time this book was prepared, illustrated reference to this somewhat isolated station is well worthwhile.

Coming from Llanidloes, 14 miles to the north, and on the long descent through the mountains from the watershed of the line at Pantydwr (7 miles), the station could be likened to a railway-served oasis—welcome to the traveller but bleak. The station buildings, large water-tank base, and the goods shed were built with large stone blocks, and the platform facings on both sides were of smaller stonework. Another feature was the low level platforms, and, apart from the recess in the main buildings, they were otherwise devoid of canopy shelter.

The sidings in the yard were laid well apart, and an unusual feature for so small a depot was that there were no less than three opportunities for 'run round', the sidings having connections into the main line at both ends.

The whole layout was hardly disturbed from that illustrated down to closure.

A curious feature of the train service at Rhayader, revealed in the summer issue of the Cambrian Railways Public Timetable for 1905, is that there were 6 trains in the 'down' direction (towards Builth Wells), and only 4 in the 'up' direction, plus a workmen's train from Llanidloes non-stop between there and Rhayader on weekdays. There was one train each way on Sundays.

The signal box was (1938) open on weekdays from 4.30 a.m. until 7.30 p.m. (after clearance of the 8.30 p.m. ex Llanidloes on Saturdays, and was closed on Sundays. The box was not provided with a switch.

FURTHER READING

R. Mag. 1907 (Vol. 21) pp. 121–127   D.A.P. Pos.
R. Mag. 1938 (Vol. 83) pp. 203–208   H.D.A.P.M. & pp. 355–360   H.D.A.P. Pos.
R. Mag. 1963 pp. 82–88   H.A.P.M. Pos.   p. 283 Letter re Mid-Wales opening
"Forgotten Railways of North & Mid Wales" by R. Christiansen.   David & Charles
"The Cambrian Railways" by R. W. Kidner.   Oakwood Press
"The Cambrian Railways" by R. Christiansen & R. W. Miller.   David & Charles

RHAYADER

DIAGRAM "A"
APPROX. SCALE: 160 FT. TO 1 INCH

Rhayader. General view North towards Llanidloes. *O.P.C.*

Rhayader. A view from the South end of the main platform looking towards Builth Wells. *O.P.C.*

Rhayader. A view through the station towards Builth Wells. *Lens of Sutton*

Rhayader. Looking North. *O.P.C.*

153

ST. AUSTELL

Origin: Cornwall Railway
Leased from opening to the G.W.R., B. & E., & S.D.R.
Absorbed by the Great Western Railway in 1889

Opened: 4 May 1859 (P)
10 Oct. 1859 (G)

Closed:
Plan date: c. 1908

The name of St. Austell has always been coupled with "china clay," and the station was one of the busiest in this area for the handling of china clay trains.

The line from Par to St. Austell was doubled and brought into use on 15 Oct. 1893, and similarly thence to Burngullow on 26 Mar. 1899. The privately leased line from St. Austell to Pentewan was opened in 1829 for goods traffic only and closed on 4 Mar. 1918 having been worked by horse-traction until the mid 1870's, when the use of locomotives was authorised.

Diagram "B", which shows the main line layout before the 1960's rationalisation, reveals some interesting alterations since the survey in Diagram "A". In late 1931, the goods depot had been transferred from its original position on the south-west side of the passenger station to the north-east side of the main line some distance beyond the road overbridge leading to Polkyth, with a more elaborate layout. In Diagram "B" the lead into the new goods depot is shown off the goods loop to the right of the footbridge by the ground frame. In 1932, the road into the old goods shed was lifted. The siding immediately outside the old shed (Diagram "A") curving away the other side of the yard crane, became No. 2 siding (Diagram "B") and this lasted down to 14 Mar. 1965 when it, too, was lifted.

When the new depot came into use, the trailing crossover between the platforms at the western end was moved eastward slightly to trail into the up main beyond the road-bridge with another (facing) crossover giving direct access from the up main beyond the road-bridge with another (facing) crossover giving direct access from the up main to the goods loop.

Prior to 1925, the old trailing lead from the down main, across to the dock and cattle pen road, had been abolished (leaving the short siding butting on to the signal box) trailing into the up main. When it was decided to extend the up platform westward, this siding had to come out and was removed in March 1971.

The level crossing by the signal box was closed on 21 Sept. 1931 during the course of the goods depot alterations already referred to.

St. Austell signal box was (1938) open continuously on weekdays, and only closing for an hour in the morning and an hour in the evening on Sundays. It was provided with a switch.

FURTHER READING

R. Mag. 1911 (Vol. 29) pp. 181–188; 382–388   D.A.P.M. Pos. + grade profile.
R. Mag. 1960 p. 482 Pos. (with train)
R. Mag. 1970 p. 270 Pos.
"The Railways of Cornwall, 1809–1963" by C. R. Clinker.   David & Charles
"The Great Western at the Turn of the Century" by A. R. Kingdom.   O.P.C.
"The Story of Cornwall's Railways" by A. Fairclough.   Tor Mark Press, Truro
"Reg. History of the Railways of Great Britain." (Vol. 1) The West Country
by D. St. J. Thomas. Phoenix

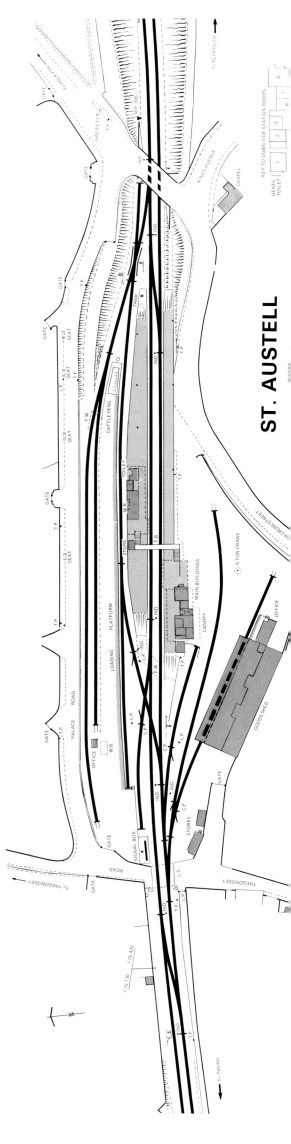

ST. AUSTELL

St. Austell. Towards Truro showing the whole station and the goods yard on right.

O.P.C.

St. Austell. Looking towards Truro from the down platform.

Lens of Sutton

St. Austell. An old picture looking West towards Truro. Probably at about the turn of the century.

Lens of Sutton Collection

St. Austell. View of the up-side platform and station buildings.

Lens of Sutton

ST. AUSTELL

DIAGRAM "B"
(NOT TO SCALE)

To PLYMOUTH

GOODS LOOP

SELECTED

UP MAIN TO GOODS LOOP START

UP MAIN START

DOWN MAIN INTERMEDIATE HOME

UP

DOWN MAIN

F.B

PASSENGER STATION

DOWN MAIN INNER HOME

SIDING

No. 1 SIDING

RELEASED BY KEY ON WOODEN TRAIN STAFF

S.B

DET

DET

No. 2 SIDING

UP MAIN HOME

To TRURO

– ELECTRIC CONTROL INSTRUMENT IN SIGNAL BOX RELEASES KEY RELEASE INSTRUMENT IN TRENANCE Jc. GROUND FRAME & LEVER No. 43.
– DETONATORS WORKED BY SMALL 2 LEVER FRAME

To PLYMOUTH

UP MAIN OUTER ADV. START

MAIN

UP

DOWN MAIN TO LOOP HOME

GOODS LOOP HOME

DOWN MAIN HOME

7

POINTS 7 & 10 WORKED BY MOTOR

SPRING POINTS

7

10

10

A

A

A

UP MAIN ADV. START

(CONTINUATION EASTWARDS)

GROUND FRAME
WORKING POINTS & DISC. "A"
INTERLOCKING LEVER FOR
GOODS LOOP No. 13.

G.F.

X

X

X

X

DOWN MAIN START

SPRING POINTS

TRENANCE Jc. GROUND FRAME
WORKING SIGNAL, DISC. AND
POINTS "X". KEY RELEASE INSTRUMENT.

To TRURO

(CONTINUATION WESTWARDS)

ST. AUSTELL

DIAGRAM "C"
(NOT TO SCALE)

To PAR

UP START

7

5

DOWN HOME

3

4

CATCH SIDING

WEIGHTED POINTS

13

SIDING

UP

MAIN

DOWN

2

3

1

S.B.

2

12

13

11

12

11

GOODS SHED

6

DOWN START

LEVEL CROSSING

10

UP HOME

9

8

To TRURO

POINTS & SIGNALS FULLY NUMBERED

ST. IVES

Origin: West Cornwall Railway
Absorbed by the Great Western Railway on 1 Aug. 1878
Opened: 1 June 1877
Closed: 9 Sept. 1963 (G)
Plan date: c. 1912

St. Ives. Main buildings looking towards terminus.

Lens of Sutton

St. Ives. A general view from 'dead end'. 27 Sept. 1956.

H.C. Casserley

To the railway enthusiast, the natural appeal of St. Ives station probably has its foundations in its snug compactness nestling into the hillside, on a graceful curve. For the modeller, it is an ideal prototype to follow, for it lends itself to being accommodated in the corner of a room—and there is (or rather, WAS) not too much of it to model.

The steeply graded 4m. 18c. branch from St. Erth ("St. Ives Road" until opening of the branch) on the main line, was the last broad gauge branch to be built. The gauge was mixed from St. Erth to Lelant Quay in Oct. 1888, and the whole branch was converted to standard gauge on 20—23 May 1892. The engine shed road and connection became redundant on 8 Sept. 1963 (although the engine shed itself had been closed since Sept. 1961), and lifted 7 weeks later. The station 'run-round' loop had a similar fate towards the end of Oct. 1963, but was not lifted until Jan. 1966, the goods shed and dock roads being lifted at the same time.

However, the big crunch came on 23 May 1971 when use of the main station was discontinued, and a new platform was brought into use adjacent to and on the south side of the former goods shed.

Down to post 2nd War times, St. Ives had dealt with considerable passenger traffic, particularly in the summer periods, and even on Sundays, before the War, the branch enjoyed a service of 8 trains each way.

In the summer period of 1938, the signal box was open from 6.45 a.m. until 11.15 p.m. (or as soon as the last train had cleared) on weekdays, and on Sundays from 9.30 a.m. until 10.55 p.m. with breaks between 2.45 and 4.40 p.m., and between 6.0 p.m. and 7.20 p.m. The box was not provided with a switch.

The branch was worked by Electric Train Staff with no intermediate crossing place. The maximum speed restriction was 30 m.p.h.

FURTHER READING

R. Mag. 1924 (Vol. 55) pp. 337—339 H.A.P. Pos.
M.R.N. 1947 p. 94 Short desc. of branch. St. Ives layout and Pos. (2)
T.I. 1952 pp. 203—207 D.A.P. Pos.
T.I. 1954 p. 5 Pos. (part)
R. Mag. 1955 pp. 70—71 Historical para. on branch
M.R.N. 1965 pp. 108—111 D.A.P. Pos. (S.B. & gds. shed), layout
R. Mod. 1970 p. 355 S.B. Diagram

"Great Western Engine Sheds, 1947" by E. Lyons. Oxford Publishing Company
"Great Western Branch Lines, 1955—1965" by C. J. Gammell.   O.P.C.
"The Railways of Cornwall, 1809—1963" by C. R. Clinker.   David & Charles
"Reg. History of the Railways of Great Britain." (Vol. 1) The West Country
by D. St. J. Thomas. Phoenix

"The Story of Cornwall's Railways" by A. Fairclough.   Tor Mark Press, Truro

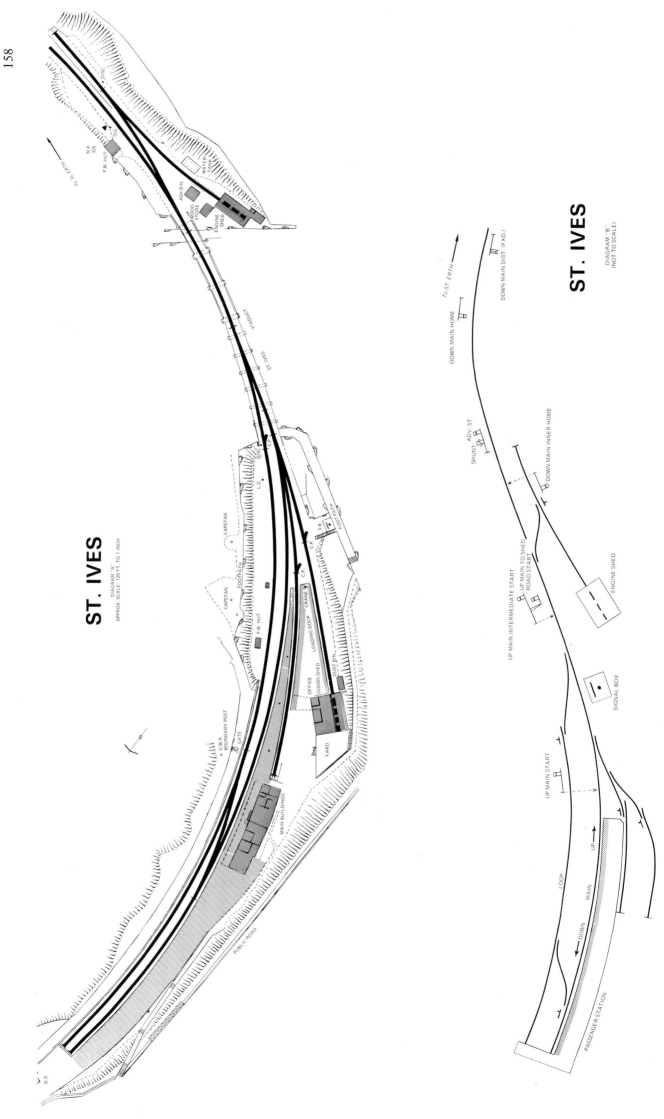

ST. IVES

DIAGRAM "A"
APPROX. SCALE: 120 FT. TO 1 INCH

ST. IVES

DIAGRAM "B"
(NOT TO SCALE)

Saltash. Looking 'down'. *O.P.C.*

Saltash. Looking towards Plymouth. May 1956. *R.H. Clark*

SALTASH

Origin: Cornwall Railway
Leased from opening to G.W.R., B. & E., and S.D.R.
(Absorbed by G.W.R. on 1 July 1889)

Opened: 4 May 1859
Closed: 9 Sept. 1963 (G)
Plan date: 5 Aug. 1910 (Signalled diagram—c. 1950)

With the exception of the catch point arrangement at the goods yard exit to the main line, the track layout at the station remained unaltered from Diagram "A" to Diagram "B" and beyond, down to post-Beeching rationalisation.

The station was rebuilt in 1880 and extended after the approach to the Royal Albert Bridge had been altered in 1908.

Beyond the western limit of Diagram "A", there was a 'down' refuge siding which was extended to rejoin the 'down' main line near Wearde signal box (33c. west of Saltash S.B.) making a 'Goods running loop' (Diagram "B").

Space considerations mainly precluded the expansion of the little goods yard, and facilities were therefore confined to the bare essentials, viz.—a dock road, a goods shed of modest proportions, and a short 'loop' siding.

The western connection into the down main line from No. 1 siding, the nearby cross-over, and the goods yard sidings (Nos. 2 and 3), were all discontinued from October 1972, and the signal box on the platform was closed and replaced by a ground frame (near the former yard siding connection to the 'up' main) on 2 July 1973.

Saltash signal box was (Summer 1938) open continuously, and there was no switch provided.

FURTHER READING

R. Mag. 1902 (Vol. II) pp. 441–447; 536–541   H.A.P. + Grade profile
"Victorian & Edwardian Railways" by J. G. Spence (Photo 35) Batsford
"The Story of Cornwall's Railways" by A. Fairclough.   Tor Mark Press, Truro
"The Railways of Cornwall" by C. R. Clinker.   David & Charles
"Reg. Hist. of the Railways of Great Britain" Vol. 1. (The West Country)
by D. St. J. Thomas. Phoenix

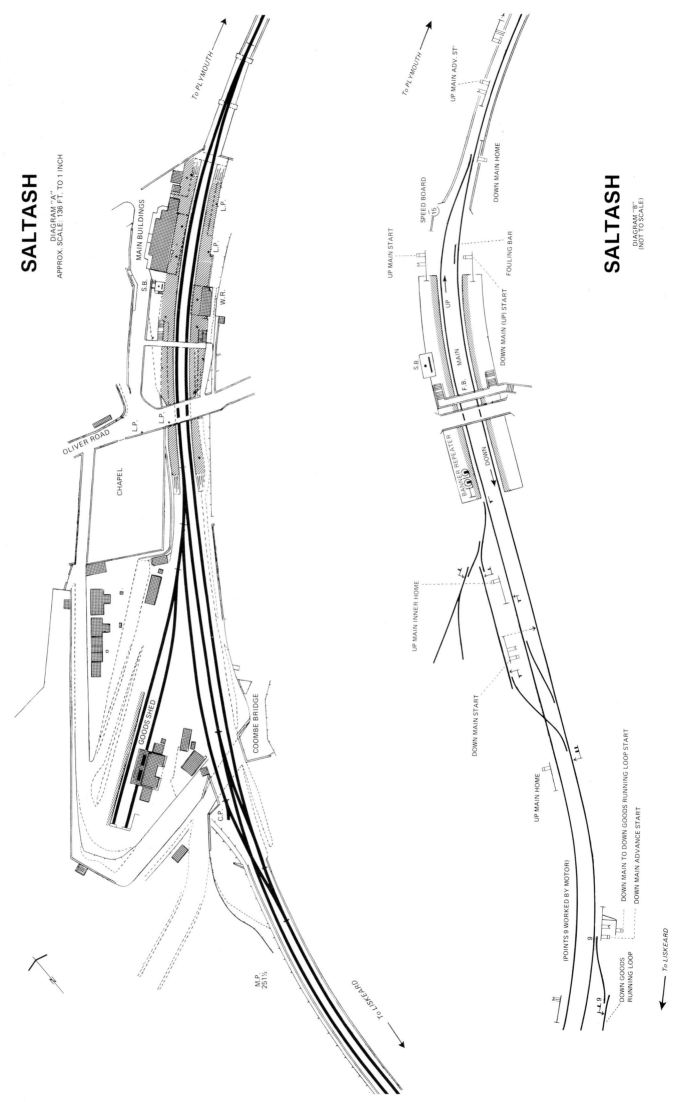

SALTASH

DIAGRAM "A"
APPROX. SCALE: 136 FT. TO 1 INCH

To PLYMOUTH

MAIN BUILDINGS

S.B.

L.P.

L.P.

W.R.

L.P.

OLIVER ROAD

L.P.

L.P.

CHAPEL

GOODS SHED

COOMBE BRIDGE

C.P.

M.P. 251½

To LISKEARD

SALTASH

DIAGRAM "B"
(NOT TO SCALE)

To PLYMOUTH

UP MAIN ADV. ST'

DOWN MAIN HOME

SPEED BOARD

15

UP MAIN START

S.B.

UP

MAIN

F.B.

DOWN MAIN (UP) START

FOULING BAR

BANNER REPEATER

DOWN

UP MAIN INNER HOME

DOWN MAIN START

UP MAIN HOME

(POINTS 9 WORKED BY MOTOR)

DOWN MAIN TO DOWN GOODS RUNNING LOOP START

DOWN MAIN ADVANCE START

9

DOWN GOODS
RUNNING LOOP

9

To LISKEARD

SANDFORD & BANWELL

Origin: B. & E.
          (Absorbed by G.W.R. in 1876)
Opened: 3 Aug. 1869 (Opened as "Sandford")
Closed: 9 Sept. 1963 (P)
          10 June 1963 (G) (Except for P.S. traffic, since withdrawn)
Plan date: Diagram "A" c. 1912

The station was 4½ miles from Yatton on the Cheddar Valley line of the G.W.R., the branch being built by the Bristol & Exeter as broad gauge, and opened as far as Cheddar on 3 Aug. 1869.

The whole branch between Yatton and Wells was converted to standard gauge on 15/18 Nov. 1875.

The buildings at "Sandford" were similar in material construction to those at Cheddar (see Vol. 1) and other stations on the line, with a large through road goods shed, which was about twice the size of the main station buildings.

The original signal box on the platform was closed, and a new box opened (in the position shown on the diagram) on 12 Dec. 1905 and at the same time the crossing loop was opened for traffic.

Except for the addition of private sidings (in later years) the basic track layout did not alter down to July 1964, when the loop and back siding became redundant.

In 1938, the box was open on weekdays for the first train, and closed after the last train had cleared. In the working timetable for summer 1938, the box opening period on Sundays was somewhat loosely described as being "During train service". There was no switch provided.

Sandford & Banwell.   A train arriving from Wells. Note the station master's house in the background on the extreme left. 28 Aug. 1958.   *M. Hale*

Sandford & Banwell.   Looking towards Wells.   *Lens of Sutton*

FURTHER READING

R. Mag.   1950 pp. 224–227; 234   H.A.P.M.
R. World   1958 pp. 308–310   H.A.P.M. Pos.
T.I.   1961 pp. 276–281   H.A.P.M.

161

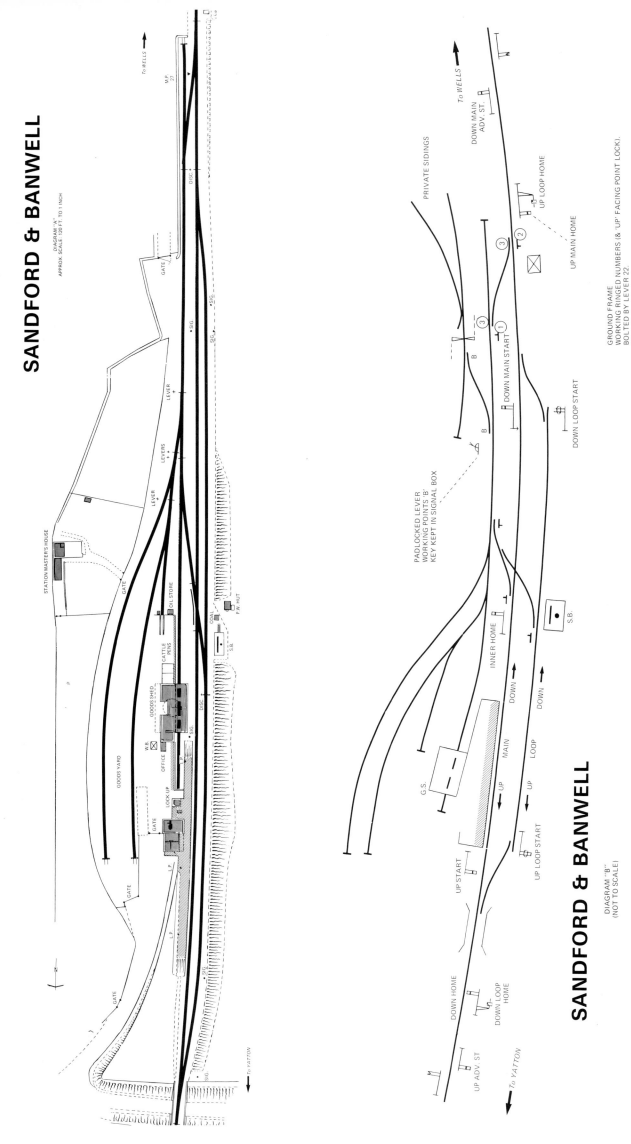

SANDFORD & BANWELL

DIAGRAM "A"
APPROX. SCALE: 120 FT. TO 1 INCH

To WELLS

M.P.
27

DISC.

SIG.

SIG.

SIG.

GATE

LEVER

LEVER

LEVERS

LEVER

GATE

STATION MASTER'S HOUSE

OIL STORE

CATTLE
PENS

GOODS SHED

COAL

P.W. HUT

S.B.

W.B.

DISC.

SIG.

OFFICE

LOCK UP

GATE

GOODS YARD

GATE

L.P.

L.P.

L.P.

SIG.

SIG.

DISC.

To YATTON

N

SANDFORD & BANWELL

DIAGRAM "B"
(NOT TO SCALE)

To WELLS

PRIVATE SIDINGS

DOWN MAIN
ADV. ST.

UP LOOP HOME

3

2

UP MAIN HOME

3

B

1

DOWN MAIN START

B

DOWN LOOP START

PADLOCKED LEVER
WORKING POINTS 'B'
KEY KEPT IN SIGNAL BOX

GROUND FRAME
WORKING RINGED NUMBERS (& 'UP' FACING POINT LOCK).
BOLTED BY LEVER 22.

INNER HOME

DOWN

DOWN

S.B.

G.S.

UP
MAIN

UP
LOOP

UP START

UP LOOP START

DOWN HOME

DOWN LOOP
HOME

UP ADV. ST

To YATTON

SAUNDERTON

Origin: G.W. & G.C. joint
Opened: c. 1899
Closed: 1 Mar. 1965 (G)
Plan date: c. 1910

The scaled plan of Saunderton does not reach to the limit of the layout at the "country" end, but the arrangement of connections and crossover was similar to that shown in Diagram "B". The signal box was well away from the station for the convenience of being near to the points under its control, thereby reducing lengthy point-rodding.

Being within the London commuter belt, the platforms were longer than would have otherwise been the case, but it was not considered necessary to make it a 4-road station as in the case of Gerrards Cross, and Princes Risborough.

As will be seen, the layout did not alter at all from opening to the 1960's rationalisation, which started with the lifting of the long crossover from the 'down' siding to the 'up' main. The siding itself was taken out of use from 21 Nov. 1965, together with the connection to the main line and cattle dock, and the trailing crossover between the 'up' and 'down' main line became redundant from 5 Feb. 1967. The signal box itself was closed on 16 Nov. 1975.

In the summer period of 1938, the signal box was open continuously from 5.30 a.m. Mondays until 6.0 a.m. the following Sunday morning, re-opening from 8.0 p.m. to 10.0 p.m. Sunday evening. The box was provided with a switch.

FURTHER READING

R. Mag. 1933 (2) pp. 157–164 H.A.P.M. and 321–326

Saunderton.   Looking towards Princes Risborough.

Lens of Sutton

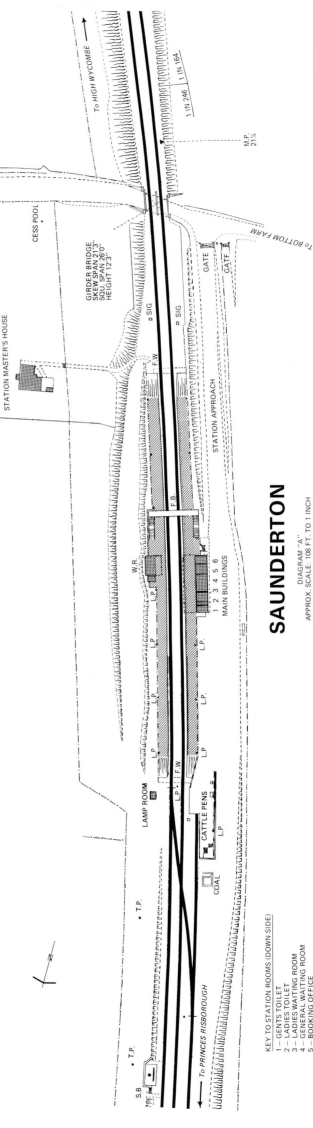

SAUNDERTON

DIAGRAM "A"
APPROX. SCALE: 108 FT. TO 1 INCH

KEY TO STATION ROOMS (DOWN SIDE)

1 – GENTS TOILET
2 – LADIES TOILET
3 – LADIES WAITING ROOM
4 – GENERAL WAITING ROOM
5 – BOOKING OFFICE
6 – PARCELS OFFICE

SHRIVENHAM

Origin: Great Western Railway
Opened: 17 Dec. 1840
Closed: 7 Dec. 1964 (P)
            4 Oct. 1965 (G)
Plan date: c. 1935 (Signalled diagram c. 1959)

The broad gauge main line of the G.W.R. was extended from Steventon to Faringdon Road (later "Challow"), and opened on 20 July 1840, and thence to Hay Lane (2½ miles west of Swindon) on 17 Dec. 1840.

In Feb. 1872, the line was converted to mixed gauge, and was finally converted to standard gauge on 20—23 May 1892. The line was quadrupled through Shrivenham station in May 1933.

In late Victorian times, there were two short dock sidings on the north side with a wagon turntable connection to the goods shed and crossover

connection to the up platform line. These had gone by the end of the 1st. War, but the date is not known. There were some sidings put in for the use of ambulance trains, at the back of the eastern end of the up platform, and trailing into the up line. These were brought into use on 30 Apr. 1944, and lasted until 11 Dec. 1949 when they were lifted.

A new signal box was opened on 18 Sept. 1932, and this was closed on 5 June 1966. The old signal box was off the western end of the 'down' platform, between the 'down' siding and the platform line.

The 1960's rationalisation programme took heavy toll of the layout with alterations too numerous to list here until, today, nothing remains except the 'up' and 'down' main lines.

In 1938, the signal box was open from 6.0 a.m. Mondays until 7.0 a.m. the following Sunday morning, re-opening at 1.0 p.m. until 11.40 p.m. with an afternoon break between 3.20 p.m. and 5.40 p.m. The box was provided with a switch.

Shrivenham.   Looking towards Swindon.   *O.P.C.*

Shrivenham.   Close-up of the main buildings, platform side.   *O.P.C.*

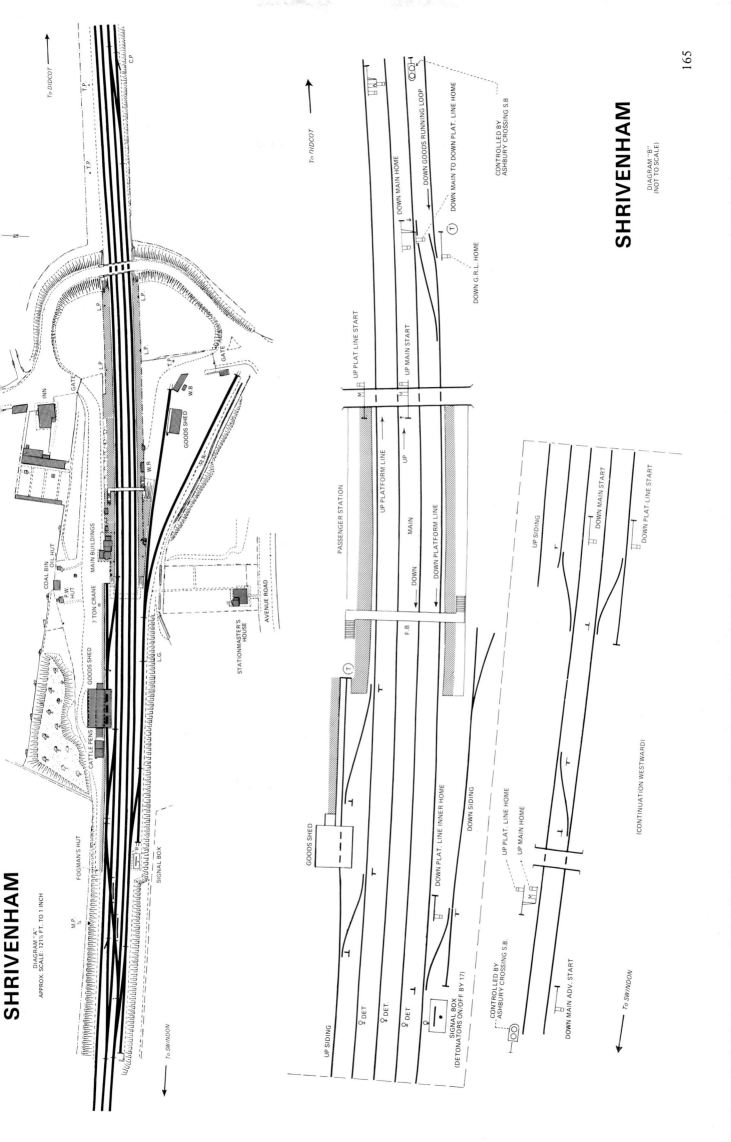

SHRIVENHAM

DIAGRAM "A"
APPROX. SCALE: 121½ FT. TO 1 INCH

SHRIVENHAM

DIAGRAM "B"
(NOT TO SCALE)

165

Silverton. Looking towards Taunton. View of the up platform, station buildings and signal box. 8 July 1959. *H.C. Casserley*

Silverton. Looking towards Exeter. *Lens of Sutton*

Silverton. Looking towards Exeter. *O.P.C.*

SILVERTON

Origin: G.W.R. (Bristol & Exeter)
Opened: c. 1876 (First appeared in 1877 Handbook of Stations)
Closed: 5 Oct. 1964 (P)
3 May 1965 (G)—Except for private siding traffic, since gone.
Plan date: Diagram "A" c. 1917   Diagram "B" 1928

This small 'staggered platform' country station built on the broad gauge main line between Taunton and Exeter, underwent some alterations during its life. In the latter part of the broad-gauge era it had only a trailing crossover at a point where the two platforms came nearest to each other, and a trailing 'down' siding. It is interesting to note also, that from the outset, the station had a 4-ton fixed crane in spite of the fact that it was rated solely as a "passenger" station. By the end of the 1st. War, the layout had acquired an 'up' refuge siding, a 'down' loop siding, against which was a small goods shed (with the 4-ton crane!), and a private siding which led to a mill.

By 1928, the station had lost its crossover between the platforms in favour of one further up the line with a single slip to provide connection to the shed road and private siding. The shunting neck was extended to form a 'down' siding on 21 Nov. 1928. On this date also, a new signal box was opened (Diagram "B") to replace the old one which had been on the 'up' platform.

The 1960's rationalisation programme brought about the closure of the whole station, ultimating in that of the mill siding. The 'up' refuge siding was first removed on 1 Sept. 1964 together with the removal of the 'down' trailing connection into the 'down' main line opposite the 'up' platform. The remainder of the sidings and connections became redundant from 4 Dec. 1967. The crossover and single-slip connection were lifted in April 1968.

The signal box opening hours in the summer of 1938 were:—

Mondays to Fridays: 7.30 a.m. until 9.0 p.m.
Saturdays: 7.30 a.m. until 10.0 p.m.
Sundays: Closed.

FURTHER READING

"The G.W.R. in the 19th. Century" by O. S. Nock.   Ian Allan Ltd.

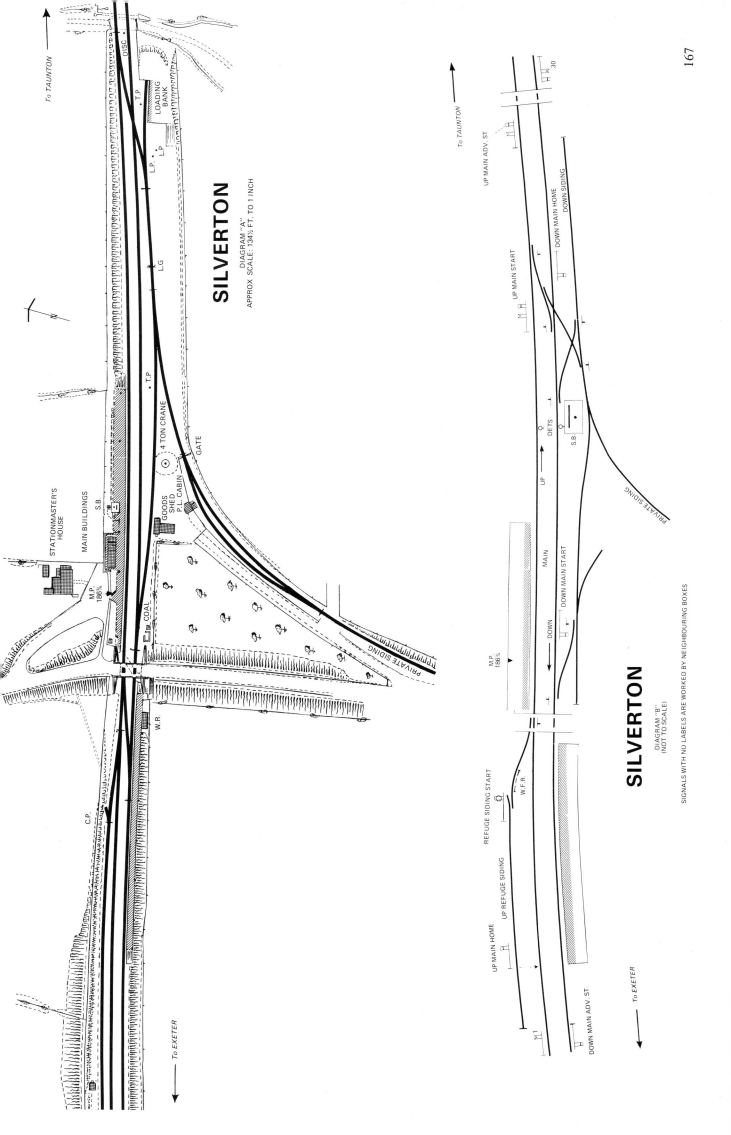

SILVERTON

DIAGRAM "A"
APPROX. SCALE: 134½ FT. TO 1 INCH

To TAUNTON

LOADING BANK

T.P.

L.P.

L.P.

L.G

T.P

4 TON CRANE

GATE

GOODS SHED

P.L. CABIN

PRIVATE SIDING

STATIONMASTER'S HOUSE

MAIN BUILDINGS

S.B.

M.P. 186¾

COAL

W.R.

C.P.

To EXETER

DISC

SILVERTON

DIAGRAM "B"
(NOT TO SCALE)

SIGNALS WITH NO LABELS ARE WORKED BY NEIGHBOURING BOXES

To TAUNTON

30

UP MAIN ADV. ST

DOWN MAIN HOME

DOWN SIDING

UP MAIN START

UP

DETS

S.B.

PRIVATE SIDING

MAIN

DOWN

DOWN MAIN START

M.P. 186¾

REFUGE SIDING START

W.F.B.

UP MAIN HOME

UP REFUGE SIDING

DOWN MAIN ADV. ST.

To EXETER

167

SPARKFORD

Origin: Great Western Railway
(by absorption of the Wilts., Somerset & Weymouth on 14 Mar. 1850,
confirmed by Parliament in 1851)

Opened: 1 Sept. 1856

Closed: 3 Oct. 1966 (P)
7 Jan. 1963 (G)

Plan dates: Diagram "A" May 1911   Diagram "B" c. 1950

Sparkford was on the broad gauge line of the Frome–Yeovil section, which was
opened on 1 Sept. 1856, the station being opened with the line.

Referring to Diagram "B", Raymond's siding was opened on 16 Feb. 1929, the milk
sidings on the up side beyond the road overbridge in 1932, and the War Department
sidings and north ground frame were added in May 1944, together with the northern
crossover on the main line. By 1963, the War Dept. sidings had gone, and in December of
that year, the following tracks became redundant, viz. the north crossover, the goods shed
road, dock road and shunting neck, and the milk sidings. No. 2 (down) siding was disused
from 27 July 1964, and the signal box was closed on 30 Nov. 1966, together with the
crossover in front of it. Ultimately, on the 12 May 1968, the main line was singled.

The signal box opening hours in the summer period of 1938 were:–
Mondays, 6.45 a.m. (Tues.–Fri. 7.0 a.m.) until 11.0 p.m. On Sundays, the box was open
from 11.0 a.m. to 6.30 p.m. with an interval between 1.30 p.m. and 3.0 p.m. The box
was provided with a switch.

FURTHER READING

"Reg. Hist. of the Railways of Great Britain" Vol. 1. (The West Country)
by D. St. J. Thomas. Phoenix

Sparkford.   A general view through the station towards Castle Cary.   *M. Hale*

SPARKFORD

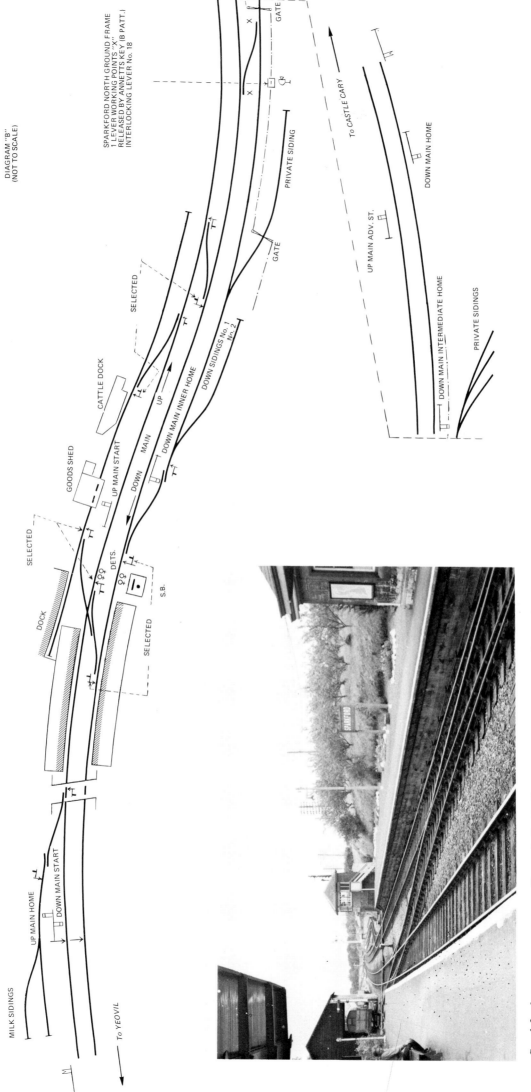

SPARKFORD

DIAGRAM "B"
(NOT TO SCALE)

SPARKFORD NORTH GROUND FRAME
1 LEVER WORKING POINTS "X"
RELEASED BY ANNETTS KEY (B PATT.)
INTERLOCKING LEVER No. 18

GATE

X

X

PRIVATE SIDING

GATE

To CASTLE CARY

DOWN MAIN HOME

UP MAIN ADV. ST.

SELECTED

DOWN SIDINGS No. 1
No. 2

DOWN MAIN INTERMEDIATE HOME

PRIVATE SIDINGS

CATTLE DOCK

UP

DOWN MAIN INNER HOME

GOODS SHED

UP MAIN START

DOWN   MAIN

SELECTED

DOCK

DETS.

S.B.

SELECTED

UP MAIN HOME

DOWN MAIN START

MILK SIDINGS

To YEOVIL

Lens of Sutton

Sparkford.   Towards Castle Cary.

169

STEVENTON

Origin: Great Western Railway
Opened: 1 June 1840
Closed: 7 Dec. 1964 (P)
             29 Mar. 1965 (G)
Plan date: c. 1935

The Great Western's broad gauge was extended from Reading to Steventon on 1 June 1840, and thence to "Faringdon Road" (later Challow) about 7 weeks later, on 20 July 1840. The line became mixed gauge between Didcot and Swindon in February 1872, and was converted to standard gauge only, when Brunel's broad gauge was finally abolished on the weekend 20–23 May 1892.

Thus, Steventon survived for 124½ years as a passenger station, but in the meantime underwent some track alterations and additions which may be worthy of note.

The up and down goods running loops (the point for which may be seen on the extreme right of Diagram "A") were opened on 16 Sept. 1907 and 20 Feb. 1916 respectively.

The station signal box (but not necessarily the same structure) changed status no less than four times, thus—from "Stocks Lane" S.B. to ground frame during the last World War, then to "Steventon" signal box on 1 April 1928, then reverting to "Stocks Lane Ground Frame" on 17 May 1965, and finally becoming redundant in January 1974.

The up siding (leading into the goods shed road) was taken out in May 1963, and all remaining sidings became redundant on 17 May 1965.

Steventon signal box was (1938) not provided with a switch.

It is worth recording here that for a brief period of about 6 months, Steventon became the centre of administration for the Company, the offices being contained in a large house near the station. This was in 1842, but in the early part of 1843, Authority moved to London.

FURTHER READING

"Reg. Hist. of the Railways of Great Britain" Vol. 1. (The West Country) by D. St. J. Thomas. Phoenix

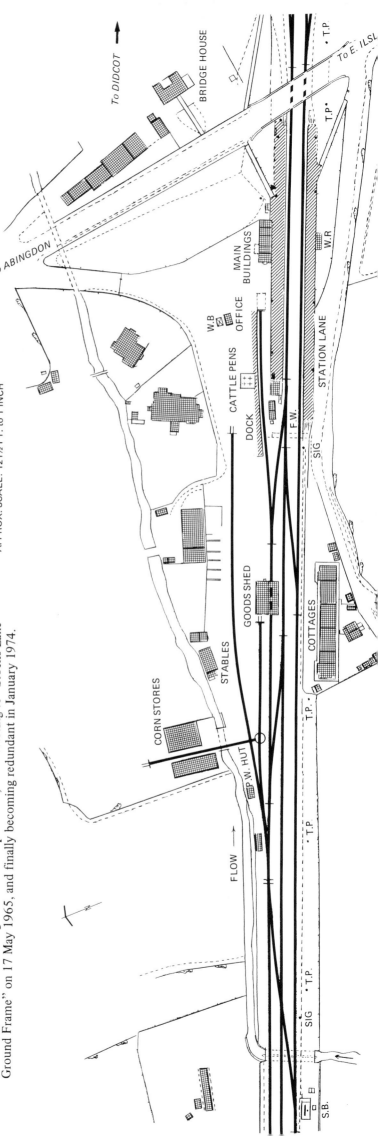

STEVENTON

DIAGRAM "A"
APPROX. SCALE: 121½ FT. to 1 INCH

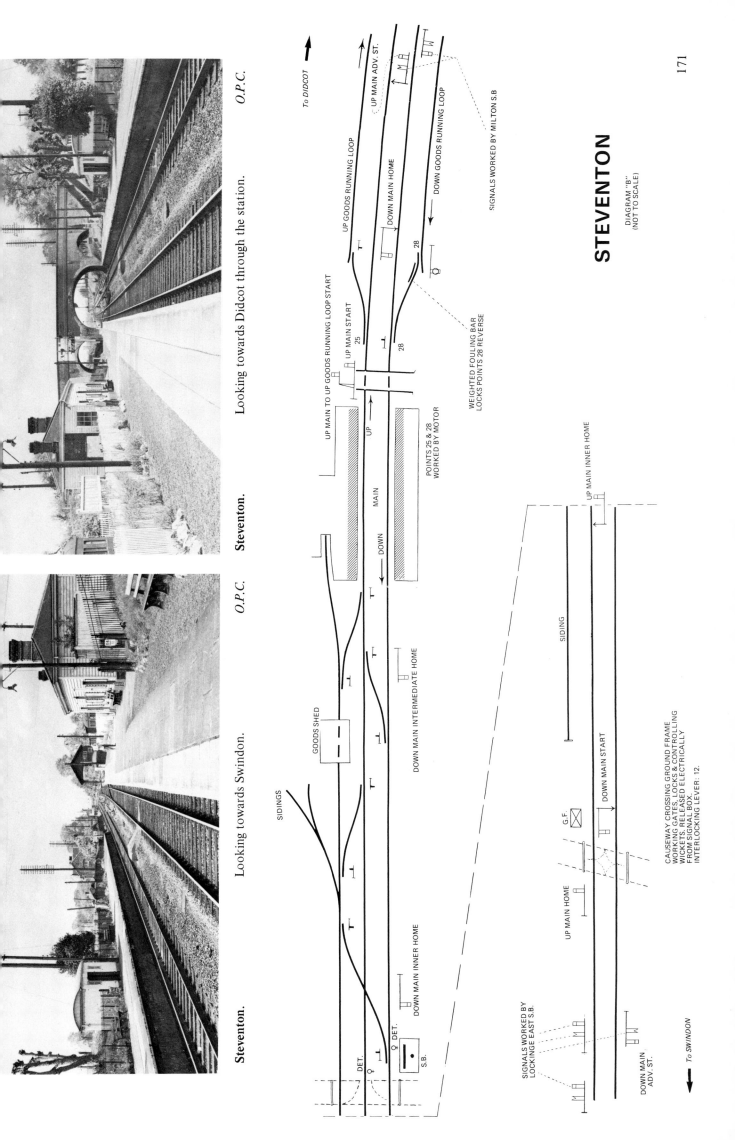

Steventon.   O.P.C.   Looking towards Didcot through the station.   O.P.C.   Steventon.

Looking towards Swindon.

SIDINGS

GOODS SHED

UP MAIN TO UP GOODS RUNNING LOOP START

UP GOODS RUNNING LOOP

UP MAIN ADV. ST.

DOWN MAIN HOME

DOWN GOODS RUNNING LOOP

SIGNALS WORKED BY MILTON S.B

UP MAIN START
25

28

28

WEIGHTED FOULING BAR
LOCKS POINTS 28 REVERSE

POINTS 25 & 28
WORKED BY MOTOR

UP

MAIN

DOWN

DOWN MAIN INTERMEDIATE HOME

UP MAIN INNER HOME

SIDING

DOWN MAIN INNER HOME

DET.

DET.

S.B.

CAUSEWAY CROSSING GROUND FRAME
WORKING GATES, LOCKS & CONTROLLING
WICKETS. RELEASED ELECTRICALLY
FROM SIGNAL BOX.
INTERLOCKING LEVER: 12.

G.F.

DOWN MAIN START

UP MAIN HOME

SIGNALS WORKED BY
LOCKINGE EAST S.B.

DOWN MAIN
ADV. ST.

To SWINDON

To DIDCOT

STEVENTON

DIAGRAM "B"
(NOT TO SCALE)

171

TAUNTON

Origin: Bristol & Exeter Railway
           Amalgamated with the G.W.R. 1 Aug. 1876
Opened: 1 July 1842
Closed:
Plan date: c. 1908

The first station at Taunton was built to Brunel's "one-sided" design which was also used at Exeter, Reading, and Slough. This consisted virtually of two separate stations on the same side of the main line, the one on the London side being used for the 'up' trains. Between the platform ends, the 'up' and 'down' lines crossed each other to gain access to their respective platforms, re-crossing again to assume their correct positions, at the London end.

The whole passenger station was on the 'town' side of the line, thus obviating the necessity for passengers to cross the tracks, but operationally inconvenient. Opposite the 'down' station was the carriage shed, and opposite the 'up' station stood the goods shed.

The Bristol & Exeter Co. eventually replaced this station and layout, with a much larger 'single' station of more orthodox design, with an overall roof in August 1868.

In 1895, the G.W.R. considerably extended the platforms, and added the bay platforms on each side at both ends. The goods avoiding line to the south of the station was opened on 1 Nov. 1896.

Although improvements and extensions on the layout continued from time to time during the next 34 years, the real re-building programme did not start until September 1930, and by 11 Oct. 1931 the new West Junction and goods lines had been re-aligned. On the 13 Dec. 1931 the track from Creech Junction to Taunton East Junction was quadrupled, and by mid-January 1932 the overall roof had been removed. On the 7 Feb. 1932 the two pairs of through platform lines were open between the East and West junctions, and the line thence to Norton Fitzwarren was quadrupled and opened on 4 Feb. 1932.

Opening and Closing dates of the signal boxes are as follows:—

Signal Box title	Opened	Closed
West Junction (new)	17 Jan. 1932	
West Jc. (converted to G.F.)	6 Dec. 1970	21 Feb. 1971
East Junction (new)	13 Dec. 1931	
West Loop (new)	18 Oct. 1931	12 Sept. 1965
(with the opening of the west yard)		(West yard closed June 1965)
East Loop (new)	30 Aug. 1931	24 July 1963
West Station (new)	20 Dec. 1931	
East Station		10 Apr. 1932

A new goods shed was brought into use on 20 Feb. 1932.

In the 1896 rebuilding, a new engine shed was provided, from which steam locomotives were withdrawn in Oct. 1964.

During the early 1930's, there was considerable addition to, and extension of the sidings, and modifications of connections and crossovers, and even as late as Sept. 1944

sidings had been added in the West yard. By the end of the late War, the layout had reached its maximum, but by the end of 1956 track started to disappear. Yet even in the course of the 1960's rationalisation programme, the coal concentration scheme was adopted and opened (near the East Junction signal box) on 1 June 1964. However, between 1962 and 1968, whole clusters of sidings disappeared reducing Taunton's layout (excluding the passenger station) to a mere skeleton of its former shape.

Below are a few notes relating to the scaled Diagram ("A")—

The 'dots' on the platforms, other than those beneath the overall roof are identified thus:— Large dots are verandah-roof supports, the small dots (between every other support) are lamp posts. In all other cases, lamp posts are indicated by "L.P.".

Owing to the considerable amount of detail incorporated in so confined an area, the usual platform shading has been omitted, for the sake of clarity. For similar reasons, the 'broken line' indication of track which is totally under cover has not been followed within the loco shed. The "W.C's" (Water Cranes), two on the 'up' main platform one on the 'down', and one off the end of the 'stops' at the western end of the middle road, are indicated by the ringed dots, not by those immediately adjacent to them.

The 'ticks' shown against some points indicate that these points are hand-lever operated on site. The four cranes shown inside the goods shed are each of 2-ton capacity.

In the summer period of 1938, the opening hours of the 5 signal boxes were as follows:—

Signal Box	Opened	Closed	Switch	Remarks
East Junction	Continuously		No.	
West Station	Continuously		No.	
West Junction	4.0 a.m. (Mons.)	4.0 a.m. (Mons.)	Yes.	Or on completion of yard shunting.
East Loop	3.15 a.m. (Mons.)	10.0 a.m. (Suns.)	Yes.	Or on completion of yard shunting.
West Loop	5.0 a.m. (Mons.)	6.0 a.m. (Suns.)	Yes.	

The signalled diagrams B, C, D, E, and F relate to the layout after final rebuilding, and are complementary to each other. Diagram "G" (Taunton East Station signal box) relates to the eastern-side station layout before rebuilding, and it is regretted that complementary diagrams thereto are not, at present (1978) available.

FURTHER READING

R. Mag.   1934 (Vol. 75) pp. 263–270   H.A.P.M. (Taunton–Minehead)
T.I.   1951 pp. 272–274   H.D.A.P.
R. Mag.   1954 pp. 118–126   H.A.P.M. (Taunton–Chard)
T.I.   1957 pp. 543–549   D.A.P. + Layout plan. Pos.
R. Mag.   1957 pp. 371–376   H.A.P.M. (Taunton–Barnstaple)
R.W.   1963 pp. 176–179, 196   H.A.P. (Taunton–Chard)
"Great Western Engine Sheds, 1947" by E. Lyons. Oxford Publishing Company
"Great Western Broad Gauge Album" by A. K. Steele. Oxford Publishing Company
     (p. 68—'Last broad gauge train at Taunton, 20 May 1892')
"Reg. History of the Railways of Great Britain" Vol. 1 (The West Country)

Taunton. Old station looking East.

Taunton. After reconstruction.

Taunton. During final reconstruction.

Taunton. After reconstruction.

TAUNTON

To TAUNTON STATION

M.P. 163½

WEST S.B.

SIG.

SIG.

T. SIG.

T. SIG.

DISC.

L.P.

L.P.

WATER CRANE

F.B.

F.P.

40' CULVERT

T.P.

T.P.

SIG.

SIGS

T.P.

To Minehead Barnstaple

To NORTON FITZWARREN

To TAUNTON

N

TAUNTON

DIAGRAM "A" (1)

APPROX. SCALE: 12½ FT. TO 1 INCH

KINGSTON ROAD

THOMAS STREET

WILLIAN STREET

RAILWAY STREET

HERBERT STREET

TAUNTON EAST STATION BOX

GATE

OFFICE

W.C.

W.B.

L.P.

L.P.

L.P.

L.P.

L.P.

L.P.

L.P.

L.P.

L.P.

L.P.

L.P.

L.P.

L.P.

L.P.

L.P.

L.P.

L.P.

L.P.

L.P.

UP SIDE APPROACH ROAD

DOWN SIDE APPROACH ROAD

HOTEL

STATION ROAD

CRANE SINGLE CHAIN

3 TON DOUBLE CHAIN

5 TON SINGLE CHAIN

W.B. & OFFICE

OFFICE

GOODS SHED

TAUNTON WEST STATION BOX

DISC.

DISC.

W.C.

W.C.

W.C.

W.C.

W.C.

DISC.

LOCO DEPOT

COAL STAGE

WEST LOOP S.B.

To NORTON FITZWARREN

N

TAUNTON

DIAGRAM "A" (2)

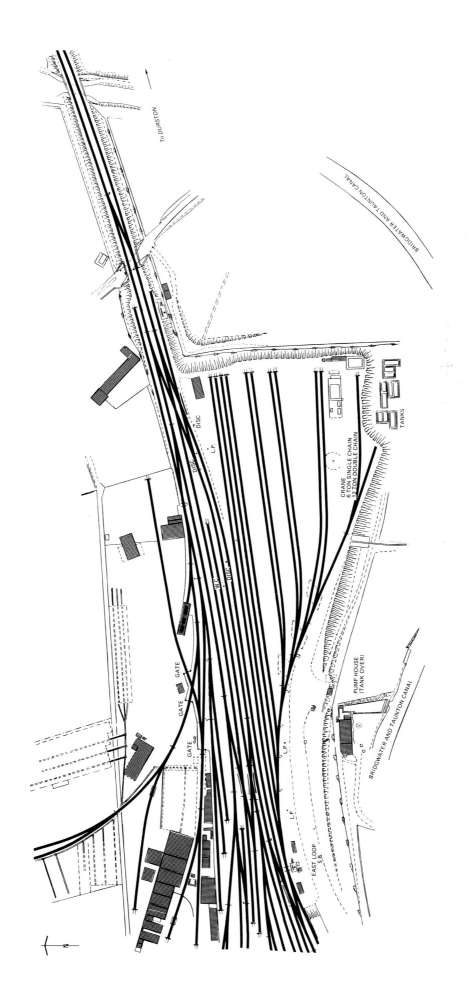

TAUNTON

DIAGRAM "A" (3)
APPROX. SCALE: 121 FT. TO 1 INCH

To DURSTON

BRIDGWATER AND TAUNTON CANAL

DISC
DISC
L.P.
DISC
W.C.
DISC

CRANE
6 TON SINGLE CHAIN
12 TON DOUBLE CHAIN

TANKS

GATE
GATE
GATE
GATE
GATE

L.P.
L.P.
L.P.

PUMP HOUSE
(TANK OVER)

BRIDGWATER AND TAUNTON CANAL

EAST LOOP
S.B.

N

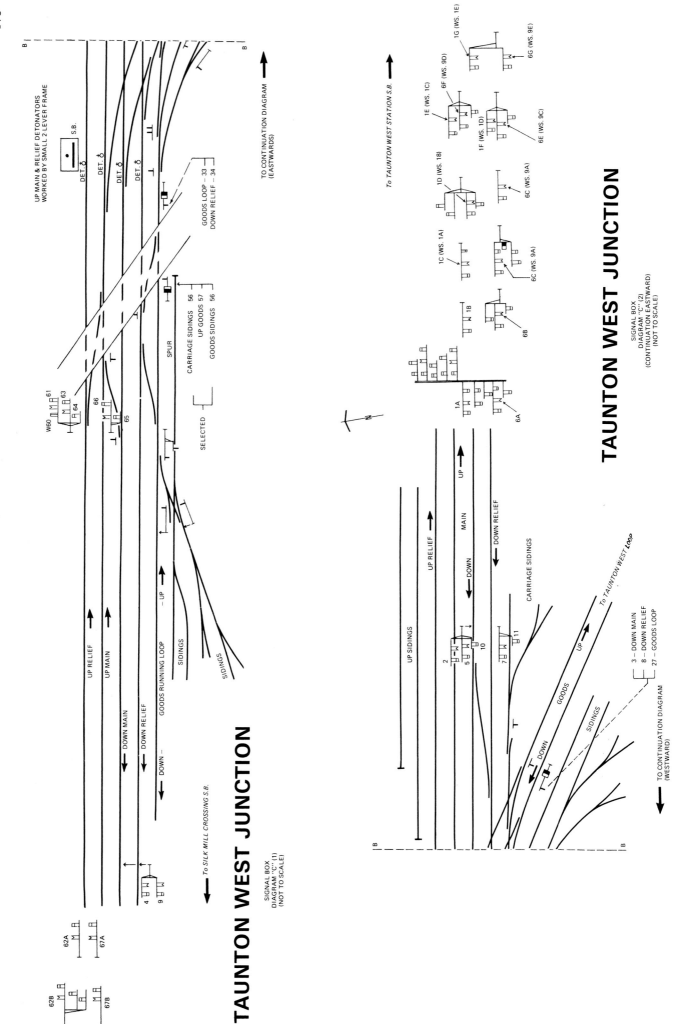

TAUNTON WEST JUNCTION

SIGNAL BOX
DIAGRAM "C" (1)
(NOT TO SCALE)

UP MAIN & RELIEF DETONATORS
WORKED BY SMALL 2 LEVER FRAME

S.B.

DET.

DET.

DET.

DET.

UP RELIEF

UP MAIN

DOWN MAIN

DOWN RELIEF

DOWN — GOODS RUNNING LOOP — UP

SIDINGS

SIDINGS

To SILK MILL CROSSING S.B.

GOODS LOOP – 33
DOWN RELIEF – 34

SPUR

CARRIAGE SIDINGS   56
UP GOODS   57
GOODS SIDINGS   56

SELECTED

TO CONTINUATION DIAGRAM
(EASTWARDS)

W60

61
63
64
66
65

62A
67A

62B
67B

4
9

TAUNTON WEST JUNCTION

SIGNAL BOX
DIAGRAM "C" (2)
(CONTINUATION EASTWARD)
(NOT TO SCALE)

To TAUNTON WEST STATION S.B.

1G (WS. 1E)
6G (WS. 9E)
1F (WS. 1D)
6F (WS. 9D)
1E (WS. 1C)
6E (WS. 9C)
1D (WS. 1B)
6C (WS. 9A)
1C (WS. 1A)
6C (WS. 9A)
1B
6B
1A
6A

UP SIDINGS

UP RELIEF

UP

MAIN

DOWN

DOWN RELIEF

CARRIAGE SIDINGS

GOODS   UP

DOWN

SIDINGS

To TAUNTON WEST LOOP

2
5
10
7
11

3 – DOWN MAIN
8 – DOWN RELIEF
27 – GOODS LOOP

TO CONTINUATION DIAGRAM
(WESTWARD)

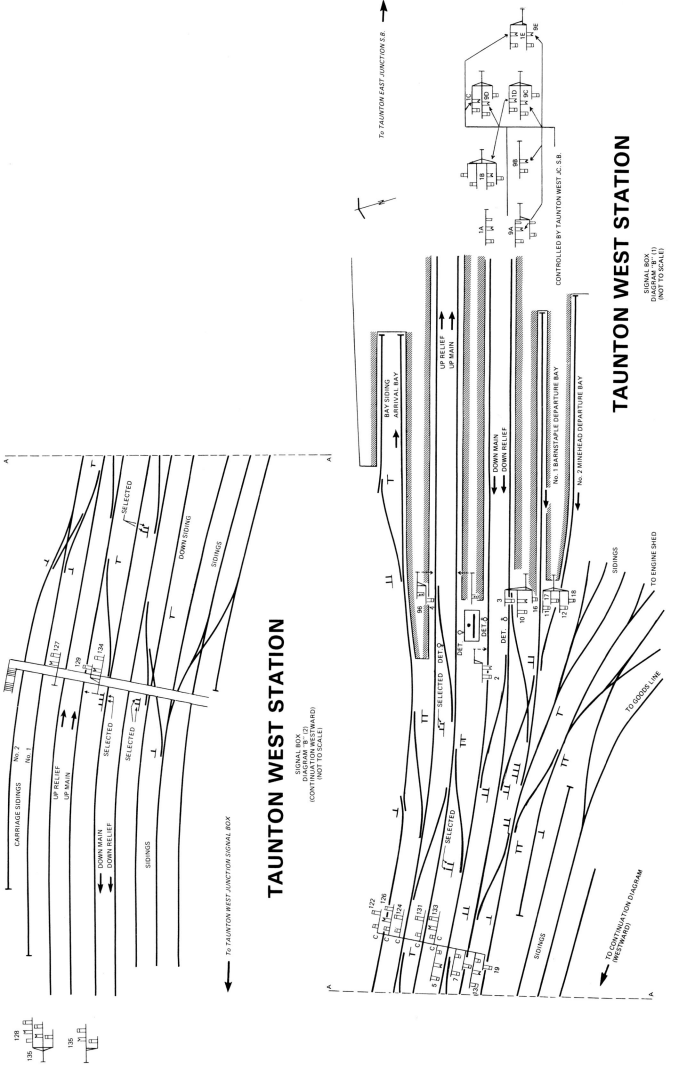

TAUNTON WEST STATION

CARRIAGE SIDINGS   No. 2   No. 1

UP RELIEF
UP MAIN

SELECTED
SELECTED

DOWN MAIN
DOWN RELIEF

SIDINGS

SELECTED

DOWN SIDING

SIDINGS

To TAUNTON WEST JUNCTION SIGNAL BOX

SIGNAL BOX
DIAGRAM "B" (2)
(CONTINUATION WESTWARD)
(NOT TO SCALE)

127
129   134

128
135

135

TAUNTON WEST STATION

To TAUNTON EAST JUNCTION S.B.

N

1E   9E

1C   9D   1D   9C

1B   9B

1A   9A

CONTROLLED BY TAUNTON WEST JC. S.B.

SIGNAL BOX
DIAGRAM "B" (1)
(NOT TO SCALE)

BAY SIDING
ARRIVAL BAY

UP RELIEF
UP MAIN

DOWN MAIN
DOWN RELIEF

No. 1 BARNSTAPLE DEPARTURE BAY

No. 2 MINEHEAD DEPARTURE BAY

SIDINGS

TO ENGINE SHED

TO GOODS LINE

SELECTED   DET.
DET.
DET.
DET.

96
4

2

3
10   16
11   17
12   18

SELECTED

122   126
124   131
133
19
5
7
13

SIDINGS

*TO CONTINUATION DIAGRAM
(WESTWARD)*

A

A

177

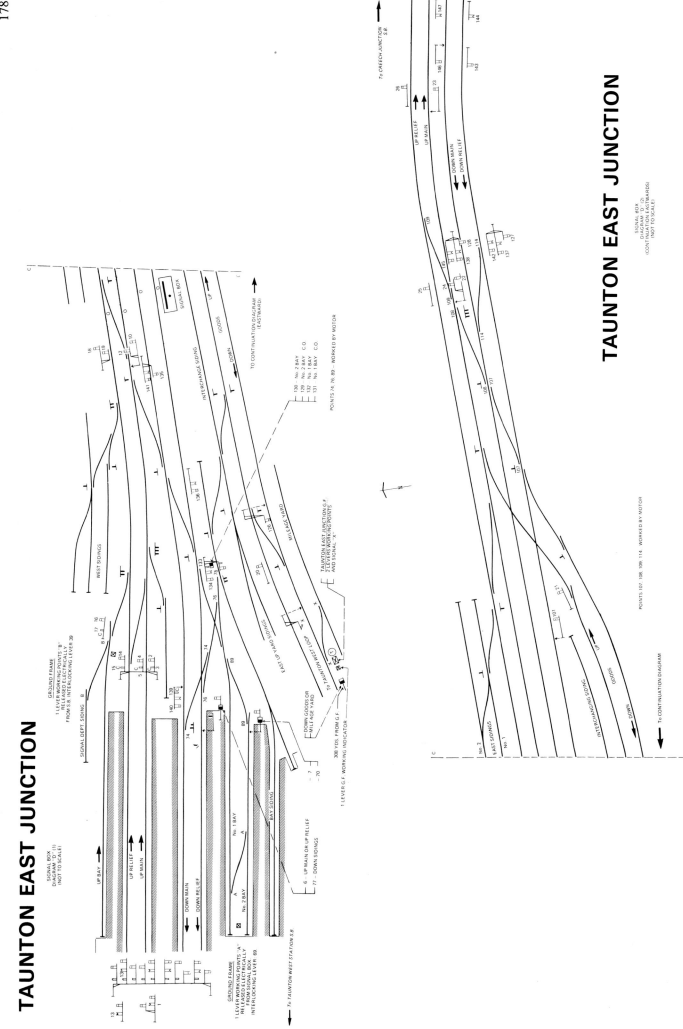

TAUNTON EAST JUNCTION

SIGNAL BOX
DIAGRAM "D" (1)
(NOT TO SCALE)

UP BAY

UP RELIEF
UP MAIN

DOWN MAIN
DOWN RELIEF

No. 1 BAY
A

A
No. 2 BAY

6 — UP MAIN OR UP RELIEF
77 — DOWN SIDINGS

GROUND FRAME
1 LEVER WORKING POINTS "A"
RELEASED ELECTRICALLY
FROM SIGNAL BOX
INTERLOCKING LEVER 69

To TAUNTON WEST STATION S.B.

GROUND FRAME
1 LEVER WORKING POINTS "B"
RELEASED ELECTRICALLY
FROM S.B. INTERLOCKING LEVER 39

SIGNAL DEPT. SIDING B

WEST SIDINGS

BAY SIDING

7
70

308 YDS. FROM G.F.

DOWN GOODS OR
MILEAGE YARD

1 LEVER G.F. WORKING INDICATOR

To TAUNTON WEST LOOP

EAST UP YARD SIDINGS

TAUNTON EAST JUNCTION G.F.
2 LEVERS WORKING POINTS
AND SIGNAL "X"

MILEAGE YARD

SIGNAL BOX

INTERCHANGE SIDING

DOWN

GOODS

UP

TO CONTINUATION DIAGRAM
(EASTWARD)

130 No. 2 BAY
129 No. 2 BAY   C.O.
132 No. 1 BAY
131 No. 1 BAY   C.O.

POINTS 74, 76, 89 — WORKED BY MOTOR

TAUNTON EAST JUNCTION

SIGNAL BOX
DIAGRAM "D" (2)
(CONTINUATION EASTWARDS)
(NOT TO SCALE)

To CREECH JUNCTION S.B.

UP RELIEF
UP MAIN

DOWN MAIN
DOWN RELIEF

No. 2
EAST SIDINGS
No. 1

UP

INTERCHANGING SIDING

GOODS

DOWN

To CONTINUATION DIAGRAM

POINTS 107, 108, 109, 114 — WORKED BY MOTOR

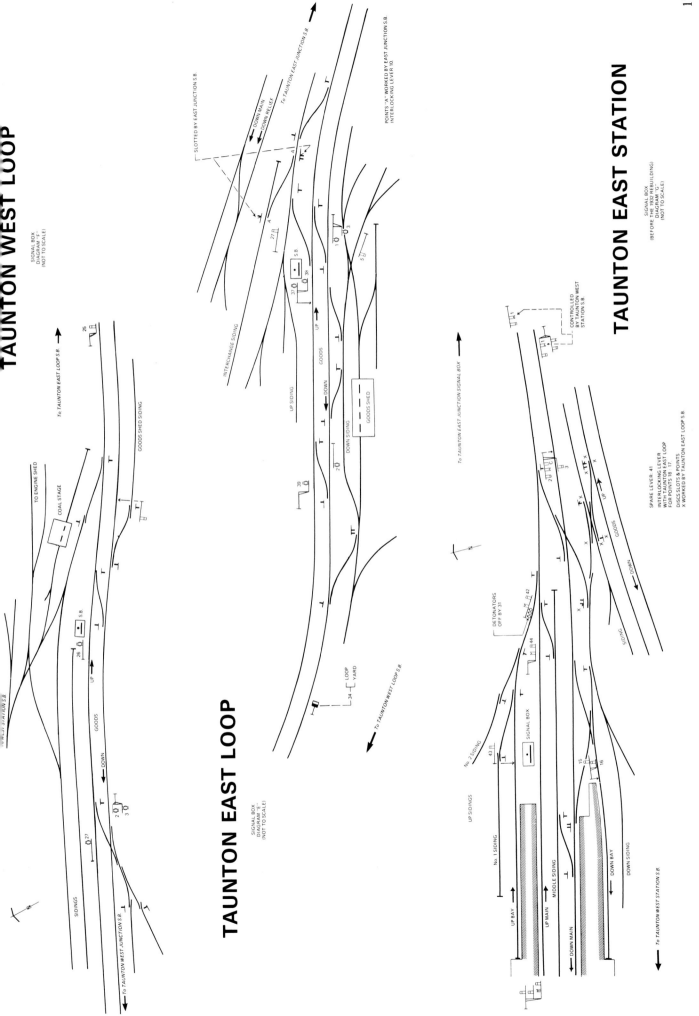

TAUNTON WEST LOOP

SIGNAL BOX
DIAGRAM 'F'
(NOT TO SCALE)

To TAUNTON EAST LOOP S.B.

TO ENGINE SHED

COAL STAGE

GOODS SHED SIDING

S.B

25

26

27

2 3

SIDINGS

UP

GOODS

DOWN

To TAUNTON WEST JUNCTION S.B.

To TAUNTON WEST JUNCTION S.B.

TAUNTON EAST LOOP

SIGNAL BOX
DIAGRAM 'E'
(NOT TO SCALE)

SLOTTED BY EAST JUNCTION S.B.

DOWN MAIN

DOWN RELIEF

To TAUNTON EAST JUNCTION S.B.

POINTS 'A' WORKED BY EAST JUNCTION S.B.
INTERLOCKING LEVER 10.

INTERCHANGE SIDING

UP SIDING

UP

GOODS

DOWN

DOWN SIDING

GOODS SHED

S.B

27

37 38

39

1

2

3

5

34 LOOP
YARD

To TAUNTON WEST LOOP S.B.

TAUNTON EAST STATION

SIGNAL BOX
(BEFORE THE 1932 REBUILDING)
DIAGRAM 'G'
(NOT TO SCALE)

To TAUNTON EAST JUNCTION SIGNAL BOX

CONTROLLED
BY TAUNTON WEST
STATION S.B.

SPARE LEVER 41
INTERLOCKING LEVER
WITH TAUNTON EAST LOOP
FOR POINTS 18 - 17.

DISCS SLOTS & POINTS
X WORKED BY TAUNTON EAST LOOP S.B.

UP SIDINGS

No. 2 SIDING

No. 1 SIDING

MIDDLE SIDING

UP BAY

UP MAIN

DOWN MAIN

DOWN BAY

DOWN SIDING

SIGNAL BOX

DETONATORS
OFF BY 31

42

43 44

15

16

1

2 3

UP

GOODS

DOWN

SIDING

To TAUNTON WEST STATION S.B.

179

TAVISTOCK

Origin: South Devon & Tavistock Railway
Absorbed by the South Devon Railway in 1865—
thence by the Great Western Railway in 1878

Opened: 22 June 1859 (P)—Date of public opening, the official opening took
place on the previous day.

Closed: 1 Feb. 1860 (G)
31 Dec. 1962 (P)
7 Sept. 1964 (G)

Plan date: c. 1912

The station was opened as "Tavistock" but shortly after Nationalisation, on 26 Sept. 1949, the title became "Tavistock South". Interlocking was introduced at Tavistock on 1 Mar. 1876.

The original station was destroyed by fire in 1887, and was rebuilt to a similar design, but using stone instead of wood.

Being a principal agricultural centre serving a wide area on the west side of Dartmoor, the town of Tavistock was a busy town long before the railways reached it, and it was, in its heyday, quite able to support the two stations of the competing L. & S.W.R. and the G.W.R. companies when they did arrive. It happened, however, that of the two, the G.W.R. station was the more conveniently situated for the town, and it took most of the local traffic, before the motor vehicle took over. Latterly, however, and by virtue of its "main line" status, it was the Southern Region station which survived (being taken into the Western Region).

Although the whole line of the former Great Western, southward to Marsh Mills was closed entirely on the day when Tavistock South lost its passenger services, the depot retained some of its freight from the Lydford direction, until this too, was finally withdrawn in 1964.

The passenger station itself, with its (once) fine overall roof, stylish footbridge, and location on the East bank of the River Tavy, has been the subject of photographic artistry on many occasions, and for many cameras, and further detailed description here would be superfluous. Suffice it to say that each photograph taken of it is a monument to a truly traditional Great Western memory.

Returning to a cooler theme, and cold facts—there was a speed restriction through the station (in either direction) of 20 m.p.h. and one of 40 m.p.h. overall, southward to Tavistock Junction, and the branch was worked by Electric Train Staff. The signal box was open from 6.15 a.m. until 12.15 a.m. (nights) on weekdays, and from 11.0 a.m. until 9.40 p.m. with two breaks, on Sundays. There was no switch provided.

FURTHER READING

R. Mag. 1908 (Vol. 23) pp. 473—479 H.D.A.P.M.
R. Mag. 1909 (Vol. 24) pp. 38—45. H.D.A.P.M. Pos. + grade profiles of Princetown and Launceston branches. (Part 2 of article above.)

R. Mag. 1959 pp. 371—377, 390. H.A.P.M. Pos.
R. Mod. 1972 p. 83 S.B. Diagram and descriptive paragraph.
"Branch Line Album" (2nd Series) by P. B. Whitehouse. Pos. Ian Allan
"Great Western Album (1)" by R. C. Riley. Pos. Ian Allan
"The Tavistock, Launceston & Princetown Railways" by G. H. Anthony. Oakwood Press
"Plymouth & Launceston" by T. W. E. Roche
"Great Western Branch Lines, 1955—1965" by C. J. Gammell. O.P.C.
"A Great Western Gallery" by B. L. Davis and A. I. Rivers. Pos. G.W. Society
"Reg. History of the Railways of Great Britain." Vol. 1. (The West Country)

Tavistock. Looking through the station towards Launceston. *O.P.C.*

Tavistock. Towards Plymouth showing layout approach. *O.P.C.*

TAVISTOCK

DIAGRAM "A"
APPROX SCALE: 120 FT TO 1 INCH

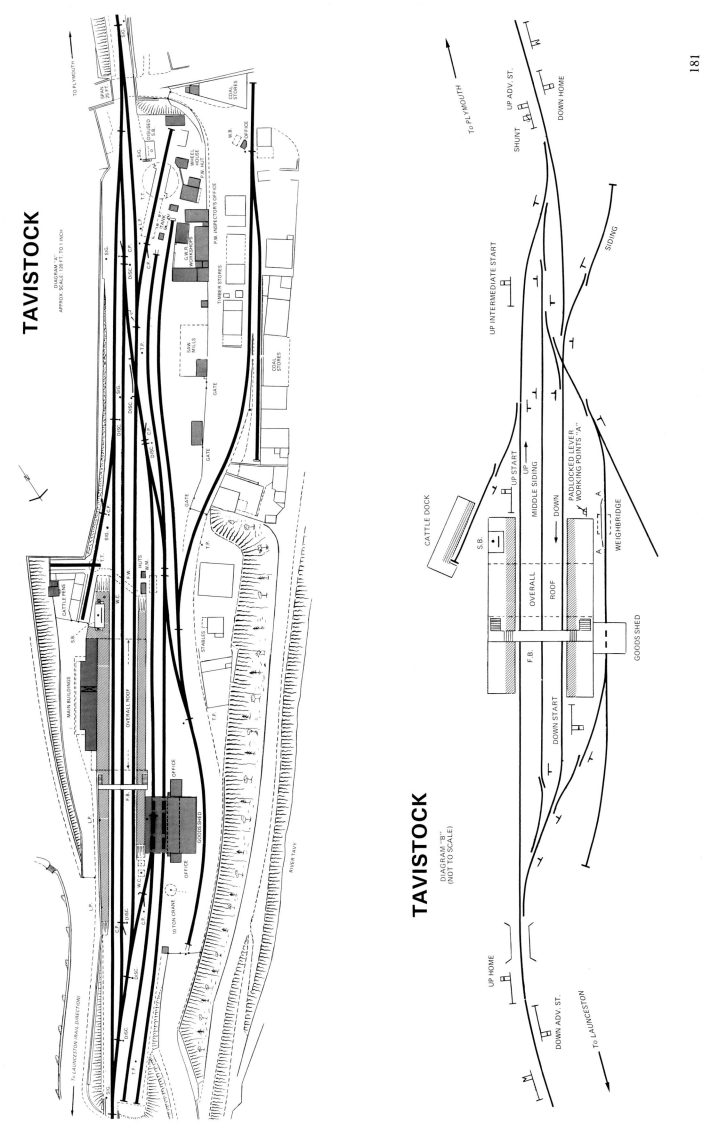

TAVISTOCK

DIAGRAM "B"
(NOT TO SCALE)

Teignmouth. Looking towards Newton Abbot through the station. *O.P.C.*
Goods yard road to the right.

TEIGNMOUTH

Origin: South Devon Railway
(Absorbed by G.W.R. in 1878)

Opened: 30 May 1846 (P) (Atmospheric trains commenced 13 Sept. 1847)
1 May 1847 (G)

Closed: 4 Dec. 1967 (Except for P.S. traffic, now withdrawn)

Plan date: Diagram "A" 21 Nov. 1912

Teignmouth (like its next door neighbour, Dawlish), in its cramped location cannot help but be convenient for its town, and the invading hordes of summer holiday makers, and, up to the end of the late War, both stations managed to deal with their own (and, on occasion, each others) goods and parcels traffic. The confined goods yard at the back of the station contained a sizeable goods shed and dock, and even workshops, and the whole layout provides an invitation to the modeller.

The dots on the platforms to the left of the F.B. are canopy supports. Those to the right hand are lamp posts.

The distance from the left hand limit of Diagram "A" to the buffer stops on the 'up' side siding is approximately 820 feet, but see unscaled continuation of layout.

The station was rebuilt (present station) in 1884.

Down to the 1960's rationalisation activities, the layout barely altered at all, except that in May 1938, the 'down' platform was considerably extended to well beyond the Dawlish Road overbridge. During rationalisation, the main line trailing crossover, between the Myrtle Hill and Dawlish Road bridges was lifted on 2 Mar. 1962, the crossover connection to the up siding was discontinued from 11 June 1965, as were the dock sidings behind the signal box, and on 1 Apr. 1968 the remaining sidings (including the goods shed road) and connections became redundant. Only the trailing crossover on the main line at the western end of the station remained.

Teignmouth signal box was open continuously, and was provided with a switch.

FURTHER READING

"Reg. Hist. of the Railways of Great Britain" Vol. 1. (The West Country)
by D. St. J. Thomas. Phoenix

Teignmouth. Looking towards Exeter through the station. *O.P.C.*

Teignmouth. Down express entering station. *O.P.C.*

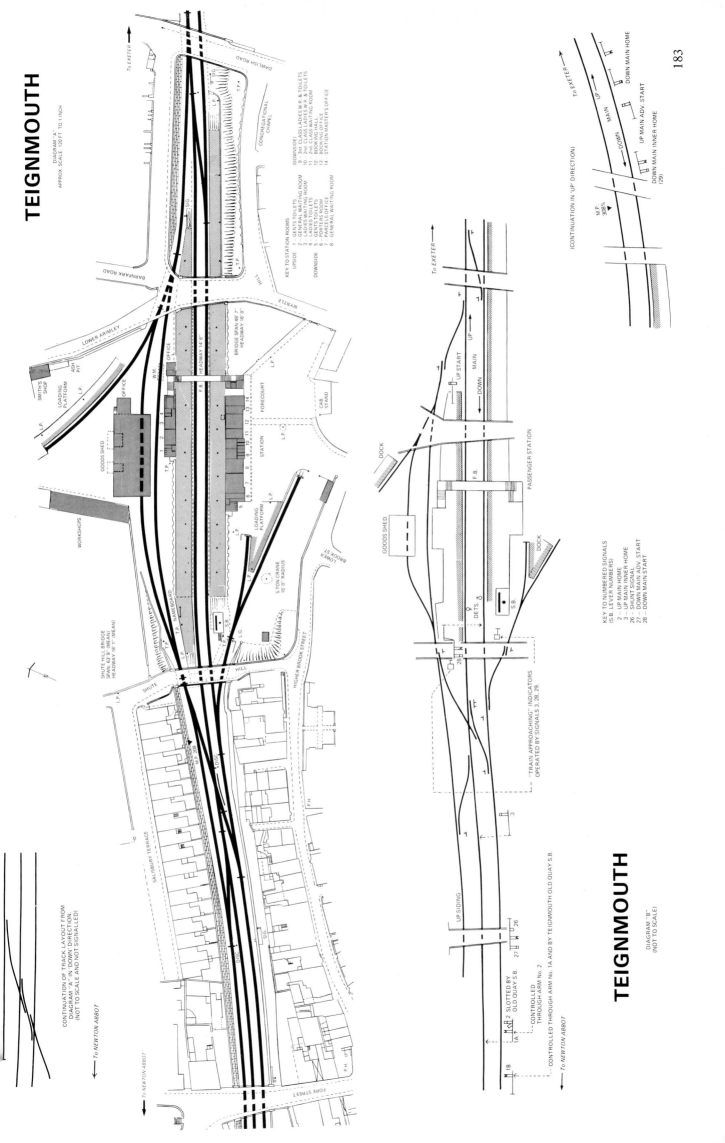

TEIGNMOUTH

DIAGRAM "A"
APPROX SCALE : 120 FT TO 1 INCH

KEY TO STATION ROOMS

UPSIDE
1 — GENTS TOILETS
2 — GENERAL WAITING ROOM
3 — LADIES WAITING ROOM
4 — LADIES TOILETS
5 — GENTS TOILETS
6 — PORTERS ROOM
7 — PARCELS OFFICE
8 — GENERAL WAITING ROOM

DOWNSIDE
9 — 3rd CLASS LADIES W.R. & TOILETS
10 — 2nd CLASS LADIES W.R. & TOILETS
11 — 2nd CLASS WAITING ROOM
12 — BOOKING HALL
13 — BOOKING OFFICE
14 — STATION MASTER'S OFFICE

CONTINUATION OF TRACK LAYOUT FROM
DIAGRAM 'A' IN 'DOWN' DIRECTION
(NOT TO SCALE AND NOT SIGNALLED)

To NEWTON ABBOT

TEIGNMOUTH

DIAGRAM "B"
(NOT TO SCALE)

(CONTINUATION IN 'UP' DIRECTION)

KEY TO NUMBERED SIGNALS
(S.B. LEVER NUMBERS)
2 — UP MAIN HOME
3 — UP MAIN INNER HOME
26 — SHUNT SIGNAL
27 — DOWN MAIN ADV. START
28 — DOWN MAIN START

"TRAIN APPROACHING" INDICATORS
OPERATED BY SIGNALS 3, 28, 29.

CONTROLLED
THROUGH ARM No. 2
SLOTTED BY
OLD QUAY S.B.

CONTROLLED THROUGH ARM No. 1A AND BY TEIGNMOUTH OLD QUAY S.B.

To NEWTON ABBOT

183

184

TENBY

Origin: Pembroke & Tenby Railway
Absorbed by G.W.R. in 1897

Opened: 30 July 1863 (1st. station)
4 Sept. 1866 (2nd. station)

Closed: 4 Sept. 1866 (1st. station)
7 Nov. 1966 (G)

Tenby was first reached by rail from a westerly direction, the single track standard gauge line being opened to a small terminus at Tenby on the site of the (later) goods yard.

The resort has always enjoyed a steady holiday traffic, and, as 'recently' as 1953, the Western Region of British Railways thought fit to introduce two named expresses to serve the branch—the "Pembroke Coast Express" and the "Capitals United Express".

Diagram "A" pre-dates Diagram "C", and between the three plans certain alterations will be noted including the rebuilding of the goods shed to take a 'through' (loop) road, the abolition of the old goods office, and the setting-back of the old signal box, to make room for the additional track. By 1896, a short siding off the end of the down platform had come into use, but was removed before the new signal box (Diagram "B") was built. On the 'up' side, a shunting neck was added to the former 'back platform road'. Apart from these alterations the basic pattern of the track layout did not alter a great deal during the period spanned by the three diagrams.

In the summer of 1938, the signal box opening hours were—Weekdays: 5.55 a.m. to after clearance of the last train, and on Sundays from 12.40 p.m. until 10.25 p.m. with an evening break from 6.50 p.m. until 8.0 p.m. There was no switch provided.

FURTHER READING

R. Mag. 1959 pp. 663–669, 724. H.A.P.M. Pos.
R. Mag. 1962 pp. 737–745 H.D.A.P.M. Pos.

Tenby. A general view looking through the station towards Whitland. *R.H. Clark* Taken in 1967.

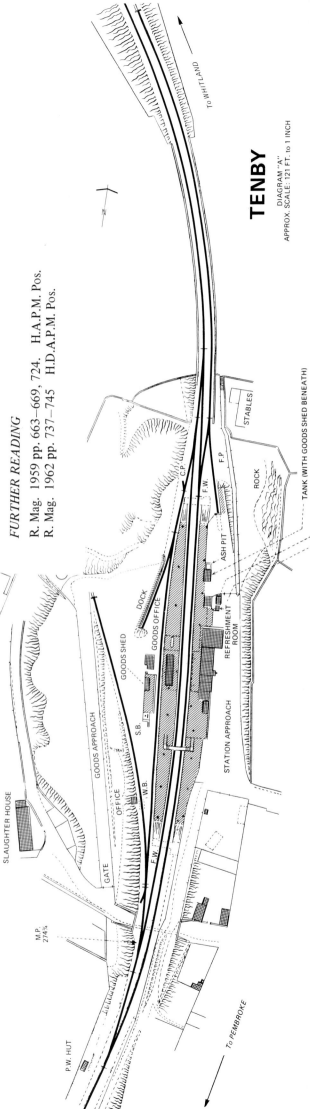

TENBY

DIAGRAM "A"
APPROX. SCALE: 121 FT. to 1 INCH

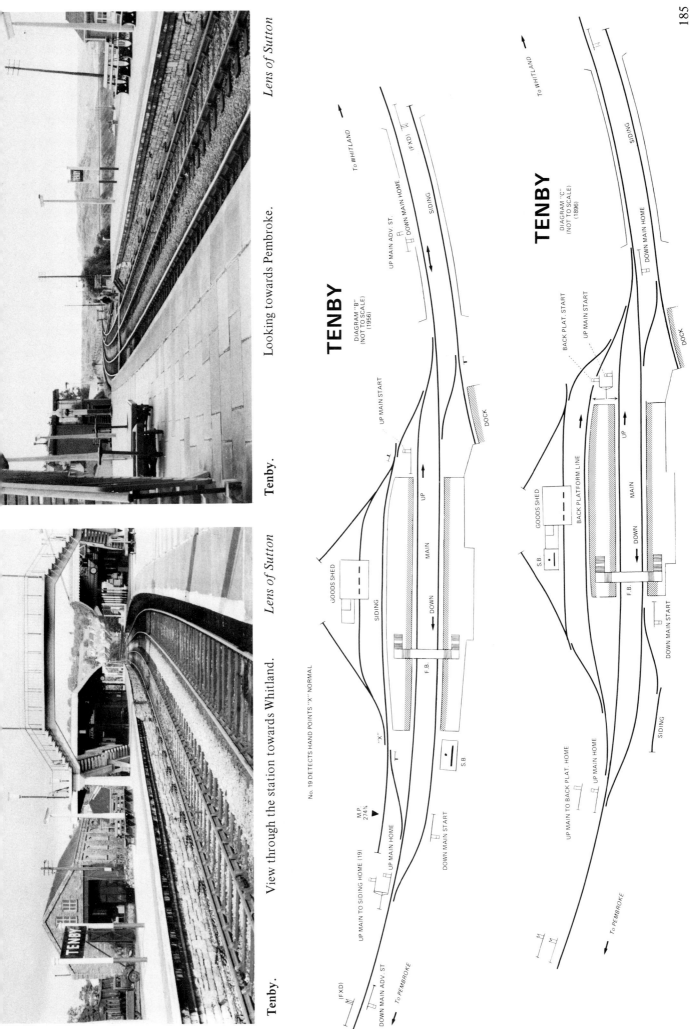

Tenby. Looking towards Pembroke.

Lens of Sutton

View through the station towards Whitland.

Lens of Sutton

Tenby.

TENBY

DIAGRAM "B"
(NOT TO SCALE)
(1956)

To WHITLAND

UP MAIN ADV. ST.

(F×D)

DOWN MAIN HOME

SIDING

UP MAIN START

GOODS SHED

SIDING

UP

DOCK

MAIN

DOWN

F.B.

"X"

S.B

No. 19 DETECTS HAND POINTS "X" NORMAL

UP MAIN TO SIDING HOME (19)

M.P.
27·4¾

UP MAIN HOME

DOWN MAIN START

(F×D)

DOWN MAIN ADV. ST

To PEMBROKE

TENBY

DIAGRAM "C"
(NOT TO SCALE)
(1896)

To WHITLAND

SIDING

DOWN MAIN HOME

BACK PLAT. START

UP MAIN START

DOCK

GOODS SHED

BACK PLATFORM LINE

UP

S.B

MAIN

DOWN

F.B.

DOWN MAIN START

SIDING

UP MAIN TO BACK PLAT. HOME

UP MAIN HOME

To PEMBROKE

185

THATCHAM

Origin: G.W.R.
         (by absorption of the Berks. & Hants Railway in 1846)

Opened: 21 Dec. 1847

Closed: 1 July 1970 (G) Except for P.S. traffic

Plan date: c. 1924

The style of station buildings was similar in most respects to those at Aldermaston (dealt with earlier in this book).

It is unfortunate that the official scaled plan available does not show the whole track layout, but Diagram "B" offers some compensation in that the layout had altered but very little down to 27 Aug. 1940, when the up goods loop was opened, with additional neighbouring W.D. sidings in October 1943, together with new main line connections thereto.

Before Diagram "A" the old station signal box was on the 'up' side of the main line, and this was replaced in 1921 by a new box almost opposite, on the 'down' side. The siding eastward from crossover No. 28 (Diagram "B"), and the crossover itself was opened to a private siding in 1923.

Although it is not shown in Diagram "A", the yard siding was there, nevertheless.

There was a short-lived "Thatcham West Signal Box" from 19 July 1940 until 2 Jan. 1966 (direction-indicated on the signal box diagram, but not shown on Diagram "B").

The shed road leading to the down siding was cut back short of the level crossing, and was discontinued (together with the crossover trailing into the 'down' main) in Nov. 1967.

In the summer period of 1938, the signal box was open continuously, and was *not* provided with a switch.

An old photo looking towards Reading.
Note the oil-lit platform lamps.

H.C. Casserley
Collection

Thatcham.

Thatcham.   Looking towards Newbury.
Goods yard in background.   *Lens of Sutton*

THATCHAM

DIAGRAM "A"
APPROX. SCALE: 120 FT. TO 1 INCH

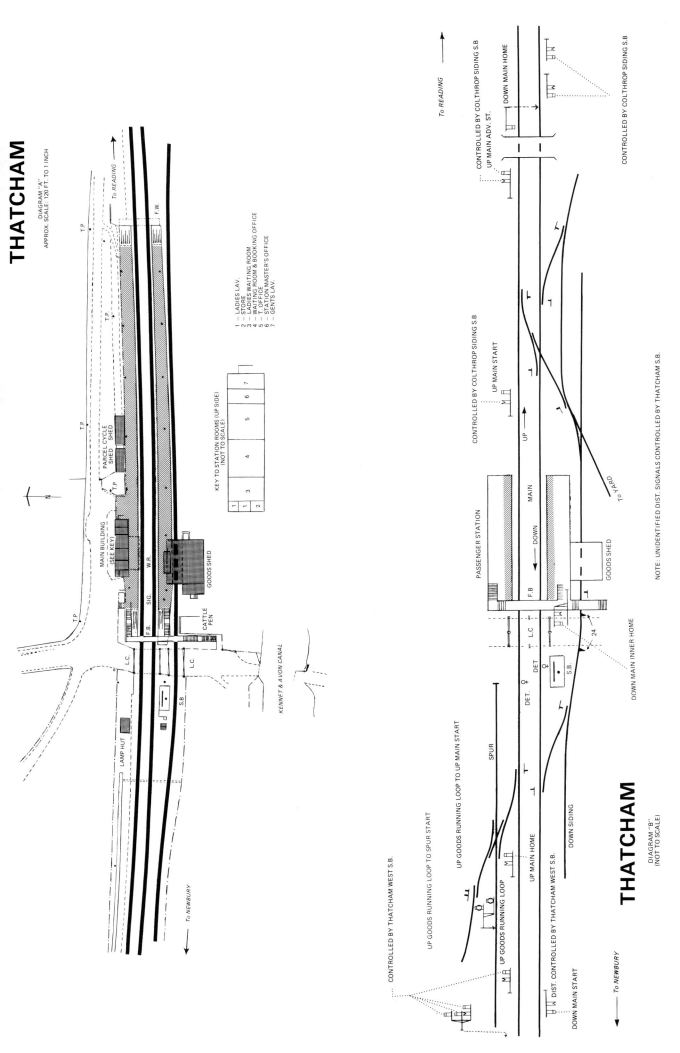

To READING →

← To NEWBURY

KEY TO STATION ROOMS (UP SIDE)
(NOT TO SCALE)

1	1	3	4	5	6	7
	2					

1 — LADIES LAV.
2 — STORE
3 — LADIES WAITING ROOM
4 — WAITING ROOM & BOOKING OFFICE
5 — T. OFFICE
6 — STATION MASTER'S OFFICE
7 — GENTS LAV.

KENNET & AVON CANAL

THATCHAM

DIAGRAM "B"
(NOT TO SCALE)

To READING →

CONTROLLED BY COLTHROP SIDING S.B
UP MAIN ADV. ST.

DOWN MAIN HOME

CONTROLLED BY COLTHROP SIDING S.B

CONTROLLED BY COLTHROP SIDING S.B

UP MAIN START

UP

DOWN

MAIN

PASSENGER STATION

F.B

L.C

GOODS SHED

To YARD

DOWN MAIN INNER HOME

24

S.B.

DET.

DET.

NOTE: UNIDENTIFIED DIST. SIGNALS CONTROLLED BY THATCHAM S.B.

CONTROLLED BY THATCHAM WEST S.B.

UP GOODS RUNNING LOOP TO SPUR START

UP GOODS RUNNING LOOP TO UP MAIN START

SPUR

UP GOODS RUNNING LOOP

UP MAIN HOME

DIST. CONTROLLED BY THATCHAM WEST S.B.

DOWN SIDING

DOWN MAIN START

← To NEWBURY

187

TORQUAY

Origin: Dartmouth & Torbay Railway

Opened: 2 Aug. 1859 (P)
              1 Apr. 1861 (G)

Closed:

Plan date: c. July 1915

The broad gauge branch from Torre to Kingswear was owned by the Dartmouth & Torbay Railway, and was worked from the outset by the South Devon Railway, who leased the line from 1 Jan. 1866 until the S.D.R. finally absorbed the Dartmouth and Torbay Company in 1872.

Torquay station has been confined to handling passenger and parcel traffic from the outset down to recent times, Torre taking care of the goods traffic in addition to its own passengers.

About the spring of 1912, the platforms were extended northwards, and the three short dock sidings on the up side (connected to the running line by a wagon turntable) had been removed. At the same time, the longer double dock siding was widened to two roads. Reference to the pre-1912 arrangement can be made to a photo in the January 1913 issue of the Railway Magazine, p. 258, which illustrates the old layout. It is clear that the published picture was taken before the alterations were even started.

The facing crossover at the north end of the layout was installed in March 1925, the old trailing one being removed, but the trailing crossover at the south end lasted until 28 Sept. 1975 when it was lifted. The middle and dock sidings (see Diagram "B") were disused from 14 Apr. 1970, the middle siding connection to the 'up' main having been lifted on 14 Feb. 1965.

The three short dock sidings on the 'down' side, shown in Diagram "A" (which were similar to the 'up' side ones referred to above), lasted well into the 1920's.

In the summer period of 1938, the signal box was opened on weekdays at 6.30 a.m. and closed at 10.30 p.m. (11.30 p.m. Fridays), opening again at 5.0 a.m. Saturdays. On Sundays it was opened from 7.30 a.m. for 2 hours when required for theatrical traffic. The box was provided with a switch.

FURTHER READING

R. Mag.   1913 (Vol. 32) pp. 46–50   H.A.P. Pos.
R. Mag.   1930 (Vol. 66) pp. 253–265   H.D.A.P.M. Pos.

R. Mag.   1933 pp. 253–264   H.A.P.M. Pos.
T.I.   1952 p. 225 Pos.
T.I.   1958 pp. 360–373   H.A.P. Pos.
"Reg. Hist. of the Railways of Great Britain" Vol. 1. (The West Country) by D. St. J. Thomas. Phoenix

188

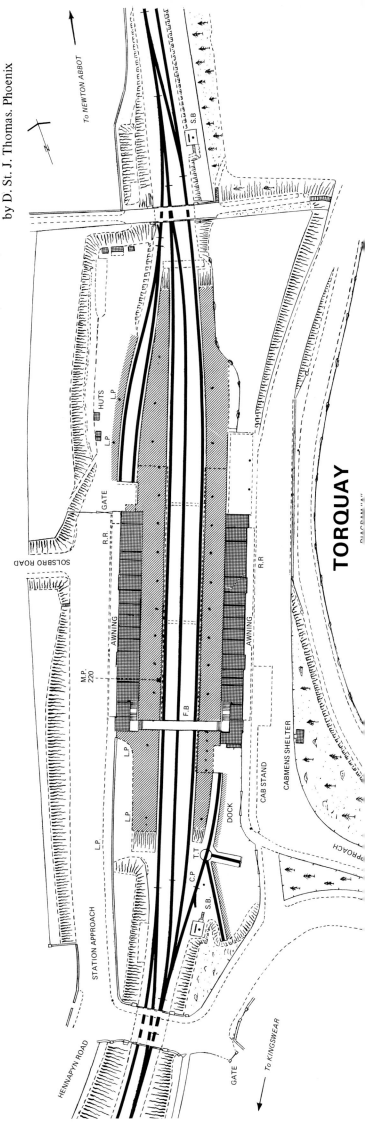

TORQUAY

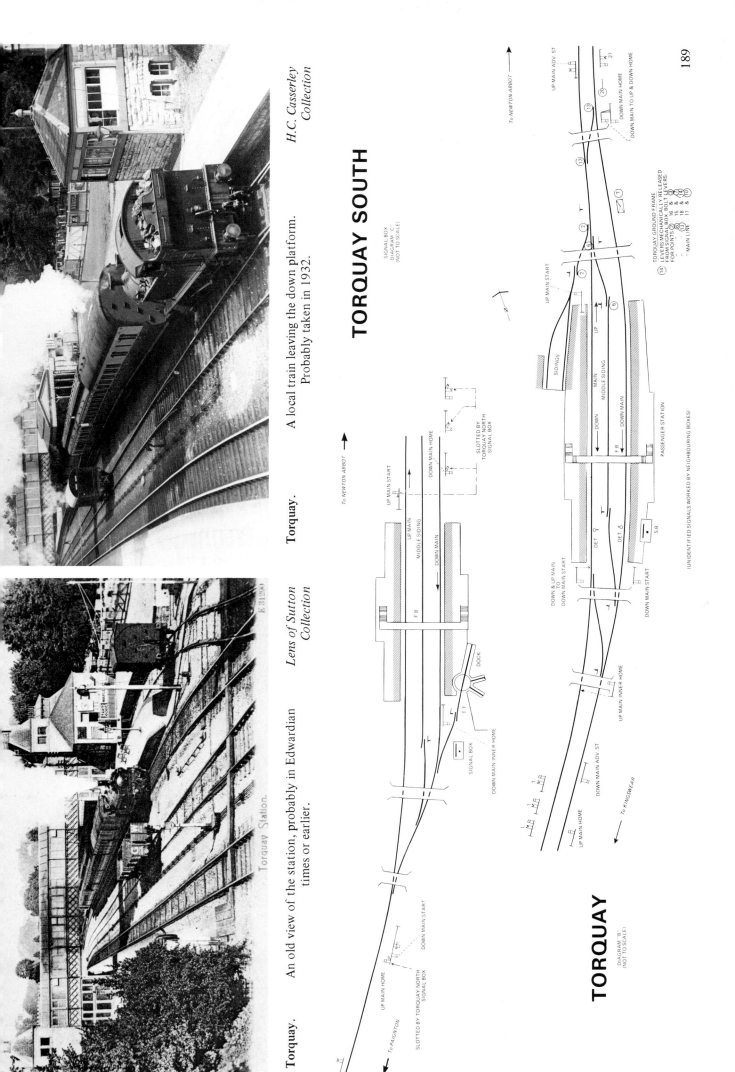

Torquay. An old view of the station, probably in Edwardian times or earlier.

Lens of Sutton Collection

Torquay. A local train leaving the down platform. Probably taken in 1932.

H.C. Casserley Collection

TORQUAY SOUTH

SIGNAL BOX
DIAGRAM 'C'
(NOT TO SCALE)

To NEWTON ABBOT →

UP MAIN START

UP MAIN

MIDDLE SIDING

DOWN MAIN

DOWN MAIN HOME

SLOTTED BY
TORQUAY NORTH
SIGNAL BOX

F B

DOCK

T T

SIGNAL BOX

DOWN MAIN INNER HOME

UP MAIN HOME

SLOTTED BY TORQUAY NORTH
SIGNAL BOX

TO PAIGNTON ←

DOWN MAIN START

TORQUAY

DIAGRAM 'B'
(NOT TO SCALE)

To NEWTON ABBOT →

UP MAIN ADV ST

DOWN MAIN HOME

DOWN MAIN TO UP & DOWN HOME

UP MAIN START

SIDINGS

UP

MAIN

MIDDLE SIDING

DOWN

DOWN MAIN

F.B.

DET

DET

S.B.

PASSENGER STATION

TORQUAY GROUND FRAME
LEVERS MECHANICALLY RELEASED
FROM SIGNAL BOX BOLT LEVERS.
FOR POINTS

MAIN LINE

(UNIDENTIFIED SIGNALS WORKED BY NEIGHBOURING BOXES)

DOWN & UP MAIN
TO
DOWN MAIN START

UP MAIN INNER HOME

DOWN MAIN ADV ST

UP MAIN HOME

To KINGSWEAR ←

DOWN MAIN START

189

Gt. Western Station.

Truro.

Lens of Sutton Collection

Truro. An old picture across the station. Note the old 4-wheeled carriage in the centre.

The Railway Station, Truro.

Lens of Sutton Collection

Truro. An interesting picture from an old postcard looking towards St. Austell. Falmouth bay to right.

TRURO

Origin: Cornwall Railway
Leased jointly to the G.W.R., B. & E.R., and S.D.R. in 1861
Absorbed by the G.W.R. in 1889

Opened: 4 May 1859 (Opened from Redruth to Truro (Higher Town) on 25 Aug. 1852.)

Closed: 3 Oct. 1859 (G)

Plan date: c. 1912

Truro was first reached by the standard gauge line of the West Cornwall Railway at a temporary station at Higher Town, which was closed on 16 Apr. 1855, when the line was extended to a terminus at Newham. This terminus lasted (for passengers) until 16 Sept. 1863, although most West Cornwall trains had been diverted to the Cornwall Railway's Truro station since 11 May 1859, a week after its opening.

The short section from Truro station to Penwithers Junction was doubled in 1893, and from Truro Viaduct into the station on 15 May 1904. Three months earlier, on 14 Feb. 1904, the old viaduct was replaced by a new one which carried a single track until doubling was completed in the following May.

Up to the 1 May 1897, there was a ticket platform east of the station.

Although the basic station layout remained down to the present time much the same as it was in the scaled diagram, in the meantime there were considerable additions to the marshalling sidings to the north of the layout, with corresponding alterations to the associated pointwork. These were effected by the mid-1920's.

The 1.1m. 68c. broad gauge single line branch of the Cornwall Railway from Truro to Falmouth was opened on 24 Aug. 1863 for passengers, and on 5 Oct. 1863 for goods traffic. The branch was converted to standard gauge on 20—23 May 1892.

By the end of 1971, most of the western side sidings had gone, as well as some of the eastern additions. The engine shed was closed in November 1965, together with the West signal box.

In the summer period of 1938, both the East and West signal boxes were open continuously, and there was no switch provided in either. Penwithers Junction signal box was opened on weekdays at 5.45 a.m. and closed at 10.15 p.m. (or after clearance of the last train), and closed on Saturdays at 11.25 p.m. On Sundays, the box was open from 6.30 a.m. until 10.15 p.m., with a morning break from 7.10 a.m. to 9.30 a.m. The box was provided with a switch.

FURTHER READING

R. Mag. 1908 (Vol. 22) p. 302 Pos.
R. Mag. 1909 (Vol. 25) pp. 479—487. D.A.P.M. Pos. (3)
M.R.C. 1936 p. 328 (Prototype layout, modified—wrongly captioned as "Taunton").
"The Story of Cornwall's Railways" by A. Fairclough. Tor Mark Press
"Great Western Engine Sheds, 1947" by E. Lyons. Oxford Publishing Company
"The Railways of Cornwall, 1809—1963" by C. R. Clinker. David & Charles
"Reg. History of the Railways of Great Britain" Vol. 1. (The West Country) by D. St. J. Thomas. Phoenix

Stations included in this survey. Key to page and map numbers.